Pragmatism
versus
Marxism

Pragmatism *versus* Marxism

An appraisal of John Dewey's philosophy

George Novack

Pathfinder

New York London Montreal Sydney

George Novack (1905–1992) joined the communist movement in the United States in 1933 and remained a member and leader of the Socialist Workers Party until his death.

As national secretary of the American Committee for the Defense of Leon Trotsky, Novack helped organize the 1937 International Commission of Inquiry that investigated the charges fabricated by Stalin's Moscow trials. In the 1940s Novack was national secretary of the Civil Rights Defense Committee, which gathered support for leaders of the SWP and of the Midwest Teamsters strikes and organizing drive who were framed up and jailed under the witch-hunting Smith Act. He played a prominent role in numerous other civil liberties and civil rights battles over subsequent decades, including the landmark lawsuit against FBI spying and disruption won by the Socialist Workers Party in 1986. He was also active in defense of the Cuban revolution and against the war in Vietnam.

His works include: *An Introduction to the Logic of Marxism; Genocide against the Indians; The Origins of Materialism; Existentialism versus Marxism; Empiricism and Its Evolution; How Can the Jews Survive? A Socialist Answer to Zionism; The Marxist Theory of Alienation; Democracy and Revolution; Understanding History; Humanism and Socialism; The Revolutionary Potential of the Working Class; Polemics in Marxist Philosophy;* and *America's Revolutionary Heritage.*

Copyright © 1975 by Pathfinder Press

ISBN 0-87348-453-3 paper; ISBN 0-87348-452-5 cloth
Library of Congress Catalog Card Number 75-10032

Manufactured in the United States of America

First edition, 1975

Third printing, 1997

Cover painting: Robert Motherwell, *Joy of Living,* 1943, Collage of oil and paper on board, 43½ x 33¾ in./110.5 x 84.5 cm. © 1997 Dedalus Foundation/Licensed by VAGA, New York, NY

Cover design: Eva Braiman

Pathfinder

410 West Street, New York, NY 10014, U.S.A.
Fax: (212) 727-0150 • CompuServe: 73321,414
Internet: pathfinder@igc.apc.org

PATHFINDER DISTRIBUTORS AROUND THE WORLD:

Australia (and Asia and the Pacific):
 Pathfinder, 19 Terry St., Surry Hills, Sydney, N.S.W. 2010
 Postal address: P.O. Box K879, Haymarket, N.S.W. 1240

Canada:
 Pathfinder, 851 Bloor St. West, Toronto, ON, M6G 1M3

Iceland:
 Pathfinder, Klapparstíg 26, 2d floor, 101 Reykjavík
 Postal address: P. Box 233, 121 Reykjavík

New Zealand:
 Pathfinder, La Gonda Arcade, 203 Karangahape Road, Auckland
 Postal address: P.O. Box 8730, Auckland

Sweden:
 Pathfinder, Vikingagatan 10, S-113 42, Stockholm

United Kingdom (and Europe, Africa except South Africa, and Middle East):
 Pathfinder, 47 The Cut, London, SE1 8LL

United States (and Caribbean, Latin America, and South Africa):
 Pathfinder, 410 West Street, New York, NY 10014

Contents

It is still possible to defend the old society with the material and intellectual methods inherited from the past. It is absolutely unthinkable that this old society can be overthrown and a new one constructed without first critically analyzing the current methods.

Leon Trotsky, *In Defense of Marxism*

If the ruling and the oppressed elements in a population, if those who wish to maintain the *status quo* and those concerned to make changes, had, when they became articulate, the same philosophy, one might well be skeptical of its intellectual integrity.

John Dewey, *Philosophy and Civilization*

Introduction

This book is a critical examination of a man's work, a method of thought, a profession, a social grouping, a period in American life, and a stage of capitalist society.

The man is John Dewey, the method of thought is pragmatism or instrumentalism, the profession is academic philosophy, the social layer is the intellectual middle class, the time is from the Civil War to the aftermath of the Second World War, and the phase of capitalism is its transformation from competition into monopoly and imperialism.

This critique is made from the theoretical standpoint of Marxism, from the social viewpoint of the working class, and from the political position of the movement for socialism.

Pragmatism—or its parent, empiricism—is the philosophy of many relatively enlightened upholders of bourgeois society among the English-speaking peoples. A generalized view of the world such as this, incorporating a special method of thought, is the supreme product of a civilization—or of a distinctive stage and grouping within it. But while it occupies the summit of cultural activity, it does not stand in splendid isolation. Every durable philosophical school is connected by multiple living fibers with the whole social organism and with one or another of its contending forces.

The main ideas contained in a philosophic system and formulated in its method are outgrowths of the mental processes appropriate to its society and its leading class. These find concomitant expression in many other pursuits, such as religion (or lack of it), the arts, science, literature, and morals. These diverse aspects of cultural life are organically connected, reciprocally influencing and reinforcing one another.

The traits and tenets of a philosophical school reflect the psychology and sentiments of a specific set of people imbued with a definite collective will and animated by hopes, fears, sympathies, antipathies, and illusions of a specific kind. Their forms of consciousness, their passions, their inclinations have grown out of the social surroundings which molded them as individuals and conditioned their development in particular ways. These in turn form part of their total response to that environment.

Since civilized societies are split into contending class formations, each different system or trend of ideas necessarily represents the standpoint, interests, aims, and outlook of a distinct segment of society, though often under the guise of speaking for society as a whole. Thus each significant contemporary school of philosophy becomes identified with a correlative political tendency and social program. Pragmatism in particular has been bound up with Progressivism, liberalism, and the reforming of capitalism.

Finally, each stratum of society grows out of an economy based on a given type of property and mode of production. When the totality of its phenomena is probed to the bottom, an unbroken chain of causation can be disclosed between the heights of philosophy and the material substructure. New modes of economic activity change the circumstances of life and the everyday relations of people. These give rise to new needs, interests, and habits, new impulses, new forms of popular and class consciousness. However vague and uncrystallized at first, these are at variance with established ways of thought, feeling, and action. Such stirrings in the bosom of the old order generate new social struggles, oppositional religious and political movements, different moral standards, rebel tendencies in the arts, innovations in the sciences. All these currents in the culture of the people provide the elements and the impetus for the individual and collective philosophizing which converts them into broader and deeper abstract ideas. Through these generalizations, the premises, positions, and perspectives of the movement of this or that class are rendered more clear and explicit and finally fabricated into an all-encompassing world view.

The problem of the relations between philosophy and economy

is made complicated and difficult by the many intermediate links at work between these extremes of social life. Their ties are far from simple or direct.

A new social class does not come into existence with a ready-made view of the world corresponding to its real conditions and constitution. Quite the contrary. At the beginning this budding formation may have as distorted and inadequate a picture of the social setup and its position and prospects in it as a child does of the world around it. The class's distinctive conceptions have to be elaborated in the course of its activities and evolution by specialists in that line. In the broad social division of labor under capitalism, that is the function of professional ideologists like John Dewey.

In his *Notebooks* the Italian Marxist Gramsci emphasized that the function of eminent middle-class intellectuals was to elaborate a view of the world that would enable the ruling class to win the allegiance and assent of the lower orders to the institutions under which they live. Thus Croce's idealist philosophy of history, which translated the outlook of the dominant class into speculative language, bolstered the intellectual and moral hegemony of the Italian bourgeoisie and justified the moderate reformism of its liberal state. Dewey's instrumentalism played a comparable role in the very different setting of the United States.

Each fresh trend of thought starts by subjecting the preexisting stock of ideas to a critical dismemberment. Its developers ignore or entirely reject certain traditional propositions. They take over others, recasting them into new forms and imbuing them with a changed content. These acquisitions from the past are fused with the discoveries and demands of the rising class until a qualitatively new combination of conceptions has been created. Thus pragmatism came to terms with earlier American schools of thought, with the British empirical tradition, with European positivism, with Kant, and, through Dewey, to some extent with Hegelianism. It was heavily influenced by Darwinism and modern science. In part it represented a reaction against certain aspects of these lines of thought, in part a continuation and extension of them.

All these various strands were woven together and cut to the measure of the reformist elements of the American middle class, whose requirements shaped the essential substance of pragmatism and marked out its path of evolution. Different social forces in different circumstances can employ the same philosophies, or portions of them, for different ends. Consider the very different uses that have been made of Hegel's philosophy in England, Italy, Germany, and the United States. The neo-Hegelian philosophers of the English universities in the late nineteenth century used what they took from Hegel to prop up an ethical idealism in philosophy and conservatism in politics. They have been aptly characterized as "Hegelian water-colorists." Croce adapted Hegel's ideas in his spiritualistic historicism to serve constitutional liberalism in Italy. In that very same period Dewey was reshaping his borrowings from Hegel to suit the doctrines of instrumentalism and middle-class Progressivism in American politics. Before him Marx and Engels had turned the Hegelian dialectic right side up to serve materialism and the aims of the revolutionary working class.

A philosophy which stems from and fills special class needs does not become a passive byproduct or epiphenomenon. Engendered by given historical, economic, political, scientific, and intellectual conditions, it becomes in its turn an influential cause which stamps its imprint upon an entire culture, inspires the thinking of large layers of people, and guides their conscious conduct. Entering as an active factor into social life, it serves as a weapon in the struggles of contending class forces. In our time, this has been the role of pragmatism in the United States, existentialism in Western Europe, and Marxism on a world scale.

A set of ideas conforming to the requirements of a certain class itself becomes modified during its development by contact with other conceptions and other social forces. If pragmatism originated in repulsion from outworn aristocratic and crudely plutocratic modes of thought, it later recoiled from the Marxism which consistently put forward the claims of the revolutionary workers. The oscillations in the positions of pragmatism as it evolved were not only, as its proponents sincerely believed, the outcome of unprejudiced researches into reality, but also of varying class attractions and repulsions. These mirrored the agitations of middle-class elements who were caught between the plutocracy and the proletariat and tried to find positions at variance with those taken by the representatives of these polar forces.

Finally, a philosophy shares the destiny of the class formation it services. Born and bred from the needs of that class, it grows in power and popularity along with it. As the circumstances and prospects of its sponsoring class change, its theoretical outlook likewise becomes altered in content and in function.

A decline in the influence of its doctrines goes hand in hand with the ebbing power of its supporting social forces. But this is no automatic and impersonal procedure. The clash of rival theories is intermingled with the harsh and unremitting conflict of classes, parties, political programs, and even with controversies between individuals. False, one-sided, and outmoded ideas do not simply wither away. They have to be criticized, exposed, combatted, and uprooted, or else they continue to litter the ground, reinforcing obscurantism, causing confusion, and impeding progress.

*   *   *

These general propositions of historical materialism have guided my examination of pragmatism, its special place in American culture, and the evolution of its philosophic thought.

Most historians take a purely empirical approach to American philosophy. They simply describe the differing ideas of individual thinkers or tendencies and assign them to one kind of philosophy or another according to their predominant features. But they do not find any persistent and consistent line of development in American philosophy as a whole.

Nevertheless, the course of American thought has not been totally haphazard and erratic. It is possible to trace an essential continuity in its growth, provided one looks in the right place and with a correct method of analyzing the movement of American civilization as a whole.

The mainstream of our national thought since the eighteenth century has flowed through the channel of bourgeois democracy. This set of ideas has passed through three principal stages. The democratic creed first blossomed on American soil during the Age of the Enlightenment in the form of the rationalism, empiricism, and anti-Calvinist Deism, shading off into materialism, which attended the first American revolution. In its second phase it became revitalized in the fountain of Transcendentalism fed by the social conflicts which were to erupt in the Civil War. The pragmatic school—culminating in Dewey's instrumentalism, which arose as the philosophical rationale for middle class liberalism at the turn of the century—was its third incarnation.

The subordination of theory to action is a theme common to the most eminent representatives of all three schools: Franklin, Emerson, and Dewey. But these successive stages in the growth of the bourgeois-democratic creed did not all stand upon the same theoretical premises. The eighteenth-century democrats and republicans (these were revolutionary appellations then!) were mostly empiricists and rationalists, whereas the New England Transcendentalists were intuitionists and spiritual idealists. Despite these differences in their theories of knowledge, both found their chief social support in the more radical elements among the small proprietors in the cities and countryside. They shared common assumptions derived from the Declaration of Independence and the Declaration of the Rights of Man, and fulfilled similar historic functions as theoretical voices of progressive social forces and democratic political movements pitted against decadent regimes. In these capacities each in its own time propelled American thought and culture forward.

When pragmatism is viewed as the intellectual consummation of this bourgeois-democratic tradition in American life, the historical necessity for its emergence and endurance becomes plain. It was not an aberrant or accidental product of American culture but the appropriate philosophical expression of middle class liberalism between the close of the second American revolution in the 1860s and the end of the second imperialist world war in the 1940s. As Santayana wrote, Dewey's pragmatism "is the pragmatism of the people, dumb and instinctive in them, and struggling in him to a labored but radical expression" (*The Philosophy of John Dewey,* p. 248).

This book aims to ascertain the background of pragmatism, the motive forces in its development, the reasons for its peculiar traits, and the causes of its rise to supremacy. We have distinguished its good points from the bad, indicating in what respects instrumentalism promoted the progress of American thought and wherein it failed to do so. We have sought to do justice to its achievements and weigh its claims to distinction without prejudice.

That is one part of our undertaking. Another is more important and imperative—the criticism of its errors and shortcomings. Deweyism still stands close to the center of the stage in American thought, despite the protests of ultrareactionaries in the field of education and competition in academic circles from logical positivism, linguistic analysis, and existentialism. But the basic ideas of this "progressive" philosophy can less and less satisfy the aspirations and aims of the most progressive forces in our country. They do not correspond to the real conditions of the national and international situation today nor give a correct accounting of them. As a method of thought and a movement of ideas, instrumentalism is out of step with the march of world events and has more and more fallen behind the latest developments in science and society, above all in the science *of* society. It is now an obstacle instead of a spur to critical thought.

Dewey's work pushed the fundamental notions of the liberal middle-class outlook as far as they could go within the boundaries of American capitalism. In the twentieth century, even in the politically retarded United States, the left wing of liberalism became a bit tinted with social-democratic hues as a refraction of the impact of labor and the influence of Marxism upon middle-class circles. But, if instrumentalism did brush socialism at certain points in its most leftward flights, it never failed to return to its nesting place.

If American thought is to go forward by crossing over to proletarian socialism, it will have to depart from Deweyism, which is anchored in middle-class liberalism. The ordinary educated American as well as the professional philosopher will find it hard to accept such a conclusion. The values of democracy in its petty-bourgeois guise were established so early in the nation's history, have been fixed so firmly in our cultural life, and lasted so long, that they appear beyond question in theory and beyond challenge in practice. Any defiance of their supremacy or criticism of their essential content is likely to be regarded as outlandish, if not downright reactionary.

Americans mistakenly assume that their current views in philosophy, sociology, and politics are as modern as their color television sets or jet planes. In reality, the United States has the most antiquated positions in these fields of any Western nation—and is much less up to date than many otherwise backward peoples of the East.

Recognition of this fact is the beginning of understanding how American thought can be saved from stagnation and retrogression and move forward to higher ground. It is imperative to expose the errors and shortcomings of instrumentalism not only for the sake of theoretical truth but also in the interests of social action and political advance.

The ideological representatives of the working class should know what the pitfalls of pragmatism are and be made to see the need for a superior method of thought which harmonizes with the new conditions of American life and the higher historical tasks of American labor and the oppressed. Further affirmation of the teachings of pragmatism, however sincerely motivated, is an impediment to the progress of American thought.

Dewey himself defined philosophy as a criticism of criticisms. Here, then, is a Marxist criticism of his instrumentalism and his liberal-reformist critique of American life. Creative forces in American society once found it necessary to adopt pragmatism as their guide. The march of events has now made it equally necessary to reject pragmatism and replace it with dialectical materialism. Such is the gist of the present turning point in the development of philosophic thought in the United States.

*   *   *

This work is the long-overdue fulfillment of a request made by Leon Trotsky in 1940 to his cothinkers in the United States. In connection with a deep-going struggle and split in the Socialist Workers Party, which raised for consideration many fundamental issues of philosophic method and its relation to revolutionary politics, he stressed the urgency of undertaking a thorough critique of pragmatism from the Marxist standpoint.

It has taken over thirty years for me to realize his recommendation. However, there may be compensations for the delay. The disenchantment with capitalist liberalism which helped produce a new generation of American radicals in the 1960s may assure greater receptivity to a Marxist appraisal of Dewey's philosophy than would have been the case during the Second World War or its cold war aftermath. This rejection of the politics of liberalism can be strengthened by reappraising the mode of thought that has best set forth its outlook and provides its most general rationale.

George Novack
May 1975

1

Pragmatism: America's National Philosophy

Many people will be surprised at the designation of pragmatism as the national philosophy of the American people. The United States has an official flag, a national anthem, a president, two houses of Congress, a Defense Department, and a Forest Service but when, they may ask, did it acquire a philosophy of its own?

Of course, pragmatism is not an official philosophy taught as a compulsory subject in the schools and universities, like Catholicism in Spain or what has passed for dialectical materialism under Stalin and his successors in the Soviet Union. It has not even been ratified as the theoretical foundation of any powerful institution, as the Catholic Church has endorsed Thomism.

But what is not validated by government decree is not thereby deprived of effective influence. The most important institutions of our country were never formally legislated into existence. Capitalist relations, for example, emerged before the present republic was founded. No law was ever passed ruling that the majority of the population has to earn its living by working for wages for employers who own the means of production. Yet this type of economic organization is today the basis of American life—and American law as well.

So the mere fact that pragmatism has never been crowned king of philosophy, or been elected to its exalted post by any vote, doesn't abolish its actual preeminence in American thought.

As the reigning philosophy in the United States, pragmatism has up to now had no serious rival. The popularity of Marxism lies in the future; its influence, though growing, is still restricted to small groups of radicals. The challengers and critics of pragmatism have been confined to coteries of learned men in the universities. Interest in the numerous varieties of positivism, in linguistic analysis, and in phenomenology is virtually an exclusive preserve of professional philosophers, among whom pragmatism is no longer so fashionable. Existentialism has had a broader influence, especially in its artistic and cultural expressions. Yet its ideas do not extend much beyond certain circles of the educated middle classes and have had little popular impact.

The scholastic philosophy taught by Catholic educators is tethered to their own seminaries and priesthood. The bulk of the faithful, including the highest church administrators, conduct themselves far more by the habits of pragmatism than by the rules of formal logic dispensed in Catholic classrooms. One of the basic tenets of Catholicism, for example, has been the submission of the state to the Church. In past centuries great religious wars were fought in Europe around this issue. However, it would not be possible for the Catholic Church to thrive as it has in the United States if the Vatican insisted, either in theory or in practice, upon this principle, which is enforced in Franco's Spain. Accordingly, the hierarchy of the American Church has decided to sacrifice this dogma for the sake of its survival and revenues. This is not orthodox Catholicism—but it is pragmatism in practice.

Washington politicians are not noted for either their intellectual abilities or their theoretical expertise. The statesmen of the capitalist class manage their affairs along the opportunist lines proper to pragmatism.

A biographer of William James noted: "The most significant application of James's ideas was made by President Franklin D. Roosevelt. Pragmatism supplied the philosophy and then helped shape the program of the New Deal. The New Deal assumed society to be plastic, and environment to be amenable to change. It adopted the theory of social experiment, and it justified experiments by their expediency and their results. It held that social, political and economic institutions are primarily instruments, and that they are subject to deliberate control and may be altered when found defective" (Lloyd Morris, *William James*, p. 84). Roosevelt himself pointed out the aim and result of New Deal experimentation: "Liberalism becomes the protection of the far-sighted conservative."

Eisenhower's avowal that he was the defender of democracy and the foe of totalitarianism did not deter him from concluding alliances with Franco of Spain and other military dictators. To this pragmatic president the principles of democracy were readily shelved whenever they conflicted with the diplomatic and military needs of American imperialism.

His Democratic and Republican successors in the White House have behaved no differently. Their courses of action in domestic or foreign affairs have been guided, not by any principles they profess to hold, but by whatever expedients serve their immediate interests. Thus, in his record of the Kennedy years, the historian Arthur M. Schlesinger, Jr., one of Kennedy's advisers, testified: "The administration itself expressed the spirit of liberal pragmatism; and other liberal pragmatists in Congress and elsewhere urged only that it do so with greater audacity and force" (*A Thousand Days,* p. 741).

And *New York Times* Washington reporter Warren Weaver observed in a September 21, 1969, article: "The hallmark of the Nixon administration, as its spokesmen from the President on down like to say, is pragmatism. The standard applied to a program by the pragmatist, Nixonian or otherwise, is not so much 'Is it good or bad?' or 'Is it liberal or conservative?' but 'Will it work?'"

*   *   *

What is pragmatism? First, pragmatism is what pragmatism does. It is the habit of acting in disregard of solidly-based scientific rules and tested principles. In everyday life, pragmatism is activity which proceeds from the premise (either explicit or unexpressed) that nature and society are essentially indeterminate. Pragmatic people rely not upon laws, rules, and principles which reflect the determinate features and determining factors of objective reality, but principally upon makeshifts, rule-of-thumb methods, and improvisations based on what they believe might be immediately advantageous. Such is the kind of practice out of which the theorizing of pragmatic philosophy has grown.

The huge Mobil Oil corporation pithily formulated this attitude in an advertisement in the *New York Times,* August 29, 1974: "Businessmen are pragmatists, and with their daily feedback from the marketplace, they readily abandon dogma whenever their survival instinct tells them to. It has become less and less a question of what they *want* to do or might *like* to do, but of what their common sense and survival instinct tell them they *have* to do" (italics in the original).

*　　　　*　　　　*

If the United States had a philosopher laureate, as England has a poet laureate, no one would have deserved the honor more than John Dewey, the chief representative of pragmatism. Morris Cohen, a fellow philosopher who did not share Dewey's views, stated that "John Dewey is unquestionably the pre-eminent figure in American philosophy; no one has done more to keep alive the fundamental ideals of liberal civilization; and if there could be such an office as that of national philosopher, no one else could properly be mentioned for it" (*American Thought: A Critical Sketch,* p. 290).

Dewey did not acquire that eminence solely because of superior personal abilities. Other philosophers of his time, like Santayana, had a more seductive prose style or, like Morris Cohen himself, presented their views with more clarity. Dewey became the outstanding philosopher of his age primarily because the content of his theoretical position and the angle of his outlook corresponded to the needs of the American people, or more precisely, to a significant section of them.

Every philosophy has to fight its way to the top against influential predecessors and energetic rivals. There must have been very powerful and persistent reasons why pragmatism, and John Dewey along with it, were lifted into first place in the minds of their contemporaries. What were the specific historical circumstances that shaped this way of looking at the world and dealing with it? What were the principal social forces that enabled pragmatism to become the sovereign theory of the American people?

The roots of pragmatic behavior lie in the origins of American civilization. Its elements have been accumulated over many generations and deposited like bedrock in the minds of the American people. Operating below the threshold of consciousness, these pragmatic bents of mind condition the outlook and activities of the entire nation. The average citizen takes pragmatic methods for granted. They appear to belong among such unquestionable values as individual business enterprise, monogamy, the two-party system, and big-league baseball.

The pragmatic viewpoint emerged organically from the special conditions of American historical development. It came to flourish as a normal mode of approaching the world and reacting to its problems because the same social environment that shaped the American people likewise created an atmosphere favoring the growth of pragmatism. It permeated the habits, sentiments, and psychology of the American people and their component classes long before receiving systematic formulation by professional philosophers. In fact, these philosophers were as much influenced by those surrounding conditions of life which gave rise to pragmatism as the fellow citizens they thought and spoke for.

The United States has been the most favored of all the major nations of the modern world. It was blessed with a protected yet strategic geographical location in the middle of North America, flanked by two oceans, and it was endowed with immense natural resources. This land came to be populated by peoples of diverse cultures. Above all, the nation grew to maturity at an exceptionally propitious juncture of history when world capitalism was ascending and in need of the products America's labor force was able to supply.

The United States is distinguished from the other great powers by the meagerness of its precapitalist past and the fullness of its capitalist development. Precapitalist institutions have had far less importance and capitalist ones far more profound effects on this country than elsewhere. Since the coming of white civilization from Western Europe, the social structure of North America has been raised almost entirely on bourgeois foundations.

This does not mean that other forms of social organization and their customs did not exist or exert influence. Indian tribal life, feudalism, and slavery all played their parts in the formative stages of the nation. But these became subordinated to capitalist forms and forces and were ultimately crushed and eliminated by them.

This central fact has up to now shaped the whole development of the American nation, from its ways of work to its trends of thought. American life, American character, American ideas have been thoroughly impregnated with the substance and spirit of capitalism. The predominance of Protestantism, that form of Christianity most suited to the bourgeois epoch of economic evolution, is a reflection of this.

However, capitalism has had a different path of development in America than elsewhere, and has acquired some very pronounced peculiarities. Until recently, the United States has been a land of pioneers and innovators. Immigrants with energy and enterprise, whether arriving voluntarily or under coercion, confronted a virgin continent largely free of precapitalist encumbrances and long-settled institutions. Those Old World traditions that were carried over had to be recast to fit the novel conditions of life and labor in the New World.

This held true in regard to the institutions of capitalism, which developed their potentialities to the full. The Americans struck out boldly onto new paths, improvised ingenious ways of achieving their ends, and projected wider ambitions for themselves. Having severed traditional ties, they quickly became used to trying new things and modifying old ones in many fields. American life on the whole has been marked by an exceptional freshness, variety, originality, and spontaneity, however much standardization and conformism have subsequently been imposed under monopolist capitalism. This can be noted in American speech, which is richer, more inventive, more hospitable to newly minted terms than the English mother tongue.

The United States, as the melting pot of Europe, became a happy hunting ground for adventurers, innovators, enterprising individuals on the move and on the make. The spirit of initiative, the willingness to disregard routine and try something new to see what comes out of it, is a deep trait in the American character. This readiness to cast aside the past on quick notice and forge fresh precedents is markedly present in the plebeian segments of the population. It has passed into folklore through Steve Brodie, who jumped off the Brooklyn Bridge on a wager, saying: "I'll try anything once." Americans have built new types of bridges, as well as leaped from them, in a similar spirit of experiment.

Yankee inventiveness, the American talent for improving appliances and adopting novel techniques, is justly world-famous. This has been most dramatic in industrial production. But it has been no less significant in agriculture, which in Asia and Europe was the nesting place of archaism. From early days the American farmer has been unusually progressive in using the most up-to-date tools and techniques. This release from archaism and routinism was accompanied by industry and thrift in the lower classes. Whoever would not get to work was suspect; whatever could not be put at once to practical use was derogated. This attitude of utilitarianism was summed up in the popular habit of asking: What's it good for?

Whereas the heights of feudal society had been conspicuous for extravagance and ostentation, the bourgeois of all grades in the early stages of capitalism sought to press everything from religion to recreation into the service of gainful labor. The Puritans, Quakers, and other representatives of the rising middle classes preached that work was one of the most important of God's commandments and idleness was sinful. This bourgeois gospel passed into the folk wisdom summed up in the sayings of Benjamin Franklin's *Poor Richard's Almanac,* which rivaled the Bible in popularity. He taught that the steady accumulation of wealth was the way to happiness; that God could be served and this blissful state of prosperity could be attained by diligent labor, sobriety, thrift, and the avoidance of vain pleasures.

"Time is money"—and it was best spent in productive pursuits which could be turned to material advantage. Success in life came to be measured by the accumulation of wealth which rewarded the industrious individual. Such were the beginnings of the cult of the self-made man, the Horatio Alger legend ("from rags to riches"), and the glorification of business enterprise which was crowned by the idolization of the industrial and financial tycoons.

At the same time almost all the indigenous folk heroes have been associated with some field of labor. Paul Bunyan was a lumberjack, Mike Fink a keelboatman, Kemp Morgan a mighty oil driller, John Henry a rail layer, Joe Magerac a steel roller. For multiple reasons work was respected and idleness condemned.

The quest for personal material gain was the most powerful and persistent stimulus to economic and social progress. And the urge to cut down overhead expenses in order to facilitate accumulation manifested itself in all branches of bourgeois activity. This extended to the height of philosophical thought.

Just as the bourgeoisie repudiated unproductive labor in material production, their thinkers turned away from theories which justified pursuits not immediately productive or gainful. They demanded that a philosophy prove its worth in practice. In an account of his earliest experiments Benjamin Franklin asked: "What signifies philosophy that does not apply to some use?" In the same vein Emerson wrote: "The one condition coupled with the gift of truth is its use. That man shall be learned who reduceth his learning to practice." This utilitarianism, which is the life breath of bourgeois society and can be found in Bacon and Locke before Emerson and Franklin, was carried forward and vigorously accentuated by the pragmatic philosophy.

Many of the prime peculiarities in the American character have their fundamental source in the constant revolutionizing of the means and methods of production inherent in capitalism, and the rapid changes in society that this system has brought about as it spread over the continent and passed from one stage to another. In no other great country did social relations remain fluid for so long, shift so quickly in so many parts of the land, and involve such large layers of the population. These aggregated changes culminated in two social and political revolutions: one at the end of the eighteenth century and the other in the middle of the nineteenth.

The success and sequels of these revolutions fixed the popular supposition that change for the better is or must be, despite temporary setbacks, an essential aspect of American life. Optimism about the future is a salient characteristic of the American people. They have as a rule been forward-looking, more intent upon exploiting today's chances and preparing for a better tomorrow than mourning yesteryear's lost opportunities or cultivating nostalgia for happier days. The whole march of American civilization, from its earliest settlement to its capitalist triumphs, has fostered this sentiment of uninterrupted progress, which found expression in Jefferson, Emerson, Whitman, and Dewey's optimistic outlooks.

This is an essentially healthy feeling, although it has been scorned by toplofty critics as a sign of immaturity. The immaturity is not in the sentiment, which is an evidence of vitality, but in the manner of its interpretation. Since the nation has up to this point advanced under capitalist auspices, most people mistakenly assume that this particular form of social organization is indispensably bound up with their own further advancement. They have yet to understand that the very economic system which propelled America forward so fast in the past has become the main brake upon its further advance. They have yet to be struck, either in theory or in practice, by the dialectic of capitalist evolution.

This uncritical sense of progress has been associated with a robust materialism. The spirit of American life from pioneering days to the present has been opposed to deferring happiness to an existence after death. Ascending bourgeois society concentrated attention upon the work, interests, and enjoyments of this world, here and now. This attitude has been tremendously reinforced by the voluminous outpouring of material goods from the modern productive apparatus. All the efforts of ascetic religious creeds are helpless to counteract the ingrained materialism of the masses. Today this craving for higher living standards is perverted for profiteering purposes and chains the working people to the treadmill of installment payments. But, as one of the mainsprings of their strivings, it can become a powerful stimulator of the struggle for socialism tomorrow.

Because of the exceptionally fast tempo of its development and the breadth of its social shifts, America has been preeminently a land of action, of practical achievement, not of carefully meditated theory. More than any other people, North Americans have approached their difficulties and solved their problems not by painstaking thought, not by working out theoretical conceptions in advance of events, but by plunging into a developing situation and acting under the spur of immediate necessity. The anarchic and automatic functioning of capitalist "free enterprise" immensely strengthened this tendency.

This unequal development of the practical and theoretical sides of American civilization was imposed by history and could not be avoided. The social energies poured into conquering and settling so vast a continent and building up an immense industrial and state power on capitalist foundations did not leave much surplus for cultivating the theoretical aspects of the process. Even more decisive was the fact that Americans did not have an imperative need for a comprehensive and thoroughly worked-out world view. They strove to master their fundamentally favorable external circumstances by a series of improvisations and were able to dispose of their problems piecemeal.

To be sure, they required a certain amount of social and political theory. The substance of this was supplied by the English and French ideologists of the bourgeois-democratic revolution. The founding fathers eagerly assimilated these doctrines and reshaped them for their own ends. They applied progressive ideas from overseas to the problems of their own developing revolution and very successfully too, improving and advancing them considerably in the process.

The group of men who led the first American revolution, from Benjamin Franklin to Ethan Allen, were distinguished for their theoretical contributions as well as for their achievements in action. The operation of sharp contradictions in the situation of a nation or in the lives of its people is necessary to stimulate creative thought to the utmost. The preparatory struggles and the launching of the revolution called forth intense activity in social thought and political theory.

Tom Paine's *Common Sense,* for example, which trumpeted the revolutionary call for independence, is full of highly dialectical observations. In 1775 he told the Patriots that it was time for the weapons of criticism to be superseded by the criticism of weapons. "By referring the matter from argument to arms, a new era for politics is struck—a new method of thinking has arisen," he wrote. "All plans, proposals, etc., prior to the 19th of April, i.e., to the commencement of hostilities, are like the almanacs of last year which though proper then, are superseded and useless now."

The essence of this "new method of thinking" which Paine insisted events had brought to the fore—and which had to be rigorously applied in practice—was the ideology of the democratic revolution. The basic conceptions of bourgeois democracy laid down during this period became the standard forms of thought, the ruling ideas appealed to by governors and governed alike. The victories and achievements of this first revolution, and then its successor in the nineteenth century (the Civil War), tremendously tightened the hold of this type of thought upon the minds of the American people.

Pragmatism is one of the later offshoots of this ideology. The historical roots of its principal elements are to be found in the events, forces, and views arising from the bourgeois-democratic movements of the Western world. Its empirical theory of knowledge stems from John Locke, the theoretician of the consummated bourgeois revolution in England. Its theory that society is based upon a social contract which can be reviewed and remodeled by the consent of all citizens goes back to the ideas of Roger Williams, Rousseau, Paine, Jefferson, and similar advocates of the doctrine of "natural rights." Its political program harks back to the ideals voiced by the Declaration of Independence. Its political theory does not pass beyond the general "Rights of Man" demanded by petty-bourgeois democracy.

The revolutionary period of the eighteenth century was the creative springtime of bourgeois thought in America. After independence had been won, the republic constituted, and social stability regained, radical thought itself grew stabilized and conventional. The formerly fluid patterns of bourgeois-democratic ideology became stereotyped. Meanwhile the young nation prospered; whatever adversaries were encountered in the territorial expansion to the Pacific—from France and Spain to the Indians and Mexicans—were pushed aside or crushed; the economy sped forward after every halt.

Throughout the nineteenth century the democratic ideology inherited from the revolution sufficed to answer the most serious problems confronting the republic. This was demonstrated when the progressive forces came into collision with the most formidable obstacle at home: the slave owners. The slavocracy had from the first stood in flagrant contradiction to the democratic creed. The struggle against its open counterrevolution in 1861 called for the defense of democratic institutions and the reaffirmation of the ideas of bourgeois democracy—not for their replacement by a new economic system or different ideas. Thus the defeat of the South in the Civil War awarded a complete monopoly to the democratic doctrines. Who could doubt them after they had proved their invincibility in war, their truth in national life—and their usefulness in the state papers and orations of the capitalist politicians?

Nothing is so convincing as success. What is unbeaten in practice appears equally invincible in theory. The total triumph of the bourgeois-democratic forces made it impossible for other views to find a firm foothold or get a hearing from large masses. The social situation following the Civil War likewise favored remodeling the old system of thought rather than the search for a radically new foundation to philosophy. U.S. capitalism was expanding without much hindrance from without or from within. Although there was friction and hard feeling between the plutocracy on top and the masses below, there seemed to be no irreconcilable antagonism between them.

Under these circumstances neither the spokesmen for the rulers nor the ruled felt any strong incentives for developing a wholly new mode of thought. The representatives of the moneybags and industrialists could get along with a formal nod to the old values while flouting them in practice. Their liberal and radical opponents from the middle and lower classes tried to improve the situation by reasserting and renovating the same basic democratic values, turning their still sharp edge against the aggressions of the tyranny of wealth.

The one class which could have provided polar opposition to the plutocracy, the industrial workers, had not yet become a formidable, organized social power or an independent political force. It represented no immediate threat to capitalist supremacy.

Even if the pioneer leaders of the American labor movement had been capable of filling the need for a totally different world outlook, there was no clamoring social demand for it. Thus the impulse toward broader historical generalizations and new social theory was retarded and repressed, and the uncritical attitude toward first principles and far-reaching perspectives, fostered by pioneer conditions and implanted in the formative stages of our national history, was fortified.

From the close of the Civil War to the First World War the American people built up their social structure to imposing dimensions and multiplied their productive powers. Yet they lived from hand to mouth on the theoretical acquisitions of the past. While the plutocrats accumulated and invested huge sums of capital, the nation did not bother to replenish and enlarge its stock of basic ideas.

This deficiency did not bother the bourgeois magnates, for whom any general theory was an encumbrance. The exploiters were content with the capitalist automatism which laid such rich rewards in their laps. Nor did lesser folk who were busy carving out smaller careers for themselves care to be burdened by any excess baggage of restrictive principles in their quest for the main chance. They went along with the credo of adventurers like Mike Fink, the boatman on the Mississippi, who said: "It's good to be shifty in a new country."

And the thoughtful representatives of the middle classes had more than they could handle to defend, and extend a bit, the democratic institutions which were being so recklessly abused by the oligarchy of wealth.

The inadequate production and circulation of fundamental philosophical ideas has persisted as the twentieth century has unfolded. Americans are still among the least given to theorizing of all the highly industrialized nations. Bold in action, flexible in practice, blessed with material achievements, they are timid in the domain of general theory, poor and backward in ideology, blind to this gross deficiency in their social equipment, and lazy in overcoming it. As Santayana said in another connection: "The American Will inhabits the skyscraper; the American Intellect inhabits the Colonial mansion." It would be more correct to say that capitalist America has erected a skyscraper on theoretical foundations suited for a colonial cottage.

Many of these special features of American life, crystallized in the American character, are imbedded in the philosophy of the pragmatists. Some of the most pronounced twists in Dewey's thought cannot otherwise be accounted for.

"The intellectual registrations which constitute a philosophy are generative just because they are selective and eliminative exaggerations," Dewey remarked in *Philosophy and Civilization* (p. 8). "Discuss them as revelations of eternal truth, and something almost childlike or something beyond possibility of decision enters in; discuss them as selections from existing culture by means of which to articulate forces which the author believed should and would dominate the future, and they become preciously significant aspects of human history."

Let us note a few of these "selective" exaggerations in Dewey's instrumentalism—its attitude toward the past as a factor in historical causation; its cult of experimentalism; its activism; its underestimation of the material rigidity of reality; its disproportionate individualism.

Dewey placed so high a premium on novelty that he discounted the objective material causes underlying events. This denial of the past's effect on the present is woven into the very fabric of Dewey's theory of knowledge, which construes any incident as an essentially fresh experience which may break every precedent. Here he was anticipated by Emerson who proclaimed: "No facts to me are sacred; none are profane; I simply experiment, an endless seeker, with no Past at my back."

Dewey's instrumentalism likewise approaches the present situation as though it had "no Past at its back" which determined its occurrence at a particular time and in a particular way. (The determination to proceed as though no one before had come to correct and positive conclusions and to direct one's gaze wholly toward the future is not simply a disposition arising from the New World experience; it was also a trait of the more radical philosophers who inaugurated the bourgeois epoch. The pragmatist scuttled past conclusions with the same sweeping iconoclasm as Bacon discarded the scholastic heritage of Aristotelian logic and Descartes provisionally denied possessing any certain knowledge.)

The release from routinism, the devotion to the trial-and-error method, the unbounded admiration for the conquests of science and technology raised experimentalism to the first rank in Dewey's hierarchy of values. "Probably my experimentalism goes deeper than any other ism," he wrote to Jim Cork.

This is a superb trait, as far as it goes. The human race has acquired its knowledge of the universe and control over its operations through prolonged experimentation. The child without prior experience learns by trying out whatever falls into its grasp. But human civilization has advanced far beyond the elementary point of immediate experience of all things; it has accumulated a vast store of tested knowledge which in part supports and in part supplements direct contact with the world. Even a child does not have to be burnt before learning the dangerous properties of fire; it can be taught.

These results of social experience are correlated and codified in generalizations which provide indispensable guides to practice. They culminate in theoretical conclusions which, submitted to constant tests for verification, become converted into principles. Such principles, which constitute the systematic structure of scientific knowledge, form the surest basis for effective action.

Pragmatism, however, is a theory which tends to depreciate theory as such at the expense of practice and to degrade principles below experimentation. This accords with the inclinations of Americans to try any proposition once to see what comes out of it. They will risk ten failures to reach one success. Americans do not feel the same abhorrence of bankruptcy as other peoples; such proceedings are regarded merely as tough luck, a clearing of accounts for the next venture which, if successful, can recoup the losses and erase the stigma.

The same attitude marks American inventors, who are willing to make a hundred bad tries until they come across the right combination and create a working model. It is one of the sources of their ingenuity and stamina.

This fondness for trial and error stands out in the work of Ford and Edison. In *The Legend of Henry Ford,* Keith Sward writes: "His [Edison's] test of success was frankly material. He once confided to his secretary, 'I measure everything I do by the size of a silver dollar.' From so revered a source, therefore, Ford could find a sanction for his own interest in wealth as such. What was good enough for the master was good enough for him.

"From the same ideological father, Ford discovered, in addition, a confirmation of his own lifelong habits of work. Edison arrived at most of his inventions by rule-of-thumb. Short on theory, he worked by trial-and-error. One of his favorite maxims was, 'Don't experiment with lead pencils.' He resented it whenever anyone called him a 'scientist.' He hated mathematics and record-keeping. To avoid writing out records, he once devised a special blackboard in which he merely inserted and removed wooden plugs to keep track of a certain procedure. When someone jarred the board and the pins flew out, no harm was done because an assistant in the laboratory had been keeping a separate printed record surreptitiously. Ford's dislike of the written form was quite as intense. Like his tutor, Ford exalted trial-and-error. All that Edison could transmit on this score was the stamp of authority. The pupil had come by the same intellectual processes independently" (p. 113).

Edison's crudely empirical method in the laboratory and Ford's in the factory were reflected in Dewey's instrumentalism. He disdained their worship of the dollar—but he shared their exaltation of the trial-and-error technique as the one sure road to knowledge and power.

At the same time Dewey administered a wholesome corrective to the idealistic conception that in science "mental activity and ideas are all," while instruments and their applications are essentially accessory. His instrumentalism was based upon weighty facts concerning the decisive importance of technology in the development of science. It would be difficult to determine whether the heliostatic conception of Copernicus or the telescope did more to create the revolution in modern astronomy; both were indispensable.

The progress of seventeenth-century science was conditioned on the invention of such basic tools as the telescope, microscope, thermometer, barometer, and air pump. "Historically, the thesis can be maintained that more fundamental advances have been made as a by-product of instrumental (i.e., engineering) improvement than in the direct and conscious search for new laws," writes Robert A. Millikan, pioneer in atomic physics and Nobel Prize winner, in his autobiography (p. 219). "Witness: (1) relativity and the Michelson-Morley experiment, the Michelson interferometer came first, not the reverse; (2) the spectroscope, a new instrument which created spectroscopy; (3) the three-electrode vacuum tube, the invention of which created a dozen new sciences; (4) the cyclotron, a gadget which with Lauritsen's linear accelerator, spawned nuclear physics; (5) the Wilson cloud-chamber, the parent of most of our knowledge of cosmic rays; (6) the Rowland work with gratings, which suggested the Bohr atom; (7) the magnetron, the progenitor of radar; (8) the counter-tube, the most fertile of all gadgets; (9) the spectroheliograph, the creator of astrophysics; (10) the relations of Carnot's reversible engine to the whole of thermodynamics." The radioscope and transistor could be added to this list.

Dewey's "operational" theory of knowledge correctly stressed the dependence of scientific advance on instruments and the mediating role of ideas in the practice of science. The trouble is that he viewed these too narrowly and subjectively as mere means for achieving human purposes, whereas to be effective both instruments and ideas, as well as the purposes they serve, have to conform to objective realities. Francis Bacon long ago observed: "We cannot command nature except by obeying her."

America's foremost contribution to world culture has been its development of industrial technique. Americans display unflagging interest in mechanical improvements, technical devices, gadgets. But this justified confidence in the results of natural science as applied to industry is bound up with an unjustifiable neglect of the specific property relations which encase them. Both this strength and this weakness were to be found in Dewey's thought. He admitted that the scientific, technological, and industrial advances of the twentieth century had revolutionary implications—yet he hesitated to recognize the highly revolutionary effects these must produce in the class relations of capitalist society.

The theme of Longfellow's "The Psalm of Life"—"Let us then be up and doing"—is proper for both pioneering society and capitalist society, where life is dedicated not to idle contemplation but to strenuous effort. This same message pervades Dewey's philosophy. The national spirit of practical energy pulses through his thought. Take general ideas and put them to work, he says. If they turn out well and produce fruitful results, hold on to them. If they prove ineffective, discard them and try something else. In this theory of knowledge general ideas are looked upon simply and solely as tools. But the objective material conditions that decide whether or not such tools will work, and what truth the ideas contain, are dropped by the wayside.

The American pioneer background, the constant restructuring of social relations, the advances of science and technology, the march of agriculture and industry, favored the view that all things are tentative, provisional, unfinished. This state of affairs passed into the texture of Dewey's conceptions of nature, society, and the thought process.

"It is beyond doubt," he wrote in "The Development of American Pragmatism," "that the progressive and unstable character of American life and civilization has facilitated the birth of a philosophy which regards the world as being in constant formation, where there is still place for indeterminism, for the new and for a real future" (in *Studies in the History of Ideas,* vol. 2, p. 374). Actually Dewey went beyond this reasonable observation. For him the most *fundamental* feature of nature was its contingent, not its necessary, aspect. He likewise believed that present-day society has a plasticity which permits it to be molded into a desired shape regardless of given economic conditions and class relations. He held that even the surest ideas may all of a sudden be upset by unforeseen circumstances.

"Our life has no background of sanctified categories upon which we may fall back; we rely upon precedent as authority only to our undoing—for with us there is such a continuously novel situation that final reliance upon precedent entails some class interest guiding us by the nose whither it will," he wrote in "The Need for a Recovery of Philosophy" (an essay reprinted in *On Experience, Nature and Freedom,* edited by Richard J. Bernstein, p. 69). This assertion about our "continuously novel situation" overlooked the fact that the decisive changes in American history to date have all taken place within the confines of bourgeois society in its successive phases of development. This fundamental factor has not only determined the chief characteristics and categories of our national life but fixed the limits of potential change short of social revolution.

Dewey was the most social-minded of the pragmatists and constantly stressed the social conditioning of individuals and their conduct. He combatted the "one-sided and egotistic individualism" by which the rich and powerful sought to justify their privileges. Yet he never gave up the notion that the individual was the decisive force in social life, a notion which runs through bourgeois thought. "Pragmatism and instrumental experimentalism bring into prominence the importance of the individual," he declared in *Philosophy and Civilization* (pp. 33–34). "It is he who is the carrier of creative thought, the author of action, and of its application." In the last analysis, for him, the intelligence and intervention of the individual counted for more than the collective consciousness and action of classes, i.e., groups of people tied together by common material interests.

The task of philosophers in relation to their epoch is two-sided. On the one hand they have to find place in their thought for all the positive trends in scientific and social activity. On the other, they ought to point out the deficiencies of these trends, their causes, and how to correct them. Dewey benefited by trying to make room in his philosophy for many of the most powerful and positive driving forces in American life. But in many cases he failed to recognize or to reckon with the negative and obsolescent sides of these same factors. Instead of exposing the most deep-rooted imbalances of American life in his time, he tended to rationalize and reinforce some of the most important of them.

In his criticism of the bourgeois-democratic outlook on life, Dewey did not probe very deep below the surface or go far beyond his predecessors. Accepting the basic views and values of the petty-bourgeois schools that had gone before him, he readjusted them to cope with the new conditions and problems confronting the American middle class in the first half of the twentieth century.

This required considerable effort. Pragmatism had to fight the mandarins in the universities who clung to the antiquated positions of absolute idealism congenial to the conservatives and the plutocracy. This gave its spokesmen the illusion of militancy, the feeling of being at the head of the procession.

The founders and formulators of pragmatism did not have to contend against the prejudices of the people; on the contrary, they leaned upon these prejudices for support. Their ideas were welcomed and widely adopted because the way had been prepared for them by the national past. The pragmatic habits nurtured in preceding generations blossomed to full consciousness after the Civil War. They received theoretical formulation at the end of the nineteenth century and systematization at the beginning of the twentieth through professional philosophers who were stimulated by the Progressive currents at work in the middle and lower classes. Pragmatism became the dominant philosophy of the time because it provided general solutions to the specific problems agitating the broad social movement of Progressivism.

2

Dewey and the
Progressive Movement

"Philosophers are parts of history, caught in its movement, creators in some measure of its future, but assuredly creatures of its past," remarked Dewey in *Philosophy and Civilization*. Let us apply this observation to Dewey himself. What period of American history was he part of; what movement was he caught in; what kind of past formed this philosopher?

Dewey was born in 1859 and died in 1952. He remembered reports of Lincoln's assassination. His ninety-two years extended from the Civil War to beyond the Second World War, embracing several momentous stages in the development of American society.

Dewey grew to manhood under conditions quite remote from those of today. He came out of the freehold farming community which constituted the backbone of white plebeian democracy in early America. His forebears were pioneer settlers of New England. His parents belonged to the cultured, comfortable middle class. His formative years were passed in and around Burlington, Vermont, a small farming and trading center with social stratifications but without severe class conflicts, somewhat set apart from the torrential main currents of American life.

From this environment Dewey absorbed certain basic elements of his personality. Just as the character of Calvin Coolidge embodied the harsh, narrow, stinted aspects of this Vermont breed, so Dewey exhibited many of its finest qualities: its

simplicity, its spontaneous equalitarianism, its persistent industry, and its inner equilibrium. But, as the numerous cautious
qualifications and absence of broad sweep and bold perspectives
in his writings indicate, he never rid himself of a measure of
provincialism, never adequately compensated for its lack of
dynamism, never fully overcame its peripheral relation to the
chief conflicting forces at work in the modern world.

Although his experiences and ideas were rooted in New
England, Dewey developed and perfected his thought in the
Middle West, where he taught at the Universities of Minnesota,
Michigan, and Chicago. In the eighties and nineties of the last
century this region was a foundry in which new forces in
American life were being forged.

The last three decades of the century saw the impetuous, almost
uninterrupted rise of capitalist forces in the United States and on
a world scale. Despite minor and puffed-up reforms, this was
basically a period in which political reaction replaced the colossal
revolutionary leap of the Civil War years. Throughout these
decades the triumphant plutocracy was energetically consolidat-
ing its grip over the major spheres of national life.

The ever-harsher domination of the capitalist oligarchy
encountered resistance all along the way from the mass of
Americans. These were divided into three important sections: the
small agrarian producers, the urban middle classes, and the
industrial workers. The currents of protest welling forth from the
depths of these people were mostly movements of reform which
aimed to curb, regulate, or reverse the processes of capitalist
concentration in economic, political, and cultural life. Outright
revolutionary voices were as rare as outcries from the racially
oppressed; working-class tendencies bent upon the overthrow of
capitalism were in their infancy.

The principal large-scale political struggles were waged
between the agents of the plutocracy and the representatives of
the liberal petty bourgeoisie who headed the plebeian masses.
Outside of industry itself, the proletariat was as yet a subordinate
factor in most spheres of national affairs. The mainstream of
political opposition came from the Populist-Progressive movement which had its direct social bases in the middle-class
elements of the country and the city. The proletarian currents at
various times ran parallel to this mainstream, fed, or even
emptied themselves into it.

The life cycle of the Progressive movement, its rise, its periodic fluctuations from effervescence to stagnation and back again, its decline and disintegration, can be charted in close connection with the economic development of American capitalism. The Progressive movement was a political product of the post-Civil War era. It was born during the hard times following the panic of 1873 and gained new impetus from each succeeding economic crisis.

The 1892 platform of the Populist Party, as summarized by Charles and Mary Beard in *The Rise of American Civilization*, made the following indictment of the "Gilded Age" of United States capitalism: "that America was ruled by a plutocracy, that impoverished labor was laid low under the tyranny of a hireling army, that houses were covered with mortgages, that the press was the tool of wealth, that corruption dominated the ballot box, 'that the fruits of the toil of millions are boldly stolen to build up colossal fortunes for a few unprecedented in the history of mankind; and the possessors of these in turn despise the republic and endanger liberty'" (p. 210).

The movement reached the peak of its social energy and political influence in 1896 when its aims were ostensibly adopted by the Democratic Party, and Populist-Democratic candidate Bryan led the Progressive hosts in an attempt to dislodge the finance capitalists from power in Washington. After Bryan's defeat, the Spanish-American War, and the ensuing prosperity, the Progressive movement died down except in rural districts. It was revived by the crisis of 1907 and took on several new shapes, culminating in Theodore Roosevelt's Bull Moose crusade and Wilson's New Freedom of 1912.

The entry of the United States into the First World War dealt a mortal blow to the Progressive cause but did not finally dispose of it. After a regional revival in the agrarian Northwest, the movement had a spasmodic national resurgence in the La Follette campaign of 1924, which was a belated response to the consequences of the postwar crisis of 1921. Even then the force of the movement, which had so many decades of struggle behind it and so many hopes deposited with it, was not wholly spent. In speeches against the "economic royalists," Franklin D. Roosevelt skillfully exploited Progressive sentiments and traditions to win support for his New Deal. His ex-vice-president, Henry Wallace, aided by the Communist Party, sought in vain to resurrect the corpse of Progressivism as late as 1948.

In all these incarnations, the Progressive movement was

middle class in body and spirit. In the earlier stages of its career, in the Greenback, Granger, and Populist trends of the seventies and eighties, it was based upon the small farmers of the Middle West and South, pulling behind it the radicalized workers and urban middle classes and effecting alliances with them. The programs of the Greenback, Granger, and Populist movements largely expressed the interests of these aroused and oppressed small farmers, and they were led by rural figures.

Later the Progressive movement came to lean more and more upon the city masses and the rising industrial workers. This shift in the base of the Progressive movement resulted from the diminishing importance of the rural population and the increasing power of wage labor in the American economy. The change in the social composition of the Progressive ranks was reflected in the character of its principal leaders. "Sockless" Jerry Simpson, General Weaver, Ignatius Donnelly, Mary Ellen Lease ("Let's raise less corn and more hell") of the Midwest and Tom Watson of Georgia were representative personalities of its Populist period. Robert La Follette, Sr., may be regarded as a leader who bridged the country and the city, a link between organized labor and the rural sections of the movement.

In their heyday the Populist-Progressives constituted the left wing of the capitalist regime. As a loyal opposition, they did not desire to abolish but to moderate the despotism of the plutocracy, to curtail its power, and reduce the privileges of the magnates of industry and finance. The principal planks in their economic platforms put forward the demands of various sections of the middle classes from the farmers to the small businessmen. This was true of such Populist monetary panaceas as Greenbackism and bimetallism, and of such reforms as the graduated income tax and the regulation of the monopolies.

The Progressives did not dream of going beyond restricting the power of King Capital and his monied aristocracy. To dethrone this despot by expropriation—that was regarded as socialism, anarchism, the end of civilization. Even the most radical political ideas of Progressivism did not transgress the boundaries of the bourgeois democracy which had been built upon competitive capitalism. The Progressives proposed their reforms within the framework of the constitution that had been laid down by the architects of the Republic following the first American revolution, as defended and amended by the second (the Civil War).

The Progressives sincerely believed—as their descendents still do—that the capitalist republic of the United States is the highest and ultimate form of political organization. They could not conceive that progressive humankind might desire or create any other, better kind of government. As a gauge of their provincial backwardness in this respect, when Robert La Follette went to the Soviet Union in 1922, he invited the revolution's leaders to come and repay his visit in the state of Wisconsin where, he assured them, they could see "a really progressive state"!

The Progressives wanted to cleanse the machinery of the United States government of its more glaring aristocratic vestiges and to perfect its democracy by introducing such reforms as direct election of senators and judges. They sometimes stopped halfway even in the direction of democratizing the state apparatus. They campaigned to abolish the Supreme Court's veto power over Congressional enactments but upheld the president's veto power, which is a relic of monarchical rule; they asked for direct election of senators on a state basis, but not the president on a national scale; they did not call for a single instead of a double system of federal legislative bodies. Their demands for civil service reform and for cheap, honest, efficient administration even pleased that part of the ruling class which could get along without direct corruption or coercion of their political servitors.

Armed with these programs, the Progressives vainly stormed the fortresses of plutocratic power at periodic intervals from 1872 to 1924. They did manage by tremendous exertions to exact a number of concessions and reforms from successive administrations which felt their pressure. Occasionally they even controlled some of the state governments.

Nevertheless, these gains did not result in any basic changes in American life or reverse the processes of capitalist centralization and control. In some cases they even produced consequences contrary to those expected or promised. The laws curbing or breaking up the trusts did not halt but facilitated the growth of the monopolies; the income tax which was to make the rich pay more for the costs of running the government became converted into an engine of extortion from the pay of the workers. The various electoral revisions failed to make the system more responsive to the voters' will. Instead of breaking up the party machines, the primaries gave city bosses an additional instrument for handpicking their candidates.

Why did the Progressive movement display so little stability and stamina and end up in futility? The chief factor was its class basis and social composition. The small property-owners and those imbued with their psychology could not conduct a fight to the end against big business; that would have involved abolishing the economic and social ground upon which they themselves stood.

Their interests, hopes, and outlook were bound up with the maintenance of the capitalist system, whose prosperity they wanted to share. They showed this by dropping their struggles en masse, time and again, whenever the system temporarily showed its smiling side to them. Just as every economic depression reanimated the fighting spirit of the Progressive forces, so every period of capitalist revival laid it low.

Moreover, whenever the fate of the capitalist regime was at stake, the Progressives did not intervene as an independent power but rallied to the side of the rulers. This happened at every great historical turning point from the Spanish-American War to the Korean War. John Dewey's support to the Democratic administrations in all the wars of the twentieth century was typical of the entire movement.

Progressivism, as a social movement and political force, belonged to the epoch of ascending competitive capitalism. But it was undermined and overwhelmed by the subsequent sway of monopolist capitalism in the United States. Its fortunes were bound up with the status of the middle classes which were periodically uplifted by capitalist expansion (this gave them hope) and then oppressed and ruined by the robber barons (this gave them wrath and militancy).

As monopoly capitalism grew, the plutocrats heightened their power while the numbers and influence of the industrial proletariat expanded as well. But the economic, social, and political power of the middle classes which were the backbone of the Progressive forces declined, dragging their movement down with them.

After every losing battle with the entrenched plutocracy and every ignoble surrender to its war program, the Progressives lost more of their strength, self-confidence, and mass support. Without broad historical perspectives or bold revolutionary aims, unable to grasp the dynamics of the principal forces at work in the world and in American society, the movement progressively lost whatever progressive aspects it once possessed. On the one hand, its traditions shriveled into empty phrases which served to cover the procapitalist policies of such Democratic demagogues as Franklin Roosevelt and Henry Wallace. On the other hand, whatever was vital in their proposals was absorbed by the socialist, communist, and labor movements.

The fundamental reason for the failure of Progressivism lay in the fact that it was truly progressive only in its incidental features. At bottom it was a retrograde movement which aspired to turn back the wheel of history and reverse the development of modern society. The Progressives longed for a return to the childhood of American capitalism at a time when it was maturing into imperialism. This impotent yearning for an irrecoverable past enveloped the movement in a utopian atmosphere.

The Progressives demanded greater equality, wider opportunities, peace, the extension of democracy, the sharing of wealth—all within the boundaries of capitalism. What they received was more inequality, periodic wars, a growing concentration of wealth, and political reaction. These were the natural fruits of monopolist rule and imperialism.

*   *   *

The Populist-Progressive movement had a colossal significance for the American people in the late nineteenth and early twentieth centuries. This myriad-minded mass movement of protest against the reactionary rule of big business and high finance made a deep impression upon cultural and intellectual activity. It provided the impulse for many creative forces and ideas and gave support to advanced tendencies and causes in American thought. The rebellion of the oppressed against the ideas, attitudes, and practices of the tyrannical money-masters was conducted on many fronts. This class struggle penetrated and modified not only economics and politics but the higher realms of education, morals, religion, literature, art, and philosophy.

This tremendous and sustained mass movement engrossed the services of several generations of the best minds in many fields—politicians, economists, journalists, historians, architects, writers, poets, philosophers. Indeed, in the balance sheet of the Progressive movement as a whole, its most fruitful and enduring work was accomplished in the field of general culture.

The Progressives didn't and couldn't create any lasting political party of their own. They lacked the power and the will to revolutionize either the political system or the economic structure of capitalism, or even to break with its basic ideology. But they could and did strive to push the ideas and cultural institutions of petty-bourgeois democracy to the limits of their development under the given conditions.

The expansion of free public education through the introduction of the kindergarten and the state universities; the development of progressive education; the building of free public libraries; settlement houses; extending the franchise; women's suffrage; prison reform; the renewal of realistic literature; the liberal revision of American history; the creation of pragmatism—these were accomplishments of the leading figures of Progressivism.

Dewey belongs wholly to this movement. He was a foremost participant in many of its most important enterprises. In time he became the supreme and unchallenged theoretical head of the movement. Dewey was not a leader of its plebeian legions like Weaver or La Follette. He was rather the leader of the advanced intellectuals, those who worked out the theoretical premises and formulated the views and values corresponding to the mass movement in their various spheres of professional activity. Dewey performed for the philosophy of Progressivism a service similar to that performed by Henry George and Veblen for its economics, Beard for its history, Parrington for its literary criticism, Holmes and Brandeis for its jurisprudence, Sandburg for its poetry, Charles Edward Russell and Lincoln Steffens for its journalism.

Dewey has been acclaimed as the spokesman for the "American spirit" in philosophy. There is a measure of truth in this judgment—provided it is clearly understood what part of America he spoke for and what period of our national development his ideas mirrored. Dewey certainly did not express the outlook of America's richest families with their conspicuous waste, incorrigible conservatism, and imperialist policies, their authoritarian and conformist spirit in culture. On the other hand, he explicitly and accurately disavowed identification with the industrial proletariat as a specific class.

Where, then, did Dewey stand? Viewed from the correct class angle, Dewey's entire life and thought forms a consistent whole. Indeed, it is one of Dewey's qualities that, by the act of disclaiming any class allegiance for himself or his philosophy, he expressed the formless outlook of his own social group—the intermediate classes who are not sure either from day to day or in the long run where they really stand and where they are going in capitalist society.

Dewey's philosophy was the theoretical expression of the outlook of the educated petty bourgeoisie in the epoch of the climb of American capitalism to world domination and the transformation of bourgeois democracy into imperialist reaction. This definition is the key to understanding the sociological essence of Dewey's thought, its historical function, and its class significance. It is likewise the source of its inadequacies and its ultimate frustration.

3

From Puritanism
to Pragmatism

Dewey was not a politician, although he took part in politics. He was a philosopher by inclination and profession, the most representative one America has yet produced. We have to examine what place he occupied in the evolution of philosophy, both in the United States and in the Western world. These two aspects are not necessarily identical. Because of the peculiar conditions of American development, a thinker may promote our national thought in certain respects even though his basic ideas have not caught up with the most advanced thinking elsewhere. And in fact that was the case with Dewey.

In the middle ages, philosophy was the handmaiden of theology. In early America it escaped bondage to Rome—and became instead the servant of the diverse denominations of Protestantism. It served that mistress in college and church for over two hundred years, until the scientific and secular interests of rising industrial capitalism released it from this indenture.

The first philosophers of colonial America were mostly clergymen of the Protestant sects, engaged in justifying the ways of God to man and refuting the arguments of atheists and the errors of those rationalists who were more responsive to the demands of the new age. At the same time the most influential clerical philosophers had to invoke more up-to-date arguments to support their special brand of theology. Jonathan Edwards, for instance, used the empirical argument that God must be known by a kind of sense experience in place of the old argument of

Puritan rationalism that He was known by "His ways and His works."

The colonial colleges were established as seminaries whose main purpose was to perfect their students' morals by rigid discipline and their minds by inculcation of classical learning. Philosophical instruction was entrusted to the president, himself usually a minister of the gospel, who rounded out the education of the undergraduates by giving an annual course to seniors in "mental and moral philosophy" consisting of the "evidences of revealed religion." This tradition lingered late into the nineteenth century, as illustrated by the letter of notification to William DeWitt Hyde when he was called from his pulpit in 1885 to assume the double duties of president and professor of mental and moral philosophy in the small New England college of Bowdoin: "It is necessary to combine the offices. The arrangement will give you access to the whole body of students for moral and religious influence."

The earliest efforts of American thought to escape from clerical bondage were associated with the rise of the rationalist criticism of religion and the spread of Deism in the eighteenth century, which helped prepare people's minds for the first American revolution. Some of the foremost leaders of the revolution were part of this Age of Enlightenment. They were non-churchgoers who adhered to that "natural" religion whose pillars were the Newtonian system, the writings of John Locke, and the teachings of the French rationalists. Their criticisms of official authorities in the religious realm, from the royalist Anglicans to the Calvinist theocrats of New England, trained them for contests with the civil authorities of the established order. The philosophic outlook of these rebels was inseparable from their politics. Ethan Allen, Tom Paine, Jefferson, Franklin, and even Washington turned away from orthodox systems of faith as well as against the authority of the British Crown. Moreover, the divine right of kings and the fusion of church and state had to be directly challenged by the revolutionary movement for independence.

The republican Tom Paine even turned that doctrine upside-down by ascribing devilish origins to monarchy. "In the early ages of the world, according to scripture, there were no kings," he told the colonists in *Common Sense*. "Government by kings was first introduced into the world by heathens, from whom the children of Israel copied the custom. It was the most prosperous invention the devil ever set on foot for the promotion of idolatry."

The most iconoclastic forms of this rationalism inclined toward materialism, while Deism shaded into pantheism and even atheism. But such extreme tendencies were not yet strong and influential; they were to gather strength through the following century.

Nowadays, most academicians think it proper that philosophy and politics should be total strangers; the pragmatic bourgeois politicians have no use for philosophizing. Yet during the revolutionary period philosophic thought and political activity were intimate companions in the task of social regeneration.

In America the philosophy of the oncoming revolutionary generation was not presented so systematically as it was among the French Encyclopedists. That was not because the heads of the movement did not think deeply and correctly, but rather because for them the idea was not divided from the deed or opposed to it. The French men of letters *prepared* a revolution; the American thinkers *participated* in theirs. They were not philosophers but mainly men of action: orators, statesmen, soldiers, inventors, merchants, organizers, and managers of great enterprises in diverse fields. They were many-sided personalities whose thought emanated directly from pressing social problems and was applied in action to solve the crucial issues of their time.

"Never in America were philosophical thinking and social action more closely joined. . . . Never was history made more consciously and conscientiously," observes Herbert W. Schneider (*A History of American Philosophy*, p. 35). Never before or since, it might be added, was philosophy nearer to the major concerns of the American masses. It is a sign of the degeneration, not elevation, of philosophy that it has today become so estranged from the American people. This is the very opposite of the role it played in the enlightened era of the first American revolution.

The next big push in philosophy was inspired by the ferment of new ideas among the more progressive thinkers in the Northern states in the decades before the Civil War. This movement was extremely heterogeneous, amorphous, and ideologically confused, but it was unmistakably both radical in temper and petty-bourgeois in its social content, advocating reforms in many fields from religion to the economy.

The headquarters of this movement was in New England. There it found expression in philosophy through Emerson and Alcott's Transcendentalism; in religion through Channing and Parker's Unitarianism and various brands of Perfectionism; and in sweeping proposals for social reconstruction such as Fourierism, anarchism, and abolitionism.

Transcendentalism had one of its theoretical starting points in Kant. He had split reality into two absolutely opposed domains: the noumenal, which was accessible only to the practical reason or faith, and the phenomenal, which the senses and theory dealt with. But its actual historical starting point was the frustration felt by the forward-looking middle-class and plebeian elements of the North in the years of political reaction before the Civil War. The writers and preachers who shared their moods were repelled by the ugly features of the slaveholder-capitalist regime but could see no practical way of throwing off its domination.

Whereas the patriot ideologues of the preceding century relied upon enlightened reason, looked outward, and came to grips directly with the hostile authorities around and above them, the Transcendentalists turned inward upon themselves and away from their social environment for illumination. They relied upon intuition rather than reason to reach the spiritual reality, or Oversoul, hidden behind the veil of appearances. The substance of the ideal realm they sought lay in the cherished values denied them by the crassness of a bourgeois society stained with the crimes of the slave power.

They turned against the empiricism and sensationalism of their patriot forefathers because they believed it had become degraded into an apology for slothful ease and a license for skepticism. The Transcendentalists wielded their conceptions of absolute truth, absolute justice, absolute good, which were presumably derived from direct communion with God and nature, as weapons against acquiescence in the status quo. They despised the expediencies of the careerists and asserted the power of the individual spirit to defy the gross reality around them.

In the words of Walter G. Meulder and Laurence Sears, "The Transcendentalists thought of themselves as revolutionists; they set out to make all things new. There is not a significant figure among them who was not at one time or another involved in subversive activities. Samuel May was mobbed five times within one month for preaching abolition. Thoreau went to prison rather than pay a tax to the state which countenanced slavery, and followed this protest with his *Duty of Civil Disobedience.* Parker was indicted for obstructing the Fugitive Slave Law, which he had most certainly done. Alcott hid a Negro who passed through Concord on the underground railway. Even the aloof Emerson went home with a copy of the Fugitive Slave Law in his pocket to sit down before his *Journal* and write: 'I will not obey it, by God' " (*The Development of American Philosophy*, p. 113).

The social surroundings against which the Transcendentalists recoiled were graphically depicted by Theodore Parker in a review of Emerson's writings published in the March 1850 *Massachusetts Quarterly Review*:

> You see the author lives in a land with free institutions, with town-meetings and ballot-boxes; in the vicinity of a decaying church; amongst men whose terrible devils are Poverty and Social Neglect, the only devils whose damnation is much cared for. . . . He does not worship the idols of our time, Wealth and Respectability, the two calves set up by our modern Jeroboam. He fears not the damnation those idols have the power to inflict—neither poverty nor social disgrace. . . . [He is against] commercial Boston, where honor is weighted in the public scales, and justice reckoned by the dollars it brings; conservative Boston, the grave of the Revolution, wallowing in its wealth, yet grovelling for more; seeking only money, careless of justice, stuffed with cotton yet hungry with tariffs, sick with the worm of avarice, loving money as the end of life, and bigots as the means of preserving it; Boston, with toryism in the parlors, toryism in its pulpits, toryism in its press, itself a tory town, preferring the accidents of man to man himself.

Against such reactionary material interests Parker posed "the human dream of the transcendental philosophy." He declared in *The World of Matter and the Spirit of Man*: "It looks to a future, a future to be made; a church whose creed is truth, whose worship love; a society full of industry and abundance, full of wisdom, virtue, and the poetry of life; a state with unity among all, with freedom for each; a church without tyranny; a society without ignorance, want, or crime; a state without oppression; yes, a world with no war among the nations to consume the work of their hands, and no restrictive policy to hinder the welfare of mankind."

The radical tendencies of the movements associated with Transcendentalism were certified by the hostility they aroused among the protectors of the established order. The alarmed orthodox churches united with the colleges to scotch these heretics and reformers. They pronounced as damnable to the soul all those doctrines which preached salvation through the inspiration of nature, individual reason, or personal intuition rather than through the Bible and established churches. No less dangerous was the agitation for women's rights, for extension of the vote, and against slavery, which leaned for support upon these heresies. Thinkers like Emerson and Thoreau, as well as militant ministers like Theodore Parker, were anathematized from the pulpit, press, and professorial chair and excluded from the seats of the mighty.

These unorthodox thinkers of the 1830s, 40s, and 50s helped detach philosophy from domination by the churches, cleared a path for its independent development in league with the sciences, and educated the ideological vanguard of the Northern forces who overthrew the slavocracy in the second revolution. But this historic victory had an ironic outcome. It converted many of the former radicals to respectability, since not a few of the heresies of pre–Civil War days became accepted doctrines after the war.

The grip of clerical control upon the colleges and the philosophy taught there was finally loosened and broken after the Civil War when the natural sciences were introduced into the curriculum in response to the "practical, progressive, and materialistic" demands of the time, and the leading colleges began to be transformed into universities on the European model. The turning point can be marked with accuracy as 1869, when the former professor of chemistry, twenty-nine-year-old Charles Eliot, was installed as the first nonclerical president of Harvard.

Since that date theologians have been ousted from their position of dominance in all the more enlightened centers of learning, although in 1907, 509 out of 700 colleges in this country were still under denominational control. Such phrases could be found in their catalogs as: "The biology taught at X University has no sympathy with that evolutionary theory that makes man the offspring of the animal," or: "The history of education is traced from its origin in the Garden of Eden."

Although the tradition which entrusted philosophy with inculcating religious dogma and an edifying ethic was expelled in its cruder forms from most university departments around the turn of the century, it showed strong capacities for survival and kept reappearing in more sophisticated and erudite guises. Josiah Royce of Harvard, for example, exerted his ingenuity to bolster the tattered beliefs of Calvinism. William James called upon the resources of his psychological theory to save hopes in the existence of a personal god and an afterlife. The reassuring homilies of such eminent scientists as Millikan and Compton displayed the same zeal for defending the collapsing faith in religion and in the structure of society that animated Jonathan Edwards. And even John Dewey succumbed to the pull of this tradition in his lectures expounding the value of "A Common Faith."

While in his personal life and teaching Eliot carried on the ethical traditions of Puritanism in the service of the upper classes, he had been trained as a chemist and elected by proponents of educational reform. Impressed by the methods of professional schooling, productive scholarship, and scientific research in the great German universities, he set about to reshape Harvard into a university which would equal Göttingen, Berlin, Oxford, or Cambridge. Before the turn of the century he had gathered at Harvard the gifted group of men whose work has been largely synonymous with philosophy in America: George Herbert Palmer, Royce, James, Peirce, Santayana.

Eliot's first administrative act was to shock the orthodox by inviting the young disciple of Herbert Spencer, John Fiske, to give lectures on his Positive Philosophy, which were later incorporated into his *Outlines of Cosmic Philosophy*. The report of his lectures gave the watchdogs of the faith an occasion to howl against "Harvard's raid on religion." But the unperturbed Eliot answered their outcries by asking Fiske to repeat the course the following year and to add another course on evolutionary thought.

Fiske's lectures were part of a series which formed the first course of postgraduate instruction in metaphysical topics at Harvard—an indication of the state of philosophical instruction at the most advanced center of higher learning. Emerson and Charles Peirce, the initiator of pragmatism, were among the other lecturers in the course, which lasted through the winter of 1869 and was regularly attended by three students.

The conflict between the old religious-classical and new secular-scientific trends was brought to a head with the establishment of Johns Hopkins University in 1876 as a society of scientists and scholars dedicated to the advancement of knowledge. This purely postgraduate institution signalized the emancipation of the university from the church's direct control and influence. Johns Hopkins opened its doors without benefit of clergy, inviting that arch-agnostic Thomas Henry Huxley to deliver the inaugural address. Dewey completed his doctoral studies at this institution in 1884 with a dissertation on Kant's psychology.

Until the 1880s the teachers of philosophy were not only all men but clergymen. "The supposed requirements of religion, or theology, dominated the teaching of philosophy in most colleges," Dewey recalled ("From Absolutism to Experimentalism," in *Contemporary American Philosophy*, vol. 2, p. 15).

The development of philosophy from that time forward was bound up with the expansion of the universities. The multiplication of colleges throughout the country, the growth of graduate schools, and the decay of traditional Protestantism made the teaching of philosophy attractive. Most of the leading thinkers of pre–Civil War days had been outcasts from the clerical, academic, and legal professions; they had to earn their livings through literature and lecturing (like Emerson and Phillips) or manual labor (like Thoreau).

Now, teaching philosophy offered a reputable and secure, if not lucrative, life work. The pursuit of philosophy became increasingly professionalized, specialized, institutionalized. The departments of philosophy at the larger Eastern universities—Harvard, Johns Hopkins, Columbia, Cornell, and later Chicago—were production centers and employment bureaus of instructors in philosophy to supply the demands from the rest of the collegiate community. By the end of the 1880s, Josiah Royce reported that opportunities for employment as teachers of philosophy were opening on all sides; ambitious students came to Harvard from all parts of the country to prepare themselves for such a career.

Schools of philosophy proliferated, along with magazines devoted to the more technical questions of the discipline. At Columbia in the sixties one man had taught moral and mental philosophy, English literature, history, political economy, and logic! By 1890 Columbia had opened its graduate school of philosophy, where Dewey was later to preside. In 1892 the Sage School of Philosophy was founded at Cornell with eight teachers, a journal, and both graduate and undergraduate courses in the history of philosophy, philosophical theory, ethics, psychology, and pedagogy. Josiah Royce pointed to this school as a monument to the unconquerable idealism of the time—although it owed existence to the benefactions of a tight-fisted banker and rascally manipulator of railroad stocks, Russell Sage. What other concerns were at work beside an impartial pursuit of the truth could be detected from Royce's further statement that "the academic study of philosophy is preparing the way for a needed spiritual guidance in the religious crisis which is rapidly becoming so serious."

In this way philosophy began to oust theology from the faculties and take over some of its functions. Doctors of Philosophy replaced Doctors of Divinity who were shoved off into separate seminaries. The first collection on *Contemporary American Philosophy* was published in 1930. Many of its contributors, then over forty years old and products of these schools, were sons of clergymen swayed from following in their fathers' footsteps. The academic career provided them with all that the ministry could, plus freedom to search for some truth. They found it better to retail the wisdom of the sages to undergraduates than citations from the Bible to stuffy congregations.

The breaking up of the old orthodoxies led to a diversity of ideas. The era of free competition in the economy was matched by equally free trade in the field of philosophy. At liberal Harvard, heterodoxy was countenanced and even encouraged. The more variegated their philosophies, the higher was the faculty graded. As Santayana remarked: "I believe the authorities would have been well pleased, for the sake of completeness, to have added a Buddhist, a Moslem, and a Catholic scholastic to the philosophical faculty, if only suitable sages could have been found, house-trained, as it were, and able to keep pace with the academic machine and to attract a sufficient number of pupils" (*Character and Opinion in the United States*, pp. 58–59).

Heterodoxy was not frowned upon by the authorities only so long as it was confined to the expression of individual opinion in abstract matters and sought no practical outlet other than slightly eccentric behavior. However, permissiveness had its limits. Two brands of heresy remained suspect: social-economic radicalism and moral misbehavior, which might corrupt the future leaders of society. President Eliot refused to allow Peirce to lecture to the Harvard students on account of his marital irregularity; James and Royce had to hire a hall for their students to hear him.

Horace Kallen recalled the following story about his successor, President Lowell: "An overseer had suggested the appointment of a somewhat notorious liberal to Harvard in the Department of Philosophy; and Lowell said to him, 'You know at Harvard we have academic freedom, and we have to be very careful whom we appoint'" (*Dialogue on George Santayana,* p. 87).

As the sciences shouldered religion aside, the scope of philosophy was broadened to cover a consideration of scientific method. At the same time, the professionalization of philosophy led to its differentiation into separate subjects for purposes of instruction and research. In imitation of their fellow scholars, academic philosophers sought a private province which they, as specialists, could cultivate as their own. They found this in the so-called problem of knowledge inherited from the dualism of Descartes and reinforced by the critical philosophy of Kant.

The problem was this: How can a supposedly detached mind know the world beyond it? The correct solution of the riddle had already been given for idealism by Hegel and for materialism by Marx. But their answers were either unknown or unacceptable to most American professors, who kept proclaiming that here was a puzzle yet to be solved. Like certain behaviorist psychologists who devised experiments for the express purpose of proving that purpose played no part in human life, these tireless epistemologists shuttled from the mind to the world and from the world back to the mind, to uncover what, if any, were the connections between them. The answers they came up with determined whether they should be classed among the realists, the idealists, the positivists, or the pragmatists.

As Morris Cohen remarked, one important reason for this game of intellectual blind man's buff was professional. The academic philosophers needed a specialty of their own to mark them off from other departments of the university. But there were other motives at work in this fussing with epistemological puzzles. These philosophers could not arrive at any clear and conclusive settlement of the problem of the relations between mind, society, and nature without undermining their own reasons for existence.

Finally, this divorce between mind and the external world was a symptom and outgrowth of the widening gap between philosophy and the realities of American life. By withdrawing to the cloistered campuses and remaining shut up there, philosophy became insulated from the most active sections of society. It turned inward upon itself, rather than outward toward the arena of conflicting social forces. It became pedantic and genteel, shrinking from controversy over living issues. It became obsessed with the traditional difficulties of its own past and fussed over its special techniques, slighting the great social and scientific questions of the time. As the sciences undermined the old theology, philosophy came to fill a cultural need of the educated upper classes as a minor and pallid substitute for religion, though it had little effect upon the main currents of American life.

This was the sort of intellectual environment Dewey stepped into when he decided to make the teaching of philosophy his life work after his apprenticeship at Johns Hopkins. Such was the professional atmosphere in which he had to operate at Michigan, Chicago, and Columbia. He was one of the first Americans to prepare himself for an academic career as a philosopher, and from the beginning to the end of this career it was primarily to an audience of professional philosophers that he directed his arguments. He tried to influence them; they in turn, like his colleagues on the faculty at Columbia, influenced him. He never cut the cord that bound him to this guild. He talked their language and felt at home in their presence.

But that was no more than one facet of this many-sided man. If his intellectual interests were centered on academic philosophy, they radiated widely into other fields. Once he reached maturity as a thinker, he did not permit himself to be cabined in so restrictive a milieu but reached out beyond it, both in his ideas and in his activities.

His first outward step was taken in the field nearest at hand, education. Pedagogy had been considered one of the domains of the philosopher; Dewey radically changed its methods and outlook. One of his conditions for taking charge of the philosophy department at the University of Chicago was that it should include education. There he proceeded to test, in the laboratory school he and his wife initiated, the pragmatic principle that knowing comes from doing.

He did not stop there. The momentum of his directing ideas drew him into the social and political struggles of his era. The dynamic of his pragmatic philosophy demanded that he carry into practice the theories he advocated. He did not shrink from shouldering these obligations. Public-spirited and conscientious, he directly participated in many enterprises connected with the Progressive cause. He gave an example in this respect to his fellow Americans and above all to his fellow intellectuals.

Dewey took the lead in organizing educators at all levels of the teaching profession and sought to bring these brain workers into the same movement with blue-collar workers. He urged teachers to abandon academic snobbery and recognize that they belonged to the great mass of working men and women with whom they should cooperate in their common interest. He became a charter member and vice-president of the New York Teachers Union and recommended its affiliation with the American Federation of Labor. He was the first president of the American Association of University Professors.

He was no less energetic in defending democratic rights and resisting reactionary attacks on freedom of expression in intellectual life. For many years he served on the National Committee of the American Civil Liberties Union; and, after wartime interference with academic freedom at Columbia by President Butler, he helped found the New School for Social Research in 1919 as a center for uninhibited adult higher education.

In 1937, when he was close to eighty, he undertook the responsibility of becoming chairman of the Commission of Inquiry into the Moscow Trials and was active in all its proceedings. Like his English counterpart, Bertrand Russell, he could be depended upon to his dying day to aid any cause in defense of democratic rights

For a long time Dewey headed the left wing of academic philosophy, the one that was most closely linked with the more progressive elements and causes in American life. He towered far above his fellow philosophers, not only in influence, but in moral stature. His interests expanded as theirs contracted.

But Dewey's activism with its radical twist was exceptional among the philosophers of his generation. Most of them hid from the turmoil of their time under the cover of absorption in loftier things. As the number of professional philosophers grew, their social influence diminished; it became less than that of the departments of physical science or, later, of the schools of business administration. Aloof from the masses and immured in their university cells, they transformed philosophy into a new type of scholasticism accessible only to initiates.

Although Dewey combatted this tendency throughout his lifetime, he could not counteract the fundamental demands of capitalist society. What the ruling class expected from its professors was not philosophies to justify broad reforms, let alone revolutionary changes; they welcomed doctrines of a more sedative character. From World War I on, as imperialism grew more entrenched and aggressive, not only outside but inside the universities, and as class relations became tenser, the administrators could not permit even that degree of diversity in the philosophical faculties that Harvard boasted of in the time of William James. A gray and dull uniformity settled over a field in which professors now mulled over stereotyped and sterilized ideas.

It was in the full flush of capitalist progress around the turn of the century that Dewey came forward as the bearer of a new method of thought that was to regenerate philosophy by bringing it abreast of modern thought and the demands of practical life. Deweyism represented the third great effort by radical bourgeois ideologists to throw off the shackles of the past, take into account newly acquired knowledge, and keep in step with the changes of American society. The first was the Deism and rationalism of the late eighteenth century; the second was the Transcendentalism which nourished the radicalisms of the decades before the Civil War. Although neither contributed much that was essentially new to Western thought as a whole, both invigorated American thought and saved it from stagnation.

There was a decisive difference, however, in the historical circumstances surrounding pragmatism and the first two trends of thought—and in their ultimate results. The earlier schools were expressions of social forces which went forward to engage in revolutionary battles leading to the political and social reconstruction of American life. Pragmatism was the philosophy of a middle-class movement which aspired to similar aims but failed to attain them. The first two were swept to victory on the flood tides of bourgeois-democratic revolution in the War of Independence and the Civil War. Pragmatism was to be sucked under by the ebb tide of capitalist reaction as the twentieth century unfolded.

4

Ideological Sources
of Dewey's Thought

Having situated Dewey in the sequence of American philosophy, we must note his proximate connections with the trends of thought of the Western world as a whole. His instrumentalism was compounded—in unequal measures—of empiricism, Hegelianism, positivism, and Darwinism.

Pragmatism and Empiricism

Pragmatism is, in its ideological genealogy, a belated and updated offshoot of the empirical school which has been the predominant philosophy among English-speaking peoples for over three centuries. Empiricism, pragmatism, and instrumentalism (or "operationalism," its variant in the methodology of natural science) represent consecutive phases in the evolution of the same broad tendency. Empiricism is the plasma from which pragmatism sprang, while Dewey's instrumentalism is the consummate expression of the pragmatic ideology.

Dewey explicitly affirmed this kinship. "We must not forget," he wrote, ". . . that James was an empiricist before he was a pragmatist, and repeatedly stated that pragmatism is merely empiricism pushed to its legitimate conclusions" (*Philosophy and Civilization,* p. 22).

The founders of American pragmatism did recast the positions of the classical British empiricists from Locke to Mill to suit the different conditions, needs, and outlook of the progressive middle-class citizens of their time and place. In addition to taking a new name for their doctrine, they discarded some of the outmoded and inadequate features of traditional empiricism and introduced others called for by the scientific advances of the nineteenth century.

They most extensively remodeled the epistemology at the core of empiricism. Coming after Darwin, they were imbued with an evolutionary viewpoint. They abandoned the mechanistic theory of knowledge taught by Locke and his disciples—in which impressions were made on a passive mind through the senses—and worked out a genetic-evolutionary theory which sought to show how human intelligence had grown out of animal activities and ultimately flowered into scientific thought. They stressed the practical service that ideas performed. The mind did not mirror reality but played a reconstructive role in the activities that made up experience. The origin and essence of intelligence was its usefulness in animal behavior, extending into human conduct.

In contrast to the mistaken premise of the British empiricists that sense data were disconnected from one another, the theory of perception presented by James and Dewey held that immediate sense experience contained both connections and disjunctions.

Whereas Locke had inquired into the degree of the determination of sensations and concepts by natural causes, the pragmatists turned in a different direction. They looked upon ideas as primarily purposive and prospective. Concepts do not reflect, or reproduce in special form, objective realities. They are habits of belief which provide the basis for future action and thus further the realization of human aims.

The pragmatists defined truth and error not as correspondence or lack of it with independent and prior material conditions, but as a quality which was acquired by ideas solely through their application in practice.

Dewey went the furthest in breaking with empirical epistemology by denying the cardinal proposition that sensation was the source and foundation of our cognition of the external world. For him sensations are not the most elementary form of knowledge. They are merely "natural events," which may stimulate human actions and responses but do not in themselves convey any knowledge of other things. He rejected as "outmoded" the postulate of "sensationalistic empiricism" that "ideas are copies or compounds of sensation and hence are all lacking in original and productive significance" ("William James as Empiricist," in *In Commemoration of William James: 1842-1942,* p. 50).

Unlike the original empiricists who believed that human nature had been much the same through all ages, Dewey was aware of the decisive influence that changes in historical conditions have had in shaping and reshaping human beings. Above all, he was critical of the intractable individualism which permeated the whole of classical empiricism. He counterposed to it the "social" as the central category of human existence.

"Only by whole-hearted adoption of it [the category of the social] as a ranking fact and idea can empirical philosophy come into its own, and escape the impotency and one-sidedness which has dogged the traditional sensationalistic empiricism," he wrote in "The Inclusive Philosophic Idea" (*Philosophy and Civilization,* p. 92). "The commitment of Lockean empiricism to a doctrine that ignored the associative property of all things experienced is the source of that particularistic nominalism whose goal is solipsistic skepticism. In consequence, empiricism ceased to be empirical and became a dialectical construction of the implications of absolute particularism."

While the pragmatists modified empiricism in these and other respects, they did not transcend its inherent limitations but rather reaffirmed and reinforced them in their own way. For instance, they remained attached to the idea that knowledge hinges on the way things appear to the observer, who then chooses an action to fit the circumstances. This method discouraged systematic search for the underlying causes that produce the outward appearances of things.

The prime difference between the empiricists and the pragmatists is that the latter focused attention, not upon the way ideas are produced, but rather upon their functions and consequences. This change of emphasis was clearly discernible in the address delivered by William James at Berkeley in 1898, when he recast Peirce's formula for obtaining clear ideas in these words: "To attain perfect clearness in our thoughts of an object, then, we need only consider what *effects* of a conceivably *practical* kind the object may involve—what sensations we are to *expect* from it, and what reactions we must *prepare.* Our conception of these effects, then, is for us the whole of our conception of the object, so far as that conception has positive significance at all" ("Philosophical Conceptions and Practical Results," in *Collected Essays and Reviews,* p. 411; emphasis added).

The emphasized words indicate the pronounced shift of attention from causes to consequences, from material grounds to practical effects, from determined conditions to expectation, from correspondence of ideas with realities to preparation for action. These are distinctive marks of the pragmatic theory of knowledge.

The shift in orientation between the classical empiricists and the pragmatists in testing the nature and reality of ideas stands out in the contrast between the two following statements. The first is from Hume. "When we entertain, therefore, any suspicion that a philosophical term is employed without any meaning or idea (as is but too frequent), we need but enquire, *from what impression is that supposed idea derived?* And if it be impossible to assign any, this will serve to confirm our suspicion" (*Enquiries Concerning the Human Understanding*, p. 22; italics in original).

The second is from Dewey. Pragmatism, he wrote, is "an extension of historical empiricism with this fundamental difference, that it does not insist upon antecedent phenomena but upon consequent phenomena, not upon the precedents, but upon the possibilities of action . . ." ("The Development of American Pragmatism," in *Studies in the History of Ideas,* vol. 2, p. 365). The truth or meaning of an idea is not based upon what the idea comes out of but upon where it goes and what it helps to effect.

Dewey and Hegelianism

Dewey did not begin his philosophical career as an empiricist but as something quite different. Thanks to the influence of W. T. Harris, who introduced Hegel to America, and George S. Morris, his teacher and later colleague at Johns Hopkins and Michigan, Dewey was originally a Hegelian of the Anglo-American variety. One of the functions of this idealist school was to provide new sureties for crumbling religious faith. In a biographical sketch of her father, Jane Dewey says that such a motive inclined him toward that philosophy. "From the idealism of Hegel, as interpreted by Morris, he obtained in his late adolescence that fusion of emotions and intellect for which he had sought unsuccessfully in his boyhood religious experience" (*The Philosophy of John Dewey,* ed. by Paul Schilpp, p. 17).

There is nothing exceptional in the idealist views Dewey expressed during the 1880s and '90s. He makes psychology the central science because facts and events do not merely exist but are all known. Phenomena are the result of the objectifying and

universalizing activities of the intellect and will. The individual
and the universe are united, not by material bonds, but through
"the will, the unity of psychic life." In the last analysis, "God is
the only Reality." Although Dewey shed this unabashed and
unalloyed idealism, he acknowledged late in life that acquaintance with Hegel left a permanent deposit in his thinking. This
could be seen in the amendments he made to the traditional
empiricism.

After the corrosive skeptical conclusions of Hume, British
empiricism had grown more and more dualistic, splitting the
objective from the subjective and action from thought. Dewey
sought to restore their organic unity, having learned from Hegel
that "reality is experienced and experience is reality."

Empiricism had looked upon reality as a completely given,
ready-made, fixed and final system. Hegel counterposed to this
static conception his notion of reality and life as a never-ending
process of growth. Dewey took over from him this dynamic
conception of reality as continuous development.

The logic of empiricism, especially as presented by John Stuart
Mill and Rudolf Lotze, had become more and more abstract,
separating thought from its subject matter and divorcing logic
from living reality. Although Dewey did not cling to Hegel's logic,
he recognized the need for a more concrete logic of practice which
would do justice to "the living fullness of reality" and unify the
practical with the logical.

Many of Dewey's disciples, who use Hegel as a whipping boy to
discredit dialectical logic, would be surprised at how much of
what they consider distinctive in Dewey's thought is little more
than a restatement and modification—and often a dilution and
distortion—of Hegelian notions.

Dewey made his way from absolute idealism to pragmatism
through a complicated process of intellectual conversion. These
two opposing trends of thought wrestled with each other for quite
a while in his mind during the 1880s and '90s before pragmatism
conquered. The turning point came with the publication of
Studies in Logical Theory in 1903.

Dewey's transformation from an absolute idealist into the
leader of American pragmatism illustrates in striking fashion
how social conditions and class needs operate to reshape ideas in
the minds of philosophers and can impart a new direction to
development in this highest and most abstract field of thought.
The evolution of Dewey's philosophical views is thus instructive

apart from the validity of the doctrines themselves.

Why did Dewey depart from his original idealism? (It is not the successive steps but rather the reasons for the transit that are of interest here.) Absolute idealism glossed over those characteristics of the social environment that were of utmost importance to the dissident Progressives, and it therefore provided an inadequate guide for their effective intervention in practical affairs.

Dewey attributed part of his disillusionment with idealism to the influence of his friend Benjamin Ford, a writer on the financial paper *Bradstreet's,* who discovered by personal experience that "the social structure," which was dominated by capitalist interests, "prevented freedom of inquiry." Idealism taught that the world was free. Yet it was so only in idea, i.e., in the imagination of the idealist philosopher. In reality, society was enslaved; it had to be *made* free. How could this be done? Only through practical activity.

This same discovery was being impressed in more concrete ways upon many other minds by the social struggles of the time. The promised freedoms had not been secured; they still had to be won. American society must be changed to obtain more freedom for the masses of the people.

Thus Dewey, as a sensitive indicator of the outlook of the liberal middle class, had to shift his theoretical base. Had he not done so, he might have remained merely an obscure professor of philosophy. But he did alter his basic views—and in line with the changing needs of the Progressive movement. What were these needs?

The liberal and radical petty bourgeoisie needed both an *activist* philosophy and a *gradualist* one, which fortified neither conservatism nor revolution but justified reforms and progressive change. It wanted a *hopeful* philosophy based upon the conviction that the future could be made better than the past or present. It preferred a *middle-of-the-road* philosophy, an eclectic body of ideas, neither purely idealist nor sharply materialist, yet borrowing from both.

One way in which Dewey set about to fill this collective demand was to revise his Hegelian conceptions. Here are two examples. In 1890 Dewey wrote: "There is but one world, the world of knowledge, not two; an inner and an outer, a world of observation and a world of conception; and this one world is everywhere logical" (*The Philosophy of John Dewey,* p. 74). This is pure idealist doctrine.

In passing over to pragmatism, Dewey retained this one-world conception but reinterpreted it. The world was no longer a world of *knowledge* which is "everywhere logical." It became a world of *experience* in which humans are everywhere active and practical. In this transformation Dewey did not entirely let go of his former idealism because he makes a distinction between nature and mind *within* this one world of experience, which practical bodily behavior unifies and modifies.

Materialism, too, holds that there is only one world, a world of matter in motion. But this objective world does not depend for its existence upon human experience nor is it embraced within experience. On the contrary, the world gives birth to experience at a certain stage in the evolution of life and under certain historical conditions. This independently existing, external material world is subjected to understanding and intelligent modification by human action only with the growth of society.

Even more illuminating is the shift of emphasis in Dewey's thought on what the fundamental characteristics of reality are. The idealists taught that the world was really an organic unity and a harmonious whole, whatever appearances indicated to the contrary, and that it was rational and certain in its operations. Dewey now came to single out fluidity, uncertainty, precariousness as the decisive traits of experience. These give rise to tensions and conflicts which call for adjustment. It becomes the function of thought to understand, and of intelligent action to resolve, these troubled situations.

In this philosophical evolution we can detect an accurate reflection of the "troubled situation" of the middle classes. The proposed method of solution accords with their needs and outlook. For, according to Dewey, these tensions and conflicts are rationally adjustable within a common framework, just as the differences between the plutocracy and the petty-bourgeois dissenters are reconcilable.

Dewey adapted whatever he found useful in Hegelianism to the positions of pragmatism, to the new findings of biology and psychology, and to the requirements of the American Progressives—and then completely turned his back on it. During the First World War he went so far as to write a chauvinist-tainted polemic on "German Philosophy and Politics" (which he allowed to be reprinted during the Second World War) where he implied that Hegel was to some measure responsible for Kaiserism, just as others later blamed him for Hitlerism.

In his *Logic,* published in 1938, Dewey does not even mention this eminent logician. Nevertheless, residues of Hegel remained in his philosophy and he continued to hold the German thinker in high esteem. Late in life Dewey declared: "Were it possible for me to be a devotee of any system, I still should believe that there is a greater richness and greater variety of insight in Hegel than in any other single systematic philosopher" except Plato ("From Absolutism to Experimentalism," in *Contemporary American Philosophy,* vol. 2, p. 21).

It would be hard to picture any other pragmatist making such a statement. Indeed, the "block universe" he attributed to Hegel was James's *bête noir.*

Positivism and Pragmatism

Still another offshoot of empiricism, positivism, inserted itself as a link between the classical empiricists and the pragmatists.

Positivism started from Hume's denial to causation of any direct experience, objective existence, and rational validity, and from Kant's denial that knowledge of "things in themselves" was possible. It limited knowledge to immediate impressions and direct observations of phenomena, that is, to the surface and foreground of things. It repudiated attempts to penetrate beyond phenomena and arrive at the hidden connections, the underlying motive forces, the real causes.

Positivism placed in doubt the independent existence of the external world; though this might be assumed, it could not be demonstrated by reasonable proofs. The instinctive human belief in material objects and causation which led to materialism were dismissed as "metaphysical prejudices."

Thus the aims of knowledge and science were altered. To a positivist, these do not and cannot disclose the real interconnections of events and the essential nature of things. Such a task is beyond human capacities, a relic of theological and metaphysical thought. Knowledge can do no more than note, classify, arrange, and summarize the coexistence and sequence of phenomena. This suffices to guide human conduct and get along in the world.

Two different currents of positivist thought emerged in the nineteenth century. One was French in origin, stemming from Auguste Comte and oriented toward social reform. The other was English, passing through John Stuart Mill and developed by Herbert Spencer in a spirit of extreme bourgeois individualism.

Spencer was a thoroughgoing agnostic who asserted that we can know nothing of either matter or mind in themselves and therefore materialism and idealism are equally untenable.

Later in the century a school of positivism primarily concerned with methodological problems of physical science, represented by Ostwald, Mach, Pearson, Poincaré, Duhem, Avenarius, and others, came to the fore. Basing themselves upon a theory of "pure experience," these empiriocritics maintained that scientific investigation cannot and need not disclose the real features of the external world. It can only register, classify, and correlate the sequence of observed phenomena. Scientific theories are no more than "working hypotheses," more or less convenient and practically effective contrivances for dealing with the materials given by sensation. They knocked causation, determinism, and any objective basis for lawfulness out of existence.

At one extreme this line of thought culminated in the pure "fictionalism" of Vaihinger which regarded scientific conceptions as arbitrarily chosen formulas which by some mysterious means enabled people to handle phenomena effectively in practice.

Ernst Mach was the most influential member of this scientific-positivist trend of thought. While his criticism of certain absolute concepts of the Newtonian world view helped convince theoreticians of physics like Einstein of the relativity of physical phenomena, his philosophical standpoint was retrogressive.

Here is the most flagrant example of how the prejudices of empiriocriticism ran counter to the advance of science and misinterpreted reality. Mach, like Ostwald, contended that the atom—and even the molecule—was nothing but a useful fiction, a conceptual working model for the theoretical physicist; atoms did not actually exist in the world outside. Although this deduction was consistent with his positivist theory of science, it turned out to be untrue. The people of Hiroshima can hardly be convinced that the atom is nothing but a mental construction.

The positivists and pragmatists were associated in a joint enterprise. Many of the pet ideas of the positivists were incorporated into pragmatic theory. James acknowledged his debt to Mach and Poincaré; Dewey to Comte, Spencer, and others. Later, in *The Quest for Certainty*, Dewey explicitly adopted Bridgman's up-to-date version of scientific positivism, which is labeled "operationalism."

The starting point in "pure experience"; the doubts about the independent material existence of the external world; the denial of causation, lawfulness, and determinism as intrinsic aspects of nature; the restriction of knowledge to experience of phenomena; the conception of ideas as nothing but working hypotheses which provide plans for action; the essentially practical purpose of knowing—these are common property of both schools. In addition, Dewey was inspired by Comte's efforts to substitute a religion of humanity for the old organized religions and by his insistence upon the social functions and obligations of the scientist and philosopher.

Positivism and pragmatism intersect with one another at so many points that it is sometimes difficult to draw a line between them. That is because they represent two varieties of an essentially identical philosophical position, reflecting different vocational interests of the same broad middle-class stratum in bourgeois society. From a common ideological starting point and social foundation, the positivists and pragmatists may branch off into different domains and take differing paths of development. But they are headed in the same direction and sooner or later clasp hands at their common destination.

The Influence of Darwinism

Dewey was born in 1859, the year Darwin published his *Origin of Species,* and he came to maturity when the evolutionary theory was conquering the scientific world. Dewey was deeply influenced by Darwinism and wrote a noteworthy book in 1910 on *The Influence of Darwin on Philosophy.*

Today the ideas of evolution are common property among educated people. But they do not all have the same conceptions of its meaning and application. The theory of evolution entered people's minds in the nineteenth century by two different routes and in two different forms. In the English-speaking world evolutionary conceptions were popularized through the teachings of Herbert Spencer, Darwin, and Huxley, who conformed to the native empirical traditions. On the European continent they were first introduced through the work of Hegel, then in the natural-scientific writings of men like Haeckel, and later in the materialist teachings of Marxism.

The ideas of evolution were propagated mainly in the first way in the United States. This was the form in which Dewey absorbed them—although, as we have shown, he blended them with borrowings from Hegel.

Even though thinkers bound to the empirical tradition may not recognize the fact, the dialectical definition of the evolutionary process contained in Hegel and Marx is far more correct and comprehensive and incomparably richer in content than that based upon Darwin's discoveries alone. But the very narrowness of Darwinism, plus its English origins, gave it an advantage in conquering American thought at this stage.

Darwin made the origin of new species dependent on the gradual accumulation of small variations. He minimized the importance of mutations and sudden jumps in the evolutionary process. One of his favorite sayings was: "nature makes no leaps." This strengthened the popular prejudice that gradual growth is the major, if not exclusive, mode of natural evolution. This misconception was easily extended by conservative minds to social evolution. Philosophers could use Darwin to justify the universality and—in the Fabian phrase—"the inevitability of gradualness."

They thereby identified the entire process of evolution with one of its phases: the period in which small changes are accumulated and in which gradual growth within established forms prevails. They were enabled to overlook, deny, and suppress the occurrence of sharp and sweeping changes, sudden interruptions in the continuity of things, the breakup of existing forms, and leaps from one qualitative state to an essentially new one. They could not see that continual modifications, at a certain point in their accumulation, however slow they may be and long they may take, suddenly produce qualitative discontinuities in the evolutionary process. This revolutionary side of the movement of things was formulated in Hegel's dialectical law of evolution that quantitative changes, piled up by slow and small degrees, become in the end qualitative transmutations—and that this transition proceeds by abrupt leaps and in no other way.

Everything from his personal disposition to the needs of his class induced Dewey to set aside the multi-faceted and sharp-edged definition of evolution put forward by Hegel in favor of the one-sided, rounded-off views inspired by Darwinism.

Dewey also took from Darwin the notion of adaptation and applied it to the function of the mind. "The biological point of view commits us to the conviction that mind . . . is at least an organ of service for the control of environment in relation to the ends of the life process," he wrote.

Darwin had pointed out how changes in surrounding conditions led to a selection of characteristics among animals and plants which enabled them to become better adapted to the new environment. Dewey extended this to cover humanity and its mental activities. Incessant changes in their situation compel human beings to readjust their actions and modify their ideas; this process of readjustment is the hallmark of experience, the source of progress, and the mainspring of mental functioning.

There is truth in this, though Dewey failed to carry it all the way through. For it logically follows that, if revolutionary changes in nature bring about equally revolutionary adjustments, or at least the need for them, then revolutionary changes in the economic basis of society would necessitate no less revolutionary adjustments in politics and ideology. But Dewey tended to restrict the process of adjustment in psychology and politics to the small change of gradual reforms.

This not only harmonized with the requirements of his social group, but also appeared to conform to the mainstream of American history. There had been revolutionary upheavals but these were in the past. Moreover, all the jumps in modern American history up to his time had taken place within bourgeois democracy. The significance of the profound historical and social disruption bound up with the destruction of Indian tribal collectivism and its replacement by a class-divided society was not understood; while the coming transition from class society to a new, technologically advanced communism was still below the horizon.

What the middle classes looked for was the modification of the existing setup, not its revolutionizing by violent class struggle. The doctrine of gradual readjustment was perfectly suited to these moods. Its reinforcement by Darwinism and justification by pragmatism lent assurance that they were in step with the latest word in both science and philosophy.

In Dewey's system Darwinism became a weapon against conservatism in thought and deed since it highlighted the readjustments required to respond to new needs and conditions. On the other hand, the piecemeal mode of such readjustment could serve as a defense against impatient radicalism based upon "unscientific" notions of overthrowing the foundations of the social structure.

5

Peirce, James,
and the Chicago School

There are two polar types of empiricism: idealistic empiricism (Berkeley, Mach) and naturalistic empiricism (Locke, Huxley). Like their predecessors, the pragmatists differed widely among themselves on many points of doctrine within the ambit of their common theory of knowledge. They speedily gave birth to divergent trends, one drifting toward undisguised idealism, individualism, and subjectivism, the other inclining toward a more materialist, collectivist, and objectivist interpretation. The Americans Charles Peirce and William James, the Englishman F. C. S. Schiller, and the Italian Papini belonged to the first camp; the Chicago school, Dewey, and his quasi-Marxist disciples like Sidney Hook to the second.

Charles Peirce

William James credited Charles Peirce with being the first to formulate the basic postulates of pragmatism and baptize it as a specific philosophical tendency. "The term is derived from the same Greek word *pragma,* meaning action, from which our words 'practice' and 'practical' come. It was first introduced into philosophy by Mr. Charles Peirce in 1878. In an article entitled 'How to Make Our Ideas Clear' . . . Mr. Peirce after pointing out that our beliefs are really rules for actions, said that, 'to develop a thought's meaning, we need only to determine what conduct it is fitted to produce: that conduct is for us its sole significance. . . . To attain perfect clearness in our thoughts of an object, then, we need only consider what conceivable effects of a practical kind the object may involve—what sensations we are to expect from it, and what reactions we must prepare. Our conception of these effects, whether immediate or remote, is then for us the whole of our conception of the object . . .'" (*Pragmatism*, pp. 46–47).

Peirce put forward two of the principal planks of pragmatism. He coupled beliefs and ideas with rules of conduct and identified the meaning of ideas with their conceivable practical consequences. These propositions were taken up and more fully developed by the pragmatic school.

Peirce himself pursued a different path. He was an acute and learned theoretician of logic. But his rationalistic and formalistic approach to logic and the conclusions he drew from it were fundamentally different from Dewey's. He wrote Dewey in 1905 that he was intolerant of the latter's logical theory and that its "mode of arguing that every inquiry ought to be conducted genetically is a wretched method" (*Pragmatic Philosophy*, ed. by Amelie Rorty, p. 118).

Moreover, Peirce was an absolute idealist who believed that the universe had passed from chaos to an intelligible and regular order by acquiring "habits of mind"; that matter was "effete mind"; that love or desire was the driving force of cosmic evolution which started with God, the creator, and ended with God completely revealed. His connection with the pragmatic movement, though significant at the beginning, was episodic and marginal.

William James

William James was the initiator and most ardent propagandist of pragmatism. He came to philosophy after studies in medicine, physiology, and psychology had convinced him of the biological origins of thought processes and the primarily practical, instrumental, and experimental function of ideas.

James asserted that pragmatism was "purely epistemological" and thereby compatible with any kind of theory about the nature of the universe. Just the same, his own philosophy was based upon a particular conception of reality as "pure experience."

Both materialist and idealist thinkers made a fundamental distinction between nature and humanity, matter and mind, the objective and subjective, the physical and spiritual aspects of existence. The pragmatists, beginning with James, sought to get around this dichotomy by asserting that the basic constituent of the universe is neither physical nor mental but something neutral. This is "pure experience," defined by James as "the immediate flux of life which furnishes the material to later reflection." This is the primal stuff out of which everything else is constructed. It exists before either matter or mind, which are subsequently extracted as separate functions of the raw materials of experience.

By thus placing the psychical on a par with the physical, James in effect wiped out the existential priority of the external world over the mind and the essential difference between the objective and subjective parts of experience. For him there was no external world before humankind experienced and thought about it. The world was and is created by humankind out of the plastic mass of "pure experience" which preceded all else.

This is an upside-down view of the relations between material reality and human experience. By making nature depend upon experience, and not experience upon nature, James dissolved the independent objective existence of the real world in the subjective reactions of humankind.

His theory of knowledge and interpretation of the truth flow from this. If experience preexists everything else, then the content of ideas need not copy external reality. Ideas are primarily plans of action which enable us to operate advantageously in relation to other things. They are means of orientation in the stream of pure experience which enable us to make the most of its currents.

True ideas are distinguished from false not by testing their conformity with what exists, but rather by conceiving what their effects would be and noting their consequences when they are acted upon. If an idea helps us get along successfully in the stream of experience, fulfills our needs, and satisfies our demands, then it is true, or rather it becomes true. "An idea is 'true' so long as to believe it is profitable to our lives."

This pragmatic version of the essence of ideas is bound up with a special version of the nature of human action. All activity is for James purely experimental in character, a gamble. We try out this idea or that, this line of conduct or that, and then see what happens. If it does the job, well and good; if it fails, we try something else until we hit on the right solution.

No idea possesses truth before it is validated in experience and confirmed by its results; it becomes true by virtue of our intervention in events. Truth is neither retrospective nor representative; it is exclusively bound up with the future. This is what endows all ideas with their hypothetical nature. When James and later Dewey sought to include the effects of the past in their definition of truth, this concession undermined their central argument.

For them ideas are made true by events—but since we can intervene and control the outcome of events, it is we who make ideas come true. Human action is the decisive determinant of things.

The pragmatists were extremely one-sided in hinging the truth or falsity of all ideas upon human action. However much our activities may modify things found in nature, they do not determine the nature of things in general. And the conscious intervention of people can redirect the course of social affairs only insofar as this intervention proceeds in obedience to historically given objective conditions—not in any arbitrary manner which runs counter to them.

In response to those critics who accused him of subjectivism, James protested that his theory of truth did take into account the relation of ideas to realities. For ideas to be workable, he stated, they must prove consistent with other ideas, conform to the existing facts, and submit to experimental corroboration.

This reach-out to objectivity was vitiated by the extra qualification he introduced that ideas must satisfy personal wants and desires and that the most satisfying in this respect were the most true. In practice—which is the supreme test of the meaning of ideas for the pragmatist—James assigned greater weight to the gratification of individual needs and even prejudices than to the totality of facts.

The significance of this amendment James proposed for ascertaining the truth stood out most nakedly in its application to the all-important problem of the origin and development of the universe. Thinkers have argued since the birth of philosophy over whether God or matter explained this cosmic process; idealists took one position, materialists the other. Taking advantage of his pragmatic conception of the truth, James held that both of these answers were hypothetical. Neither could find secure support in either factual evidence or the arguments of reason. Therefore the choice between the two had to be made on other grounds.

When such issues cannot be decided on an intellectual or factual basis, then "our passional nature" must take the preferable option and—since "faith in a fact can help create the fact"—make it come true, he wrote in *The Will to Believe* (p. 25).

In this case belief in God must be taken as true because it gives a fuller sum of satisfaction. It "guarantees an ideal order," whereas the materialist view denies that the moral order is eternal or unchangeable. James wrote: "Even if matter could do every outward thing that God does, the idea of it would not work as satisfactorily, because the chief call for a God on modern men's part is for a being who will inwardly recognize them and judge them sympathetically. Matter disappoints this craving of our ego, so God remains for most men the truer hypothesis, and indeed remains so for definite pragmatic reasons" (*The Meaning of Truth*, pp. 189-90). James's "predestined mission," according to R. B. Perry, was "to find a philosophic truth that should justify religion without alienating science" (*The Thought and Character of William James,* vol. 2, p. 409).

The pragmatic theory that ideas are nothing but working hypotheses and that truth is ultimately determined by the consequences of action served in James's philosophy as a springboard for his justification of religion. "We cannot reject any hypothesis if consequences useful to life flow from it. . . . If the hypothesis of God works satisfactorily in the widest sense of the word, it is true. . . ." And he found that mystical experiences afford proof that "higher powers exist and are at work to save the world on ideal lines similar to our own."

This enlightened professor plundered psychology and twisted philosophy to extort new "evidence" to bolster the shaken belief of the credulous middle classes in the existence of supernatural powers. At the same time that the Young Men's Christian Association and Christian Science came to flourish in the Boston area, the Harvard philosophical faculty boasted of a moralist who likewise exhorted young people to goodness and provided sophisticated arguments to salvage religious faith.

James became the most popular exponent of pragmatism not only because of the picturesque and flavorsome style of his writing but also because he sincerely shared and flattered the prejudices of his public. His whole cast of mind, his social outlook and political views, were relics of the outgrown America of the pioneer days, of unrestricted opportunity and free capitalist enterprise. His philosophy set out from the assumption of an abstract isolated human individual as the norm. He was as much of an individualist in his mode of thought as the average small farmer, businessman, craftsman, or professional. "He had a horror of 'bigness' as such, a distaste for all but the most local politics, a passionate hatred of imperialism," writes one of his biographers. "To the many small private struggles he was sympathetic and helpful, but toward large-scale issues and conflicts, with the exception of the fight against imperialism, he showed little philosophical concern."

"William James's *Principles of Psychology* was much the greatest single influence in changing the direction of Dewey's philosophical thinking," his daughter Jane wrote (Schilpp, *Philosophy of John Dewey,* p. 23). While this was so, Dewey moved away from the most subjectivist aspects of James's conception of truth as he developed his own instrumentalism.

While he agreed that ideas essentially refer to the future and are made true in the process of experimentation, Dewey denied that personal gratification can establish the validity of an idea, particularly where theological notions are concerned. What made an idea true, in his opinion, was not its fulfillment of moral or religious demands but rather "the advent of the object intended." This criterion brought Dewey closer to the standpoint that the content of an idea must match up with some objective reality, as opposed to James's identification of practical consequences with psychological satisfactions. Dewey eventually held that an idea is validated if it enables us to make the transit from a troubled or conflicting situation to a smooth-sailing one. Truth arises not from the gratification a belief provides, but from the effective resolution of a problematic situation.

However much Dewey owed to James, he had a different outlook in salient respects, ranging from his theory of knowledge to his social and political orientation.

Dewey and the Chicago School

Peirce and James launched pragmatism and contributed important elements to its formation; Dewey developed the line of thought as far as it could go and put its ideas into finished form. That is why this criticism of pragmatism concentrates upon his work.

Dewey came to pragmatism while teaching at the University of Chicago during the 1890s and the first four years of the twentieth century. There he was one of a group of professors with mutual interests and a shared direction of thought which they applied to various fields of the social sciences. This "Chicago school" included the sociologist Albion Small; J. H. Tufts, who wrote the textbook *Ethics* with Dewey; his fellow philosopher G. H. Mead; the ethnologist W. I. Thomas; the psychologist of religion E. V. Ames, and the economist Thorstein Veblen.

Impelled by the moods of Progressivism, these thinkers shifted the axis of their attention from the individual to institutions, from the personal to the collective, from psychology to sociology. A good example of their approach is given in Mead's conception of the social shaping of the individual. "The human animal as an individual could never have attained control over the environment. It is a control which has arisen through social organization. The very speech he uses, the very mechanism of thought which is given, are social products. His own self is attained only through his taking the attitude of the social group to which he belongs. He must become socialized to become himself" (*Movements of Thought in the Nineteenth Century*, p. 168).

The members of the Chicago school regarded themselves as consistent evolutionists. Just as the biological organism was fitted to its physical environment, so the individual and his or her social environment had to be readjusted to each other. That process, however, had to be different from the ruthless struggle for survival characteristic of big business; it was to be done through intelligent public action which would change outworn and injurious social conditions. Their theorizing became a justification for the practices of social reform.

Here is how Mead, for example, applied this approach to the problems of the class struggle. "Because the employer regards the labor union as the fixed external environment of his activity, and would have all the relations between laborer and employer determined by the method in which he bargains and does business, he becomes a narrow individualist; and because the laborer would determine these same relations by the methods which he used in building up this union, he becomes a socialist."

These equally one-sided and conflicting attitudes could be overcome if the city, state, or national government would recognize that community welfare demanded satisfaction of the needs of both sides. "If the community educated and housed its members properly, and protected machinery, food, market, and thoroughfares adequately, the problems at present vexing the industrial world would largely disappear" ("The Philosophical Basis of Ethics," *International Journal of Ethics*, vol. 18 [1908], p. 318).

Here is an embryonic theory of the welfare state. At that time it found expression in philanthropic work, community projects, settlement houses, and the like. The proposals of the Chicago school for organized collective action to better social conditions had a different orientation than James, the advocate of individual enterprise, self-help, and voluntary projects. They formed part of the powerful movement for social reform then sweeping the Middle West, notably Illinois and the neighboring state of Wisconsin

One of its principal exponents was Governor Altgeld of Illinois, "the millionaire reformer" who pardoned the Haymarket martyrs. Under his auspices many improvements were introduced to curb the most glaring social abuses. Legislation was enacted against child labor, the sweatshop system, and prolonged working hours; tax revisions, penal reforms, and state food inspection were instituted. New teachers' colleges, libraries, and museums were established and the state university fostered.

This movement enlisted a whole generation of idealistic middle-class intellectuals. They were headed by Jane Addams, pioneer of social service work at Hull House, where from two to five hours on Sunday afternoons Dewey conducted discussions with uneducated immigrants at a Plato Club. The most noted of these professionals included the attorney Clarence Darrow, defender of victims of injustice; H. D. Lloyd, the exposer of monopolies; Brand Whitlock, the author of novels of social criticism who subsequently became reform mayor of Toledo and Wilson's ambassador to wartime Belgium; and the architects Lewis Sullivan and Frank Lloyd Wright. Such Middle Western writers as Theodore Dreiser, Carl Sandburg, Edgar Lee Masters, and Vachel Lindsay derived inspiration for their novels and poetry from this mass ferment.

The left flank of this crusade tended to espouse a mild brand of socialism, which filtered into academic circles. Dewey himself eventually hovered between left liberalism and evolutionary socialism. This was a far cry from the thoroughgoing individualism of William James. Dewey absorbed from the Chicago school a firm conviction in scientifically informed intelligence as the principal means for reconstructing society around "the solidarity of the human race." This was to be supplied to the Progressive forces by advanced thinkers in the universities with their pragmatic methods and proposals for piecemeal reforms.

6

The Inconsistencies
of Instrumentalism

The spokesmen for the middle-class democratic movement in the United States have rarely been frightened by the presence of contradiction. Emerson derided "foolish consistency" as "the hobgoblin of little minds." Whitman proclaimed with aplomb: "I contradict myself. Very well, then I contradict myself. I am large. I contain multitudes."

Pragmatism shared this attitude. In a backward glance over his career Dewey observed that he appeared to himself "unstable, chameleon-like, yielding one after another to many diverse and even incompatible influences; struggling to assimilate something from each and yet striving to carry it forward in a way that is logically consistent with what had been derived from its predecessors" (Adams and Montague, eds., *Contemporary American Philosophy,* vol. 2, p. 22).

Pragmatism's view of nature and experience as basically indeterminate facilitated this hospitality toward unresolved contradictions. Experience is so fluid and unpredictable that it can encompass the most contrary juxtapositions in a single situation. No one is excluded; there is room for everyone at this inn.

At the same time the logical theory of instrumentalism stoutly denied that contradiction had any objective reality. According to Dewey's *Logic,* contradiction is a function restricted to the relations between propositions. It does not exist in things or events. It is a purely mental phenomenon without any roots or analogues in society and nature.

Moreover, even in the restricted domain of propositions, a contradiction is not essentially antithetical. "In no case of controlled inquiry," Dewey tells us, "is a flat negation of a generalization taken to be final" (*Logic,* pp. 196-97). That is to say: "either-or" is not the definitive description of any reality; a way can always be found out of the most extreme opposition without negating one of the poles.

Dewey also asserts in *Logic* that: "It is notorious that a hypothesis does not have to be true in order to be highly serviceable in the conduct of inquiry. . . . The stubborn facts . . . show that correct conclusions have been progressively reached from incorrect 'premises.'" This argument implies that truth or falsity does not determine usefulness in scientific inquiry and is not indispensable for fruitful thought. In order to arrive at valuable results, the premise need not accord with the conclusion.

Even though it refuses to recognize the objective reality of contradiction, instrumentalism is itself the most awkwardly contradictory school of American thought. It will be helpful to summarize some outstanding contradictions to be found in Dewey's thinking. (These will be more extensively discussed in subsequent chapters.)

1. In his original theory of nature Dewey stated that it was useless to inquire into nature's general traits. Such ontological observations were obsolete metaphysics. "It is hence self-contradictory for an instrumental pragmatism to set up claims to supplying a metaphysics or ontology. . . . [Instrumentalism] involves the doctrine that the origin, structure and purpose of knowing are such as to render nugatory any wholesale inquiries into the nature of Being" ("Some Implications of Anti-Intellectualism," *Journal of Philosophy,* vol. 7 [1910], p. 479).

In line with the empirical tradition stemming from Locke, Dewey claimed that instrumentalism involved nothing more than a theory of knowledge and therefore did not prejudge the nature of reality. William James declared that pragmatism was compatible with almost any theory of objective reality from idealism to materialism.

Dewey, however, did not stick to this positivist approach. He proceeded to violate his previously expressed position and indulge in "metaphysics" by setting forth in *Experience and Nature* a list of the principal traits which reality did, or did not, possess.

In 1940 he acknowledged the inconsistency in his attitude toward systematic thinking on this and other matters when he wrote: "I find that with respect to the hanging together of various problems and various hypotheses in a perspective determined by a definite point of view, I have a system. In so far I have to retract disparaging remarks I have made in the past about the need for a system in philosophy" ("Nature in Experience," *Philosophical Review*, vol. 49, pp. 244-45).

2. On the decisive question of the relation between thought and reality, Dewey could not arrive at a firm decision either that experience depended upon nature or nature upon experience but oscillated between the materialist and idealist standpoints.

3. In the pragmatic theory of knowledge, all ideas, to be fruitful, must be practical in content. Yet in his *Logic* Dewey makes mathematics purely postulational. This is not a pragmatic or even an empirical but a formalistic conception of the nature of mathematics.

4. In politics Dewey could not make up his mind which social-economic system was progressive and deserved support. At one time he favored a reconstructed capitalism, at another a socialist alternative.

5. He polemicized against Marxism on the grounds that resort to forceful actions by the masses was invariably pernicious. Nevertheless, in *Liberalism and Social Action* he conceded that under certain circumstances it was justifiable for the democratic majority to defend itself by force, if necessary, against fascist dictatorship or capitalist counterrevolution.

6. In the intervals between imperialist wars he was strongly pacifist; when a war came, he was among its supporters.

7. Dewey's views on religion clearly expose the evasiveness on fundamental issues at the core of his instrumentalism. In *A Common Faith* he denied the existence of a divine being and rejected the supernatural. Yet he refused to come out for atheism; he insisted on preserving the word "God" to denote the conjunction of human ideals with the conditions for achieving them.

Why did Dewey—unlike Freud, who dared to call religion an illusion—fear to make a clean break with the remnants of superstition? The reason he offered is that both militant atheism and traditional supernaturalism have more in common with each other than with his viewpoint because both are more preoccupied with the individual than the social.

This lame excuse for retaining relics of religion is historically and theoretically unfounded. Catholicism, as is well known, has been the arch-foe of individualism, which it correctly identifies with Protestant heresy. On the other side, atheism has no intrinsic connection with individualism; it is based upon the denial of the existence of gods in any guise.

The real reason for Dewey's reluctance was that he wanted to avoid decisive commitment to either camp in this irreconcilable dispute. How else could believers, half-believers (agnostics), and disbelievers be brought together and reconciled in "a common faith"? This very term is a misnomer. For any common faith which slurs over the fundamental issues at stake is equally offensive and displays equally bad faith toward religious people who cling to God's existence and the avowed atheists who deny it.

*   *   *

The multiple and ineradicable inconsistencies of pragmatism have been noted by many sorts of commentators. Early in pragmatism's career Professor Lovejoy pointed out that there were "thirteen pragmatisms" and asked each pragmatist to say where he stood on each of them.

One of Lovejoy's students at Johns Hopkins, W. T. Feldman, wrote a critical analysis in which he observed, on the purely theoretical level: "By what may be termed an historical accident (subjection to the particular influences which have been enumerated) Dewey has combined into one philosophy a diverse set of principles which are not completely congruous with one another and are even in some cases contradictory . . ." (*The Philosophy of John Dewey*, pp. 113-14).

These undeniable incongruities were not, as he thinks, merely the result of "an historical accident." They were not individual aberrations or merely incidental traits. The inherent and obvious inconsistencies of instrumentalism were the inescapable philosophic reflection of the unsettled situation, the zigzag course of development, the heterogeneous composition, and the wavering outlook of America's middle classes, and especially its educated professionals.

It does not suffice to show that the theoretical foundations and practical conclusions of a philosophy like instrumentalism are riddled with inconsistencies. There is more to the matter than that. It is necessary to explain where these inconsistencies came from; why they persisted; what they represented. The necessary inconsistencies in any school of thought reflect the contradictory historical circumstances in which it originated and the contradictions in the conditions of life, interests, and course of development of the social grouping that it spoke for.

We have to look into the historical situation governing the life of middle-class America in his day to find out where Dewey's persistent inconsistencies came from, why they were an essential part of his individual makeup, and why they prevented greater coherence in his thinking.

Certain class strata are inherently unsettled because they occupy indeterminate and self-contradictory places in the structure of society. This was especially true of the middle classes after the Civil War, wedged in between the ruling capitalists and the wageworkers. The pressures and counterpressures exerted upon them by these stronger, more cohesive social powers continually upset the balance of the various middle-class elements and prevented them from maintaining unambiguous positions, pursuing a consistent course, having clear perspectives, or carrying through either their ideas or their actions to logical conclusions.

The middle-class Progressives were both in conflict and in communion with the men of wealth above them. While they shared with the plutocracy a basic allegiance to the capitalist regime, they had to protest against the vicious consequences of its rule. On the other side they at times had to seek alliance with the working class—from which many in the middle classes had freshly emerged and from which they wanted to escape.

The middle layers were caught in the determinism of American capitalist development, which kept tossing them to and fro, now uplifting, now depressing them, according to the fluctuating business cycle. While increasingly maltreated by the plutocracy, they were being shoved to one side by the oncoming labor movement.

This uneasy and anomalous situation of the petty bourgeoisie was the social source of the inherent evasiveness of the pragmatists. They attempted to find positions on major issues from philosophy and logic to politics and ethics somewhere between the opposing standpoints of the two polar class antagonists. As advocates of the Golden Mean they preferred, if possible, to stand a little to the right or left of center, as their publicists phrased it, and play the middle against both ends.

The instrumentalists could not decide whether to be materialists or idealists in philosophy. The Progressives could neither live with capitalism nor live without it. They wanted its good sides without the bad and tried to avert the consequences of its essentially exploitative operation by ineffectual reform measures. The educated urban citizens who were discarding orthodox religions were yet too respectable to give up all the old religious habits and phrases—which were also handy for doping the poor.

The reformists regarded themselves as indispensable mediators between contending forces who kept the extremists of both sides within the bounds of reason. They rebuked in equal measure the aggressions of capitalist reaction and any militantly defensive actions of labor. This appeared fair. But since the preponderance of industrial and governmental power was in capitalist hands, such an attitude did not really give the workers an even break.

What should be done? The union should either come to a friendly settlement with the boss or submit the dispute to the courts or some other official tribunal. But since these agencies were controlled by men of wealth, nine times out of ten the formal impartiality of the pragmatists played into the hands of the ruling powers at the workers' expense.

This is not because, as individuals, they were unintelligent, uninformed, or hostile to labor. Their convictions and conduct were determined by their social connections and role. This same social causation is manifest in Dewey's confusions.

Even his literary style reflected this situation. Lewis Mumford aptly said that his style is "as fuzzy and formless as lint." Another critic likened it to the consistency of peanut butter. It is generally acknowledged that his writings are difficult to read and his reasoning often hard to follow. This lack of clarity and precision is dismissed as an individual failing. But his mode of expression suited the traits of thought of the amorphous middle classes, unsure of their basis and unclear in their outlook. The style is more than the man; it is the whole school, the social grouping. Dewey's confusions and cloudiness were also theirs.

Philosophers like Santayana, with a far more attractive literary style and greater clarity of thought, failed to exert a fraction of Dewey's influence. His popularity represented the triumph of an ideological content that satisfied the urgent needs of its petty-bourgeois constituency. With some grumbling, his readers were willing to overlook the inadequate form of literary presentation. The body of thought was congenial enough to offset its drab and ungainly dress.

The unsteadiness of the pragmatic viewpoint issued directly from its own elementary premises, which disavowed the necessity for resting upon any first principles. Quoting William James, Dewey said: "From a general point of view, the pragmatic attitude consists in 'looking away from first things, principles, "categories," supposed necessities; and of looking towards last things, fruits, consequences, facts'" (*Philosophy and Civilization*, pp. 22–23).

The inherent unreliability of pragmatism is glaringly exposed in this self-characterization which counterposes consequences to causes, fruits to roots, and facts to principles.

Such a separation ought to have been impermissible for a school of thought which held up Darwin as a model. *The Origin of Species* revolutionized biology by doing the opposite of what this pragmatic prescription called for. In order to explain the birth and development of species, Darwin had to look *toward* first things, go back to them, and find the intermediate links connecting the beginnings of life with its consummation in humanity. He had to deal with such real *necessities* of material life as the struggle for survival. He sought to uncover the unifying principles behind the separate and heterogeneous facts of biological observation, and found them in the unity of descent of all living things and the operation of natural selection.

This genuinely scientific procedure differed completely from Dewey's recommendation that causes be cut off from their consequences. Dewey wrongly counterposed to each other phases of development that are organically related in an integrated process. He inserted the adjective "supposed" to try to siphon all necessity out of reality.

Darwin demonstrated how changes in the relations between the organism and the environment necessarily led to the alteration of existing species and the generation of new ones from the old. He traced organs back to their original forms; the hands and feet of the human and the wings of the bird can be linked with the fins of the fish. He did not ignore the fact that the intrusion of new natural conditions and organic developments can considerably modify, distort, and even change beyond easy recognition the products of evolution. But a knowledge of the intermediate forms, together with the intervening conditions and changes, makes it possible to disclose the connections between first and last in the sequence of species. Such linking up is the task not only of biological but of all science.

Similarly, what comes out of a philosophy and what it can do during its career can be traced in large measure to its basis and point of departure. The lack of a backbone of principle and a firm skeleton of ideas—and its theoretical justification for not needing either—gave pragmatism the original flabbiness it has ever since exhibited. In the matter of sticking to principles, pragmatism differs from Marxism as a jellyfish differs from a vertebrate.

The indefiniteness of pragmatism was partially derived on the theoretical plane from its recoil against the unacceptable positions of the reigning idealist philosophy. But its aversion to inquiring into the nature of first principles in general, and its own in particular, had specific social causes. The middle classes incline to take the basis of their existence for granted. Too probing an investigation into their historical evolution would reveal their dependent and precarious status within the capitalist order and their growing weakness compared to the major class forces. Their ideological representatives prefer to concentrate on matters as they stand and see what can best be made out of the present situation without peering too far into their future or delving too deeply into their past.

Pragmatism is the most promiscuous of all doctrines. It will spend the night with any partner and feel no obligation to any one for any length of time. Donald Piatt, himself a disciple of Dewey, admitted: "The pragmatist is the least bound by prior commitments of all philosophers . . ." (Schilpp, *Philosophy of John Dewey,* p. 106). Its practitioners will borrow whatever ideas they need from next-door neighbors without a thank-you for the loan.

Pragmatism has the complexion of a chameleon; it excels in mimicry and can easily blend into any background. "Pragmatists not only will disavow the statements you criticize but will embrace as their own the very point of view from which you criticize them," remarks Barrows Dunham (*Giant in Chains,* p. 83). (For an example of this, see Dewey's answers to criticisms by Santayana and Russell, *Philosophy of John Dewey,* pp. 530-32, 544-49.)

There is a method and a meaning in this quick change of hue. Instrumentalism wishes to make no lasting commitments, to give no hostages, to be bound by no pledges which inhibit its freedom of operation and maneuver. It aspires to be "free" in the opportunist sense of adapting itself to the main chance. This is the freedom of a weather vane which is constantly being whirled about on its pivot by the strongest currents in the social-political atmosphere. Thus from 1932 to 1972 Sidney Hook, John Dewey's exegete, supported in succession the Communist, Socialist, Democratic and Republican presidential candidates.

This shiftiness permits the pragmatist to swing far to the right or left in deference to prevailing conditions. In 1935, for example, under stress of economic crisis, mass radicalism, and the onset of fascism, Dewey was half ready to acquiesce in the use of revolutionary resistance as a method of social action. Fifteen years later, although the need for such action had not lessened, he contended that this would only replace one totalitarianism with another. The Second World War and ensuing cold war's change in the political climate had brought about his reversal.

Consistency can hardly be expected of a method whose cardinal tenet asserts that there is no lawfulness in the movement of things, no intrinsic necessities in nature, society, and the human mentality. If each concrete case may be a law unto itself, no general rules govern events and no definite principles can be reliable guides to action.

But, it may be objected, do not dialectical materialists say that rules have only a relative validity since circumstances alter cases and may even transform things into their opposites? Does not Deweyism maintain this same view?

There are two major differences between these rival methods of thought on the question of lawfulness and determinism. Marxism declares that laws govern *both* the circumstances in the case *and* their most extreme alterations and transitions. For pragmatism, as Dewey says, necessities are "supposed"; they are not actually coercive.

Second, pragmatists tend to regard all the material conditions in a given situation as being equally indeterminate and as having the same weight and power. In reality some factors are always more stable and more decisive than others. All circumstances do not change at the same rate or affect other things in the same degree. While certain factors are highly determinate, others are only slightly influential in a process. A correct and comprehensive method must make room for both determinism and indeterminism in their concrete combination.

This may be so, expostulates the pragmatist, but it is not possible to tell in advance how any given situation will turn out— the candidate is not elected until all the ballots are cast and counted.

To be sure, all indetermination is not removed until the event is concluded. But in situations where the *basic* determinants can be analyzed, uncovered, and known in advance, it is possible to predict the main line of development, the general outcome, and even specific consequences. Otherwise science would be a hopeless and fruitless enterprise.

*   *   *

A mixture ranging from radical opinions to obsolete prejudices is to be found in Dewey's writings. That is why so many diverse thinkers—from moderate liberals to quasi-Marxists—have been able to claim him as their own. Each can pick out of the magpie's nest whatever consorts with their particular inclinations and purposes, especially since so few lines of his thought are drawn out to their ultimate conclusions.

It is futile to lament these equivocations. Eclecticism is ingrained in instrumentalism. In order to serve discordant social interests, Dewey had to espouse half-measures; he had to be as inconsistent in practice as in theory.

7

Dewey's Conceptions
of Nature and Science

With the publication of *Studies in Logical Theory* in 1903 Dewey definitively cast off his earlier adherence to idealism and launched his distinctively instrumentalist theory. He continued to elaborate this line of thought in various ways in many works until his death in 1952. It would be tedious to trace the windings of his thinking over those fifty years of tireless productivity. The following chapters will concentrate on analyzing his basic positions in four decisive areas of philosophy: epistemology, logic, the theory of nature, and his views of society and history.

$$*\qquad*\qquad*$$

The last chapter pointed out that Dewey held varying positions on numerous fundamental philosophical questions. His habit of taking a stand on one principle and switching to another is exemplified in his theorizing about nature. Over a span of two decades he put forward conflicting opinions on whether objective reality is subject to rational generalization.

In 1917 he wrote: "It is often said that pragmatism, unless it is content to be a contribution to mere methodology, must develop a theory of Reality. But the chief characteristic of the pragmatic notion of reality is precisely that no theory of Reality in general, überhaupt, is possible or needed" ("The Need for a Recovery of Philosophy," in *Creative Intelligence,* p. 155).

This statement is clear. "No theory of Reality in general . . . is possible or needed." The pragmatist will examine things piece by piece as they come along and take note of their specific characteristics and relations without drawing any general conclusions about the essential nature of reality from these findings. Such systematizing would be meaningless and useless.

Dewey thought the same seven years earlier when he wrote that instrumentalism "involves the doctrine that the origin, structure and purpose of knowing are such as to render nugatory any wholesale inquiries into the nature of Being" ("Some Implications of Anti-Intellectualism," *Journal of Philosophy,* vol. 7, p. 479).

Then, in 1925, Dewey flouted his explicit rejection of the need for any general theory of this kind by presenting his own conception of "the nature of Being" in the lectures later published as *Experience and Nature;* their purpose, he said, was to give a "detection and description of the generic traits of existence." What Dewey called his "naturalistic metaphysics" was a generalized account of reality and humanity's relations with it.

This inability to follow a straight course, marked out by the compass of settled principles, is typical of the pragmatic method. Without bothering to remove the guidelines they themselves have set up, pragmatists will dart off in a quite different direction than they originally projected. They have no consistent orientation.

Nature and Experience

Dewey's views on the nature of reality, or as he put it, "the nature of nature," are most fully and definitively set forth in *Experience and Nature* (1929). This is one of the twin peaks of his philosophical achievement; *Logic* is the other.

In treating the relations between nature and experience, the existential priority of the two factors has to be made clear at the outset. Which comes first? Are they to be considered on an equal footing or is one subordinate to and dependent upon the other?

Dewey tries to brush aside this question as meaningless, as the product of the artificial dualisms inherited from magic, religion, and classical philosophy. It is false to empirical observation, he says, to separate experience from nature since the two are always found together and we know nature only through the medium of experience. To divide the two and counterpose one to the other is to introduce an unwarranted breach into the continuity of existence.

This issue, however, cannot be so lightly disposed of. It is the most meaningful question confronting a philosopher because the fundamental nature of one's world outlook flows from the answer.

Materialists hold that nature existed before experience and can exist apart from it. Although experience is always bound up with nature, the latter has an autonomous existence not necessarily associated with human experience.

Natural science backs up this position. The evidence of the evolutionary process demonstrates that the universe existed billions of years before our planetary system, inorganic matter long before living beings, life before mind, and the plants and animals before humankind.

Where does Dewey stand on this key issue? It is difficult to cull an unambiguous statement or a consistent position from *Experience and Nature*. In the first chapter on method, which deals specifically with "the relation that exists between experience and nature," he goes so far as to agree that "experience as an existence is something that occurs only under highly specialized conditions, such as are found in a highly organized creature which in turn requires a specialized environment. There is no evidence that experience occurs everywhere and everywhen" (p. 3a). From this assertion it ought to be concluded that nature can and does exist independently of experience whereas experience is always dependent upon living beings. But Dewey refrains from saying so.

Instead he polemicizes against the view that nature is "complete apart from experience." This is a diversion. Of course physical nature on earth cannot be regarded as complete in and of itself once highly organized creatures emerge that are capable of reacting to their experiences. These living products of natural evolution thereupon become an integral part of reality, interacting with other less developed parts and among their own kind.

But that is not the point at issue. Is nature all there is apart from such creatures? Or was there experience before intelligent life evolved?

Dewey fiddles around with this question without giving a plain answer. His more materialist disciples and interpreters claim that he takes the materialist premise for granted and then goes ahead without further fuss to deal with more complex matters. Dewey himself several times says something of the same sort.

But it is an empirical fact that his "naturalistic" theory of experience is vague, evasive, and inconclusive on this most important aspect of the connection between nature and experience. He fails to state unambiguously whether or not there is a fundamental qualitative difference between nature and experience; he declines to say that nature is self-sustaining while experience is always derivative from it. Moreover, he equates "the purely physical side of nature" with "mathematical subsistences, esthetic essences . . . or God," as though the primordial reality of physical nature were as imaginary as nonexistent deities or as mental as theoretical abstractions (*Experience and Nature*, p. 29).

It is true that *for human beings* experience and nature are always to be found together, since experience results from the interactions between ourselves and the external environment. But what is true of human history does not apply to all existence. Nature had a development long before humankind and its experiences came on the scene. This all-important fact is left obscure in Dewey's exposition of their relations.

Dewey tries to justify his refusal to subordinate experience to nature by denying the presence of radical discontinuities in the process of being and becoming. The stated aim of *Experience and Nature* is to replace the traditional disjunction of nature and experience with the idea of continuity between them. But in carrying out this praiseworthy purpose Dewey tends to efface the essential differences between them.

Nature and experience are materially, genetically, historically united. But they constitute a unity of opposites. Their opposition does not consist in totally "separate kinds of being," as idealism contends and Dewey fears, but in their status as qualitatively different factors in the development of material existence.

Dewey distinguishes three main plateaus of being: the physical, the psycho-physical, and the mental, representing levels of increasing complexity among natural events. For Dewey these are simply differing degrees in the interaction of one thing with another, links in an uninterrupted chain. However, these levels embody not only a continuum but successively higher stages of material evolution, each involving a "quantum jump" in the total process. Dewey gives a one-sided picture of the real situation by slurring over the significance of such sharp breaks.

He writes that "breaks and incompatibilities occur in collective culture as well as in individual life" (*Experience and Nature*, p. ix). Yet he does not make room for such breaks in the phases of material development. In his scheme of things continuity takes precedence over discontinuity. "The fundamental assumption is *continuity*" (*Essays in Experimental Logic*, p. 87).

He applies this principle of continuity by submerging the essential differences between the material and the mental.

Matter and Mind

In order to establish a third position between materialism, which teaches that the physical world is the prime reality, and idealism, which claims that ideas are the essence of things, Dewey had to efface the major distinction between matter and mind and put the one on a par with the other. According to him, neither has an independent status; they are interdependent characteristics of the complex of events that constitutes nature. Matter expresses "a character of natural events and changes as they change; their character of regular and stable order;" mind is "the order of their meanings in their logical connections and dependencies" (*Experience and Nature*, p. 74).

Dewey argues against drawing any fundamental distinction between matter and mind because they are always found together. This is a misleading half-truth. Matter can exist apart from mind but mind cannot exist without matter. Dewey can existentially equate the two only by annulling this determinative difference.

Dewey's definition of matter as the regular and stable order of events is a usage of the term peculiar to him. To be sure, the concept of matter has had a changing content in the history of Western thought, and varying qualities were attributed to it according to the standpoint of the particular philosophical school.

Dialectical materialism has given the most general and adequate definition of matter. The sole property of matter which is decisive for the modern materialist is that of being the objective reality that exists outside our consciousness, whether or not it is experienced by our senses and reflected in our minds. Dewey's special conception of matter leaves out the central characteristic of autonomous existence that distinguishes it from consciousness.

The traits of regularity and order which he simplistically selects as demarcating matter from mind are not its universal and necessary qualities. Matter can be viewed as not only regular but highly irregular, not only orderly but chaotic, depending on the level of approach to its manifestations. Indeed, Aristotle and other Greek thinkers viewed it as the refractory element in the making of things, in contrast to the "forms" which gave them order, shape, and harmonious structure. Furthermore, the motion intrinsic to matter can upset established orders.

Matter can be viewed as stable or unstable, orderly or disorderly, but at all times and under all conditions it is what objectively exists, whether or not there are any minds around to explore the meaning of its movements. Dewey's notion of the relations between mind and matter obliterates the primacy of matter in reality and the priority of material conditions in the process of knowledge.

For example, he denies that matter causes mind. It is not, as materialism—and science—teaches, a product of material causes at a certain stage in the evolution of living beings. Instead of being the offspring of matter, mind is simply another way of dealing with events. For him the term "matter" covers lesser, more external fields of interaction; the mind deals with wider, more complex, more inward characteristics of events.

Dewey explicitly polemicizes against any causal connection between matter and mind. "Historically speaking," he writes, "materialism and mechanistic metaphysics—as distinct from mechanistic science—designate the doctrine that matter is the efficient cause of life and mind, and that 'cause' occupies a position superior in reality to that of 'effect.' Both parts of this statement are contrary to fact" (*Experience and Nature,* p. 262).

This is not so. Matter—by which materialists mean the independent objective conditions of existence—*is* the efficient cause of life and mind. How else have they been brought into existence, if the theory of evolution is taken seriously?

The second statement has a more complex character. It is true that mechanical thinkers have been inclined to exalt cause over effect. This is a narrow, one-sided conception of the causal relation and the reciprocal action of its two poles. The cause precedes and produces the effect but does not stand above it in reality, because the effect is essential to the cause and any cause is itself an effect of a previous cause. Moreover, in cases of progressive development, of a passage from lower to higher stages of being, the effect can stand on higher ground than its cause—for example, living beings compared with inanimate things and humans compared with animals.

This discussion leads to consideration of a chief feature of Dewey's instrumentalism and one of the paramount problems of science and philosophy. That is the place determinism and indeterminism, necessity and chance, occupy in the scheme of things.

Determinism and Indeterminism

Dewey resolutely tried to do justice to the contradictory character-istics nature exhibits. He remarked that all things are at the same time solitary and associated, particular and general, unique and exemplary, unpredictable and predictable in certain respects, immediate and mediate, inexpressible and expressible, evanes-cent and enduring, instrumental and ultimate, incomparable and commensurable, inconvertible and interchangeable, inclusive and exclusive.

"We live in a world which is an impressive and irresistible mixture of sufficiencies, tight completenesses, order, recurrences which make possible prediction and control, and singularities, ambiguities, uncertain possibilities, processes going on to consequences as yet indeterminate." "Nature is an intersection of spontaneity and necessity, the regular and the novel, the finished and the beginning" (*Experience and Nature,* pp. 47, 360).

Dewey gave a felicitous description of the interplay between the necessary and the contingent: "A world of 'ifs' is alone a world of 'musts'—the 'ifs' express real differences; the 'musts' real connections. The stable and recurrent is needed for the fulfillment of the possible; the doubtful can be settled only through its adaptation to stable objects. The necessary is always necessary for, not necessary in and of itself; it is conditioned by the contingent, although itself a condition of the full determination of the latter" (p. 65).

However, after having emphasized the interpenetration of these opposing features in nature, Dewey did not give them equal weight in the balance of his judgment. In the "union of the hazardous and the stable, of the incomplete and the recurrent" he raised the first above the second in both cases. The main characteristic of natural events is "their particular and variable, their contingent, quality" (p. xiv). Existence is primarily indeterminate. "Every existence, as well as every idea and human act [is] an experiment in fact, even though not in design" (p. 70).

There have been two main traditional opinions about chance and necessity. The strict determinists say that every event in the world is necessary and nothing is accidental. Their opposites, the indeterminists, maintain that everything happens by chance and nothing is necessary. The first position is more in line with science, whose aim is to ascertain the necessity, the regularity, the lawfulness of phenomena. It cannot be based upon the discovery of accidents—or even on accidental discoveries.

These views have contended with one another through the history of philosophy. The first clear enunciation of causal law came from the atomists, whose founder, Leucippus, stated: "Nothing happens at random; everything happens out of reason and necessity." The identification of lawfulness with necessity marked a colossal advance in exploring and explaining phenomena. It became the cornerstone of the mechanical conception of the world that was incorporated in the systems of Hobbes, Spinoza, and Holbach and found its classical physical formulation in the determinism of Laplace. However, this notion of causality was too rigid and narrow, not admitting the objective existence of phenomena that must be classified as accidental.

On the other hand, diverse schools of thought have denied that anything in objective existence is necessary. They have either made nature and history the sport of chance, as contemporary existentialists do, or have questioned the existence of cause-and-effect relations in objective reality, as Berkeley, Hume, Kant, and other skeptical and subjectivist thinkers have done.

The dialectical view of the categories of necessity and chance avoids the one-sidedness of both the strict determinists and the indeterminists. The categories of chance and necessity are not mutually exclusive. Both reflect fundamental characteristics of the objective connections in the material world. As Leucippus said, nothing happens without cause. But these causes are of different kinds: some are essential and others are non-essential to the occurrence. All events result from a combination of inner necessities and external or accidental conditions.

The whole philosophical outlook of a thinker can be shaped by the relative importance assigned to one or the other of these categories. That was the case with Dewey. His instrumentalism gave predominance to the contingent and indeterminate qualities of nature over its necessary connections and thus, as we shall see, deprived causality of its objective and universal existence.

Dewey's Conception of Causation

Dewey defined causality as simply the sequence of events. "Causality . . . consists in the sequential order itself" (*Experi-*

ence and Nature, p. 99). This view that causality involves nothing more than serial order is a shallow one. The observation of sequence is only the first step in ascertaining the content of causality.

The fact that one set of events or conditions in the past regularly precedes the occurrence of another, and that this sequence is invariable, suggests some causal connection between them. But to establish and verify the existence of such a relation of cause and effect it is essential to prove their *necessary* connection.

Mere association or concomitance is not enough. From the bare fact of succession or association the inquiring mind must go deeper into the relations of the events in order to uncover the existence of generation, production, efficacy, and power. Cause and effect are then seen to coexist not merely in the *external relation of succession,* which may have an adventitious character, but in the *internal connection of mutual determination,* which gives necessity to their affinity and determines the place of the two factors in the process.

Large-scale proof of this relation is provided by the successive stages of evolution from the physical world to humankind. Dewey correctly holds that the levels of being should be arranged in the sequence *nature-life-mind.* But why have they originated in this order, and not otherwise? Is this evolutionary sequence accidental or necessary?

Science teaches that life was not possible until chemical processes had reached a certain state of complexity and interaction; mental functioning depended upon the existence of specific biological prerequisites such as the central nervous system; human rationality grows out of social conditions.

Because of this sequence the real order of causation is not *mind-life-nature,* as some idealists would have it, but *nature-life-mind,* as the materialists present it. When Hegel postulated that world development proceeded from the Pure Idea or Spirit to nature, then through the forms of life back to mind on a higher level, he was inverting the real order of causation in history and negating the verified results of scientific knowledge in the interests of his special philosophy.

The superficial conception that causality cannot comprise more than sequence drains all the dynamism out of the interactions of things by depriving the cause-effect relation of determination, generation, and lawful necessity. While it says that cause and effect are two aspects of a single process, the one is not considered essential to the other.

Dewey's definition differs not only from the popular notion of causality but, what is more important, from the procedures of science. Science is not content with tracing out the sequence of events or the correlation of changes, as the positivists teach. It goes beyond that point of empirical observation to seek out the *necessary* connections in the complex of events. It distinguishes what is accidentally conjoined or found together from what is necessarily combined.

The production of water is a case in point. Water is a chemical compound whose molecules are made up of two atoms of hydrogen and one of oxygen. When these elements are brought together in the proper proportions and under the appropriate environmental conditions, water results. The cause–effect relation between the material components can be experimentally demonstrated by either association or dissociation. When the two gases are brought together, they combine to form water. When an electric current is passed through the fluid, it decomposes into hydrogen and oxygen.

The liquid state of water depends upon, among other things, the prevailing temperature. If the temperature is lowered beyond a certain point, the liquid turns into a solid. The change in one physical factor, the temperature, is then the effective agent of the change in the physical state of the other factor, the water. This causal connection can be tested and verified by altering the temperature in different directions and noting how the physical properties of water vary from liquid to solid and back again.

Thus "cause" and "effect" reciprocally determine each other as two sides of an interactive process—and the initiating and most determinative factor in their mutual dependence is labeled the cause. Reality does not display cause as separated from effect, although the one can be distinguished from the other in a mental analysis.

Dewey recognized this interrelation when he pointed out that "there is no exclusively one-way exercise of conditioning power" and "whatever influences the changes of other things is itself changed" (*Experience and Nature,* p. 73).

Despite his interpretation of causation as nothing but orderly succession, it will be noted that Dewey speaks of "power" in the causal situation. He states elsewhere that he does not thereby intend to assert or imply that any transmission of energy or intrinsic influencing actually takes place. But despite this disclaimer, his lapse into this reference is more than a manner of speaking; the facts keep forcing him to do so. Interactive power is so deeply lodged in causation that even positivist philosophers cannot avoid associating them. This is not anthropomorphism or a mere psychological propensity as is sometimes contended, but an irresistible acknowledgment of the pattern of objective reality.

Dewey sought to make experience continuous with nature by maintaining, contrary to traditional empiricism, that we directly experience the connections of things as well as their distinct qualities. But his conception of causation as mere sequence is taken from the skeptical Hume, who denied that causation could be shown to have any existence in nature; it was simply the habit of expecting a thing to be followed by or associated with another in the future as it had in the past.

This idea of cause is based upon the explicit presumption that phenomena are essentially detached from one another. "All events," Hume wrote, "seem entirely loose and separate. One event follows another, but we can never observe any tie between them. They seem *conjoined,* but never *connected*."

Hume derived his view of causation from this misinterpretation of nature. Although Dewey discarded Hume's picture of the world as made up of disconnected events and experiences, he retained the concept of causation corresponding to it. But if nature is a unified, coherent whole in which all objects are connected and reciprocally condition one another, then the categories of cause and effect must be regarded as reflecting their interactions.

Events in nature do not have any intrinsic causal character, according to Dewey. When events are taken as they are, he writes, "there is no event which is antecedent or 'cause' any more than it is consequent or 'effect'" (*Logic,* p. 459). Such an interpretation is purely arbitrary.

The reason he gives for rejecting "an existential or ontological interpretation" of causation and banishing it from the objective world is that every event has an indefinite number of antecedents and consequents—and therefore everything in the universe would be cause and effect of everything else. This argument dismisses the fact that, while the universe is unified and its parts are interactive, it is made up of relatively autonomous processes, trends, and formations. Only some of the infinite number of possible conditioning factors actually have determinative effects on a specific entity. The rest are practically inconsequential.

Our solar system, for example, exists as a relatively independent formation with its own intrinsic causal laws governing its movements, despite the infinite swarm of particles within it and the countless bodies outside it in the universe. These other factors do not influence the solar system enough under ordinary circumstances to upset its internal order of causation.

Such considerations did not swerve Dewey from his position. In his *Logic* he flatly declared that "the category of causation is logical . . . not ontological. . . ." It is not a property of nature which objectively exists but only a logical device, "a functional means of regulating existential inquiry" (p. 462). He shared this view with Kant, who believed that causality had an *a priori* character and was introduced into the world of phenomena by the knowing súbject.

Dewey held that one thing is taken as cause and another as effect not because they really stand in this relation, but because investigators of a particular problem find it useful to make this distinction between them. A cause for him has the same relation to an effect as a means to a consequence. "Causation in any existential, non-categorial, sense is practical and teleological through and through" (ibid.).

Dewey thereby introduced the notion of purpose into cause. This reversion to teleology, the notion of purposes at work in things, was a relapse into the prescientific concept of animism, which identified causation with intended action by some creature.

Science was put on a firm theoretical foundation only when Aristotle's view of causes as ends was excluded from nature and when it was understood that the only really existing causes were efficient ones. Final causes were restricted to the conscious behavior of the higher animals and humankind.

Dewey smuggled finality back as the essence of the concept of causation by taking causation out of nature entirely and making it a purely human activity. He started with defining cause as ordered sequences and coexistences and ended by making purposive action the source of these relations. "'Causation'," he concluded, "is a category that directs the operations by which this goal [of instituting qualitative individual existential situations consisting of ordered sequences and coexistences] is reached in the case of problematic situations" (*Logic,* p. 462).

Dewey unjustifiably claimed that his subjectivist theory of causation as a means of instituting order is consonant with the procedure of science. Scientific practice, however, proceeds from the premise that causation is not only an idea in the mind, an expedient guide to action, but corresponds to a fundamental relation in the external world. Science takes not a purely formal, positivist, and subjectivist approach to causation but an ontological, materialist, and objective one.

Dewey confused the fact of causality with the generation of the *idea* or *principle* of causality. The notion of causality arises in the mind from two sources. First, from the activities of humans who change one thing into something else. This leads to the primitive view of causation as purposive activity, the means-consequence relationship. Second, the idea is predicated on the regular sequence and cyclical character of certain natural phenomena—night following day, summer alternating with winter, etc.

However, neither of these epistemological aspects of the notion suffices to establish its validity. The objective reality of causality is proved by practice. If one thing is produced by or through another, if one change brings about another change, then these events or phenomena are causally connected. This gives proof of the reality and efficacy of causality.

Hume thought that regular connection was the sole basis for the belief in causality, which he construed as nothing but customary expectation. Dewey offered a more materialistic interpretation. He observed that "labor and the use of tools seem . . . to be a sufficient empirical reason" for belief in the principle of causation. Causal explanation is a generalization from the "procedure of the workman" (*Experience and Nature,* p. 84).

Repeated acts of labor may have germinated the idea of causation. But they do not give objective validity to it. The material foundations of the category of causation ultimately rest not upon the activities of humans in the processes of production, but upon the connections within reality itself, of which labor is an instance.

*   *   *

Science aims to discover the causes of phenomena in order to put this knowledge to effective and fruitful use. Dewey's conception of causation as purely logical, methodological, purposive, and thoroughly practical rather than existential and efficient in character is controverted by the science of medicine.

Microbiologists study the sources of the pathogens in humans, animals, and plants: their ways of transmission to the host and their characteristic behavior. The germ theory of causation is not merely a useful logical device to explain the ordered sequence of the introduction of the pathogen followed by the pathological state of the bodily tissues of the organism, as the positivists maintain. It reflects the functioning of real organisms, which the microbiologists correctly designate as the causative agents.

The eminent bacteriologist Robert Koch set forth four requirements that have to be fulfilled in order to demonstrate and verify the cause–effect relation between the pathogen and the host. These are known as "Koch's postulates." (1.) The organism must be present in every case of the disease. (2.) The organism must be isolated and grown in pure culture. (3.) The organism, when inoculated into a susceptible animal, must cause the disease. (4.) The organism must then be recovered from the animal and identified. Although not every pathogen that causes infectious disease fulfills all these postulates, these form the cornerstones of the procedures of medical microbiology.

So ingrained is this search for objectively existing organisms as causative agents among microbiologists that even when these cannot be directly observed, they are presumed to be present and active as causal agents and hunted for.

This is what led to the discovery of the filterable viruses. Although a certain group of infectious diseases required living cells for their proliferation, no bodies visible even to the optical microscope were found that could be the causative agents.

It was inferred that the cause of these cellular transformations must be extremely small particles. This hypothesis guided further and deeper investigation. They were looked for, isolated, purified, and identified as the filterable viruses. These microorganisms are clearly visible under the electron microscope. Thus the cause-effect assumption was verified in that area. This case demonstrates that the causal connection between virus and disease is not simply logical, as Dewey asserts; it is ontological, as he denies.

Human purpose enters the situation in the process of discovering the biological relation and verifying its existence. The investigators intend to discover the lawful connections of certain existing phenomena and put the results to use. Once it has been ascertained that this or that virus is really responsible for the production of an infectious disease, it is then possible to take steps to treat or prevent that disease.

This can be a two-way process. If the original path of discovery went from the effect (disease) to the cause (virus), the procedure can be reversed by going from the cause to the effect. The virus can be introduced into organisms in the laboratory to produce the disease. The causal bond can thus be tested and verified.

If the presence of the pathogen is accompanied by the characteristic symptoms and development of the disease, if this happens consistently, if these precise effects are not produced by other agents, if it proves possible to prevent the development of the disease by virus-killing agents or by removing the virus, this range of tests proves the objective reality of the causal relation. Precisely in these ways have viruses been shown to be the causative agents of pathological conditions in higher plants and animals, in various insects, in bacteria and other microorganisms.

The causation actually and effectively exists. The virus particles are within the living cells and their activities influence their vital processes. The idea of efficacy and power is as essential to the content of the cause–effect relation as the idea of sequence or regular connection. It is precisely this real, necessary connection between the virus and the host that gives the actions of the microbiologist and the physician their usefulness. If this mutual relation did not exist, or was merely "a logical device" for instituting order in a problematic situation, then the measures taken to combat the virus would be ineffective and useless.

Dewey's Version of Scientific Laws

According to materialists, scientific laws formulate objective characteristics of events, processes, and things—their intrinsic features and basic properties, their necessary connections and modes of development. They are based on recurrences of these aspects in nature, as well as in society and thought. The actual inner and essential relationships of nature are expressed in the laws of movement of the planets, the laws of diffusion of gases, laws of chemical action, heredity, organic evolution, etc.

These objective connections of the physical world exist independently of human sensation and thought. The abstractive capacity of the intellect picks out the determinative features of phenomena—setting aside what is individual, accidental, and incidental—and states them in conceptual, verbal, or mathematical forms. This conception of the content of laws as the essential and determinative features of events conforms to the practical assumptions of scientists as they carry on their work of investigating natural processes in diverse fields.

Dewey had a different view of the laws of science. For him these laws do not reflect the real relations and properties of the physical world. They are as completely conceptual and subjective in character as the causal relation itself. The laws of science, he writes, "are means, through the media respectively of operations of reasoning (discourse) and of observation, for determining existential (spatial-temporal) connections of concrete materials in such a way that the latter constitute a coherent individualized situation" (*Logic,* pp. 455–56).

His contention that scientific laws "determine existential connections of concrete materials" stands things on their head. On the contrary, it is "the existential (spatial-temporal) connections of concrete materials" which, if they are broad and necessary enough, determine the content of laws. Laws operate in the external world before their effects are observed and analyzed by us. They are discovered as the outcome of prolonged scientific investigation.

The lawful movements of the planets governed the solar system for billions of years before Kepler, Galileo, and Newton disclosed the real connections among its components and expressed these in mathematical terms. Their observations, calculations, and deductions did not determine the substance of the laws of planetary motion. That came from the solar system itself, which already constituted "a coherent individualized situation."

Dewey, however, makes the laws formulated by us the means for organizing the realities they represent. He confuses the lawfulness in the operations of nature with the understanding and conceptualization of its laws. He substitutes the growth and organization of our knowledge of nature for the composition of nature itself.

This confusion is evidenced when he discusses the predictive power that genuine laws possess. Laws function, he says, as "means of *pre*diction only as far as they operate as means of *pro*duction of a given situation . . ." (*Logic,* p. 456). Curiously, he cites the inappropriate example of an eclipse to substantiate his point. However, the observation and reasoning that precede an eclipse enable astronomers to forecast its occurrence, though not to produce it. Scientific knowledge indicates that the situation will necessarily be produced or repeated owing to the conjunctural motions of the sun, moon, and earth.

Dewey mixes up the existence and operation of a law with its testing and confirmation; he confuses the scientific knowledge and activities of the astronomers with the necessary conditions for the happening in question. Causal prediction in science fundamentally depends not upon what is done by us, but upon the regularities of the objective processes that go on outside ourselves.

Through his general theory of relativity, Einstein postulated that light would bend in the presence of a strong gravitational field. He predicted that this would account for the discrepancies observed in the movement of Mercury around the sun. When this prediction was first tested during the eclipse of 1919, it was found that the measured deflection of light at the edge of the sun corresponded to the values required. The Einstein shift has since been verified by other experimental results. The relativity theory is so powerful an instrument of discovery because it has disclosed the laws—that is, the necessary connections—that actually exist in the universe with greater precision, depth, and scope than the Newtonian laws of mechanics.

However, according to Dewey, the connections of events are not "literal constituents of the laws themselves" (*Logic,* p. 445). Physical laws are "hypothetical propositions" which "are non-existential (and hence non-temporal) in their content" (p. 453). They are "inherently conceptual in character. . . . they are *relations* which are thought not observed" (*Quest for Certainty,* pp. 206-7). He even describes causal laws as a mere "figure of speech" (*Logic,* p. 445).

Dewey thereby erases the specific difference between a hypothesis and a law. A hypothesis may or may not be applicable or valid, whereas a law is a verified regularity. Although a rational suggestion or surmise and a verified truth may have the same conceptual form, they have an essentially different content because the latter is demonstrably anchored in objective reality.

Through processes of inquiry, hypotheses are converted into laws precisely by virtue of their correspondence with the facts. The germ theory of disease was once a hypothesis. But since Pasteur and Koch it has been recognized as correct. The theory was confirmed. On the other hand, the hypothesis of the ether as the medium for the transmission of light and heat has been discarded because experiment revealed no traces of its existence. It had no material reality, and after Einstein's theory was confirmed it was relegated to the scrapheap.

Dewey's version of scientific laws conforms to his general epistemological denial that knowledge reveals the antecedent properties of reality. What knowledge gives, in his opinion, is not the content of reality but rather the means to redirect and reorganize it. The thing to be known is not "something which exists prior to and wholly apart from the act of knowing" (*Quest for Certainty,* p. 205).

This failure to differentiate between what is known and the process of knowing, between the objective and subjective elements in cognition, separates the pragmatic theory of knowledge not only from materialism but from the contemporary American realist schools of philosophy as well.

In line with his positivist outlook, Dewey denies that laws are in any sense necessary; they are only "formulae for the prediction of the probability of an observable occurrence" (ibid., p. 206). This means that all laws have a statistical character. "The net effect of modern inquiry makes it clear that these constancies, whether the larger ones termed laws or the lesser ones termed facts, are statistical in nature" (p. 248).

In reality, statistical laws that pertain to the properties of aggregates like subatomic particles—a large number of elements dependent on continually changing external conditions—are only one type of scientific law. There are in addition dynamic laws that express regular causal connections in which one state or condition determines another with more than a high degree of probability. Thus Newton's laws of motion connect the positions and velocities of all parts of a mechanical system at a given instant of time with their positions and velocities at any other moment of time.

Dynamic laws are by and large restricted to relatively autonomous systems in the domain of macroscopic physics. But within these boundaries the causal relations they describe are necessarily determinate.

Dewey's philosophy accords no place to coercive necessities, whether in nature, society, history, or the processes of thought that elucidate their events. Nothing has to take place in his world by virtue of its very nature. The lawfulness of the universe that so awed Kant looked like a relic of ancient metaphysics to the American probabilist.

Appearance and Reality

Dewey was perplexed by the relation between appearance and reality manifested in the sharp contrast between the data of direct observation and scientific ideas. What was the connection between the familiar face of things encountered in everyday experience and the conceptions and conclusions of scientific knowledge which seemingly contradicted them?

The discrepancy between the sensory and conceptual elements of knowledge is an old philosophical problem. It was implicitly posed as early as Thales, the father of rational materialist speculation in Greece, who traced all phenomena to a single substance, water. That raised the question of how what is immediately presented to the senses relates to the underlying universal substance. Which is the reality: the qualities of ordinary experience or the causal mechanisms disclosed by deeper inquiry and rational inference?

Philosophers have grappled with this enigma since the Pythagoreans taught that number was the essence of reality and the atomists counterposed the atom and the void to what we directly perceive. The specific form in which the duality between the empirical data of gross experience and scientific abstraction came down to Dewey resulted from the shattering of the medieval picture of the universe based on Aristotle's physics and the emergence of the mathematical physics of the mechanical school.

Natural scientists from Galileo to Newton divided the qualities of things into two opposing categories, the primary and the secondary; the first set was objective, invariant, and inhering in the things themselves, and the second was subjective, changeable, evanescent, and produced by the perceiver. Kepler went so far as to say that only the qualitative characteristics of the world are real. Others, like Descartes, held that only those physical properties that had extension, were measurable, and could be mathematically formulated were real and knowable.

The bifurcation of nature into primary and secondary qualities accentuated the division between the physical world described by natural science and, on the other hand, social and moral values. This division gave rise to the following dilemma: The world disclosed by natural science is alone real, but we do not directly experience it; the realm of everyday experience, morality included, is illusory, yet we are immersed in it. If what we directly experience is purely subjective, we live in a meaningless world.

The mechanical materialists and the spiritualistic idealists each upheld this dualism in their own way. The mechanists stripped nature of all its diverse qualities except quantity. External reality was made up of homogeneous masses differentiated by homogeneous motion in homogeneous space and time. Rebelling against this reduction of variegated nature to its purely mechanical aspects and metrical properties, the idealists sought to reinstate the qualitative appearances of things by making them the essential stuff of reality.

Here is how Dewey saw the problem: "If the proper object of science is a mathematico-mechanical world (as the achievements of science have proved to be the case) and if the object of science defines the true and perfect reality (as the perpetuation of the classic tradition asserted), then how can the objects of love, appreciation—whether sensory or ideal—and devotion be included within true reality?" (*Experience and Nature,* p. 135).

Dewey resolutely tried to overcome this dualism and reestablish continuity between everyday experience and scientific knowledge. He pointed to the fact that the capacity of science to give greater control over everyday things testified to the vital and valuable connection between them. But how were the two interlinked?

Physical science, he says, takes experienced objects that are qualitatively heterogeneous and expresses their properties, relations, and changes in mathematical terms. This translation of objects into measured quantities gives scientists greater control over them and more facility in changing them for given purposes.

However, it is "ridiculous" to believe that these scientific ways of thinking about objects "give the inner reality of things" and "put a mark of spuriousness upon all other ways of thinking of them, and of perceiving and enjoying them." Scientific conceptions, "like other instruments, are hand-made by man in pursuit of realization of a certain interest—that of the maximum convertibility of every object of thought into any and every other" (*Quest for Certainty,* pp. 135–36).

His interpretation of scientific ideas as human products designed to serve specific purposes contained an important negative clause. It meant that ascertaining the measurable properties of things does not give greater insight into their essential reality; such information is only a way of thinking that helps us deal more effectively with them.

This purely instrumentalist definition of science does not do justice to its truths. Consider, for example, valence, the number representing the relative ability of a chemical element to combine with others. In a molecule of water, one atom of oxygen is found combined with two atoms of hydrogen and therefore has a valence of two.

The ascertainment of the specific valences of the various elements has many uses. They are of prime importance in the writing of chemical formulas and equations. These formulas, originally based on chemical evidence alone, were long thought to be merely symbolic. But it was later demonstrated by physical methods that valence fairly accurately represented the actual arrangement of atoms in space. It has been possible to go further and explain valence itself by analyzing the electronic structure of the atom, i.e., the number and arrangement of the electrons around the nucleus of the atom. This electrochemical knowledge tells more about the inner nature of things than the immediate experience of their superficial qualities. Thus, from the standpoint of epistemology, valence gives deeper information about the nature of chemical elements.

Dewey himself likens the quantitative calculations of "objects and nature as a whole" to the prices put on commodities. This analogy from the field of economics can serve to expose the shallowness of his positivist reasoning about the relations between quality and quantity.

Commodities possess many diverse physical properties that make them useful for different purposes. These values for use that commodities have by nature are immeasurable. At the same time all commodities are commensurable and exchangeable one against the other. These quantitative values in exchange are expressed in monetary terms as prices.

What enables commodities that have very different natural qualities to be equated with one another? Dewey argues that the standard rests upon no objective basis. To say that an article is worth so many dollars and cents is simply the most effective way to think about it "for purpose of exchange" (*Quest for Certainty*, p. 134).

The notion that the value and the price of commodities are nothing but arbitrary and convenient devices was long ago refuted by economic science. Value in the exchange of commodities is not a useful fiction but the expression of an objective fact, a social property of commodities. Value is the embodiment of a certain amount of socially necessary labor time. Price is the monetary expression of value. Value is measurable and convertible because it represents a certain quantum of social labor time. Marx's analysis of the commodity, showing value to be congealed labor time, revealed the innermost nature of this unit of the exchange economy.

Dewey denies that "knowledge is possession of the inner nature of things" (*Quest for Certainty,* p. 131). Physical science does no more than disclose the connections and consequences of things, so that they can be used as means. Further, "when the physical sciences describe objects and the world as being such and such, it is thought that the description is of reality as it exists in itself" (*ibid.,* pp. 136-37). However, "the business of thought is not to conform to or reproduce the characters already possessed by objects but to judge them as potentialities of what they become through an indicated operation" (p. 137). "Ideas," he asserts, "are statements not of what is or has been but of acts to be performed" (p. 138). This, he says, is "the teaching of science" that philosophy must accept.

Is this so? Does science merely provide ideas that are useful in handling and controlling objects—or does it also inform us about the inner nature of things?

All scientific investigations into the properties and causes of nature start from immediate experience. However, as Dewey points out, the original experience which incites inquiry is far less controllable and comprehensible than subsequent experience enriched and guided by scientific knowledge. What is the reason for this?

Immediate experience gives us some elementary truths about the nature of things. People learn that boiling water may be dangerous but is excellent for making meat more palatable. However, this sort of purely empirical knowledge is superficial, fragmentary, one-sided. Appearances, the first impacts of things upon us, are both indicative and misleading. Even though they give significant clues to what things are, these outward evidences are also sometimes the very opposite of the truth. The sun looks as though it revolves around the earth. The oar in the water seems bent.

To know things more profoundly, it is necessary to seek out their connections with other things as well as the changes they undergo through time. Things are not always what they seem to be at first sight and with limited experience. They are the products of long processes, outcomes of the past with all sorts of relations in the present. They are also portents of the future, of endings that constitute new beginnings, links in a long causal chain. Moreover, the subjective components of our experience have to be separated from the objective.

The task of science is to uncover and explain these wider, deeper, more complex connections. Dewey is correct when he says that scientific concepts trace the connections between things and their characteristics, as well as in his contention that science at any given moment of its development does not give a "grasp of reality in its final self-sufficing form" (*Experience and Nature,* p. 135). Science gives provisional, partial, approximate, and conditioned accounts of reality. Novelties are incessantly coming into being and there is always more to be known.

But Dewey goes wrong in asserting that science gives no explanation of reality at all, that it is merely a useful instrument "to effect immediate havings and beings" (p. 136). The concepts, laws, conclusions of science express a fuller understanding of the nature of things, and this deeper knowledge often contradicts the immediate impressions made on our senses or the inductions we draw on too meager information. Science penetrates to deeper levels of reality and embodies more profound and comprehensive truths.

Science unites what appears to be separate (chemistry shows that the gases hydrogen and oxygen belong together in water) and dissociates what appears to be the same (biology removed the whale from the category of fishes and placed it among the mammals).

Instrumentalism asserts that scientific ideas, propositions, and theories do not reflect or reproduce any objective realities; they are simply symbolic of the relations of those realities, enabling us to regulate their changes. Dewey himself brings forward the example of water to buttress this nonmaterialistic definition of scientific concepts. "Water as an object of science, as H_2O with all the other scientific propositions which can be made about it, is not a rival for position in real being with the water we see and use. It is, because of experimental operations, an added instrumentality of multiplied controls and uses of the real things of everyday experience" (*Quest for Certainty,* p. 106).

However, the chemical formula for water is more than an additional useful device. It gives a deeper knowledge and truer understanding of the inner nature of this familiar substance. It is the greater truthfulness of the concept that makes it so useful in controlling reality.

Dewey says that the water we drink and the chemical formula are not rivals for "position in real being." But they are different dimensions of the same thing. The epistemology of science—and of materialist philosophy—says: The chemical formula gives greater insight into the constitution and behavior of this compound. Water is actually made up of two highly inflammable gases, hydrogen and oxygen, combined in the specific proportions of two atoms to one. The formula is not an arbitrary symbol but the representation of what truly exists in the world. This material composition is the cause of its properties and the source of its uses.

The scientific abstraction does not deprive water of any of the characteristics we sense: its sparkle, transparency, fluidity, etc. It aids our understanding of what these are based on and produced by, what their essential causes are, and how their existing physical state can be changed.

Dewey's definition of scientific objects as "simply conceptual means for the work of inquiry" disregards the objective content of genuinely scientific concepts and their reference to the realities of objects. Dewey rejects the Kantian notion of unknowable "things in themselves." Yet his theory of the cognition of objective reality imitates the conclusion of Kant that science organizes experience but does not and cannot enable us to know the essence of things.

Dewey attacks the view that scientific objects disclose more of reality than subjective impressions on the grounds that this assumes a transcendental reality beyond and behind experience similar to the Platonic Idea or Kant's thing-in-itself. This argumentation covers up his denial of the objective basis of ideas and his limitation of them to instrumental purposes.

Much more was learned about the reality of the air we breathe when chemists found that it was essentially a mixture of two gases with very different properties, nitrogen and oxygen, in certain proportions. This knowledge, which transcended direct experience, enabled scientists to extract nitrogen from the atmosphere for use in many industrial processes, including the manufacture of fertilizer.

Science walks on two legs. As it delves ever deeper into reality, it produces new concepts and refines old ones. Science has proceeded from analyzing diverse states of matter (solid, fluid, gas, and later plasma) to discover molecules, atoms, electrons, and elementary particles. This penetration into more fundamental levels of the material world has been reflected and formulated in the creation of new and superior concepts. The two processes go hand in hand in the advance of knowledge. Biology started with studying the organism, then its organs and their functions and interrelations, moving on to cells and then molecules—until its researches have merged with chemistry and physics.

Dewey focuses on a single side of this progress of science. He does not admit that the instrumental value of its ideas comes from their fuller and more genuine correspondence with reality and the more thoroughgoing insight they afford into the essential constituents and properties of things, their modes of generation and development, and their relations with one another. By going from the concrete to the abstract, from immediate experience to scientific generalization, thought does not get further from the reality of things but comes ever closer to it. Scientific ideas, theories, laws reflect reality more deeply, more accurately, more comprehensively as well as more comprehensibly.

The problem of appearance and reality, common sense and scientific knowledge, is inseparable from the study of the dialectical relation between the concrete and the abstract. Scientific concepts are abstractions from the everyday world we experience that disclose the hidden relations of things and probe more deeply into their essential being. For Dewey the opposite is true. Direct experiences and the immediate human responses to them are closer to reality than what he calls "scientific objects."

This derogation of scientific law in favor of immediate impressions misreads the true state of affairs. The theory of organic evolution and the discoveries resulting from it provide more truth about living beings, including our own species, than any amount of direct observation of living creatures. The general law that covers the development of all forms of life on earth stands at a higher level of knowledge than the most extensive description and exact classification of any specific living organisms. While the empirical data amassed about them was indispensable for the creation and verification of the theory, it has a lower rank in the scale of knowledge. Linnaeus, who regarded species as fixed, had less insight into their nature than Darwin, who postulated their origin and evolution.

As a logical consequence of his refusal to accord objective content to scientific concepts and his interpretation of them as purely mental expressions, Dewey grants undue objectivity to immediate experiences. If science doesn't reveal the inner nature of things, what does? Here is his answer: "The *intrinsic* nature of events is revealed in experience as the immediately felt qualities of things" (*Experience and Nature,* p. xii).

Instead of resolving or removing the contradiction between appearance and reality, between phenomenon and essence, Dewey turns it upside down. Whereas the mechanical materialists made the scientific abstractions of quantitative relations the sole objective reality and relegated sensed qualities entirely to the realm of the subjective, he takes the opposite view. "Immediate feelings" divulge the inner nature of things; scientific concepts are merely useful devices.

This conception, that what is directly experienced is the best known, is a relapse on the theoretical level from a genuinely scientific approach; it goes all the way back to the naive standpoint of the Greeks. It reinstates the dualism he set out to eliminate. Instead of showing the real connections between what is experienced and what is known on a scientific level—that one has grown out of the other and reacts back upon it—he counterposes the immediate, as that which is truly known, to scientific abstractions, which are useful in action but not true reproductions of objective reality.

He does not stop there. In his overzealous application of the principle of continuity he mixes up the objective with the subjective and fails to draw a clear distinction between what belongs to the physical world and what is added by human beings. He places all qualities present in immediate personal experience on the same level. "Empirically, things are poignant, tragic, beautiful, humorous, settled, disturbed, comfortable, annoying, barren, harsh, consoling, splendid, fearful; are such immediately and in their own right and behalf. . . . These traits stand in themselves on precisely the same level as colors, sounds, qualities of contact, taste and smell" (*Experience and Nature,* p. 96).

However, colors, sounds, and other sensations are generated by objective material causes; they are connected with the physical world in a way that emotions of poignancy or judgments of beauty and tragedy are not. Dewey expunges the distinction between the sensory and the socially conditioned elements in our experience.

Still further, he insists that "*things* are beautiful and ugly, lovely and hateful, dull and illuminated, attractive and repulsive. Stir and thrill in us is as much theirs as is length, breadth, and thickness" (ibid., p. 108). This puts aesthetic judgments and emotional responses, which are socially and historically conditioned phenomena, on a par with physical sensations—qualities generated by the properties of the things themselves.

Likewise, "dream, insanity and fantasy are natural products, as 'real' as anything else in the world" (*Quest for Certainty*, p. 243). He even views the faculty of imagination as an "organ of nature; for it is the appropriate phase of indeterminate events moving toward eventualities that are now but possibilities" (*Experience and Nature*, p. 62). Imagination is a genuine function of the human mind. But it is necessary to preserve the distinction between the natural and the human, although everything in the latter has its roots and reference in the former. In asserting that mind itself is "a genuine character of natural events" (ibid., p. xiii) Dewey erases the difference between the two.

Dewey refuses to retreat from his attribution of "secondary" and "tertiary" qualities to nature itself. In his 1939 reply to critics of his position on this point he insisted upon the genuineness of affectional and other qualities as "doings of nature." (See *The Philosophy of John Dewey*, pp. 579-80.) Ethical and aesthetic evaluations are for him as objective as weight, heat, and color.

A noise can be loud or soft, as determined by physical conditions and sensations, but as such it is not either frightful or reassuring. Such personal responses to the given sensation are located not in nature but in ourselves. The blessing of a priest may convert ordinary water into holy water in the imagination of the believer. But this religious fetish is a psychosocial phenomenon, not a physical fact.

The relation between the data of direct experience and the truths of science has an altogether different character. The wooden table that presents itself as a single substance to our senses is actually made up of molecules, atoms, and particles in motion. Both the macroscopic object we sense and handle and its microscopic constituents disclosed by scientific inquiry are real. Science informs us about relations and causes that are behind and beyond our sense impressions. Despite Dewey's disclaimer, its concepts are objectively true representations of the content of the external world.

Dewey tries to disqualify objective truth by identifying it with the idea of absolute truth. The concepts and laws of science are not absolute in the sense of being unconditioned, immutable, and eternal. Nonetheless, they are objective truths which can be amplified, amended, corrected and improved as scientific knowledge of the world advances. The usefulness that instrumentalism makes central comes from the correspondence of ideas with the facts.

For Dewey truth and usefulness are not inseparable in science. A scientific hypothesis need not correspond with reality. "It is notorious," he writes, "that hypotheses do not have to be true in order to be highly serviceable in the conduct of inquiry." Of decisive importance is not the degree of truth possessed by scientific ideas but their usefulness, or, as he phrases it, "their operational character as means" (*Logic,* p. 142).

This nonchalant dismissal of their objective truth would transform scientific laws into "useful fictions." Such a theory cannot even account for the displacement of one hypothesis by another in the history of the sciences. However convenient the earth-centered Ptolemaic scheme had been for centuries in arranging and interpreting astronomical phenomena, it was permanently superseded at the dawn of modern science by the sun-centered Copernican thesis which more accurately corresponded to the realities of our solar system. Dewey performed a disservice to the understanding of scientific method by disjoining theoretical and practical usefulness from truth. The closer a hypothesis approximates the truth, the more serviceable it is.

Empirical Naturalism and Dialectical Materialism

Experience and Nature was the nearest Dewey came to presenting a conception of reality that would be both materialist and evolutionary. He preferred to call his interpretation naturalistic and empirical. These terms were less offensive to the philosophic conventions in the Anglo-American intellectual circles where he sought acceptance for his ideas.

He identified materialism as a world view with the natural-scientific mechanical school of the nineteenth century, just as he identified dialectics with the Hegelian speculative method. Both were in disfavor among academic philosophers of his time.

His criticisms invariably pertain to that outmoded type of mechanical materialism based upon fixed and unchangeable entities. Until old age he was not well acquainted with the dialectical materialism that had transcended the limitations and errors of the mechanical school and created a higher mode of materialist thought. When he did learn something about its doctrines, he explicitly repudiated them.

Dewey also knew of dialectics primarily in its idealistic versions. After its initial attraction, this logic meant to him imposing arbitrary patterns of thought upon ever-changing situations to the detriment of their empirical features. The Marxist dialectic that saw the logic of contradiction at work in the objective facts seemed to him an absurdity that yoked incompatible opposites together.

Despite his rejection of what these terms represented, Dewey's analysis in *Experience and Nature* did contain elements of the dialectical and materialist approach to reality. But these were present in an undeveloped and haphazard form and embedded in a matrix of contrary conceptions.

Materialism regards nature as primary, and life and thought as derivative and dependent phenomena. The formation of stars and planets has to precede the formation of animate beings. Although Dewey more or less proceeded on this premise in practice, he did not stick to it consistently in his theorizing. He was erratically materialistic, pragmatically wandering onto other paths when that was expedient.

For instance, in the preface to *Experience and Nature* he said: "There is in the character of human experience no index-hand pointing to agnostic conclusions, but rather a growing progressive self-disclosure of nature itself" (p. x). This is an ostensibly materialist view. Yet it is vitiated by his denial that science discloses the real inwardness of nature and by his introjection of subjective phenomena into the physical world.

The dialectical conception of the universe is evolutionary through and through. It looks upon the world not as an assemblage of fixed objects with unchanging relations but as a complex of processes in never-ending flux and development. Nothing is everlasting, no distinctions are absolutely rigid, no divisions are insurmountable.

Dewey did his best to evolutionize all aspects of reality and overcome the hard-and-fast partitions and dualisms that afflicted the classical empiricists. "Every existence is an event. . . . The important thing is measure, relation, ratio, knowledge of the comparative tempos of change. In mathematics some variables are constants in some problems; so it is in nature and life," he declared (ibid., p. 71). These thoughts are in accord with Hegel's logic. All things are in transition from one state to another, just as humans keep passing from one situation to another. Nothing is totally fixed and final.

Dewey protested against eternal traits of reality, eternal laws of thought, eternal truths, eternal social relations, and the immutable standards of morality characteristic of many earlier systems of Western philosophy. "They have seen themselves, and have represented themselves to the public, as dealing with something which has variously been termed Being, Nature or the Universe, the Cosmos at large, Reality, the Truth. Whatever names were used, they had one thing in common: they were used to designate something taken to be fixed, immutable, and therefore out of time; that is, eternal," he remarked in the introduction to *Reconstruction in Philosophy* (p. 12).

In opposition to this metaphysical mode of reasoning, Dewey insisted that change was the most fundamental and universal feature of reality and every existing thing was historically relative to changing circumstances. His demand that philosophy do away with eternal entities, unchangeable relations, and absolute axioms in every field was progressive. However, he drew from this sound premise the incorrect conclusion that no general laws of the ever-changing processes of reality were operative and that it was unnecessary to look for them.

Being is only a phase of becoming, the ceaseless process of entering into existence, enduring, evolving, and passing away. The processes of change, no less than the products of change, are governed by objective laws that can be, must be, and have been—up to a certain point—discovered, formulated, and applied. These laws of universal becoming, which incorporate the laws of being as an integral but subsidiary part of their totality, constitute the content of dialectics.

Once the thoroughgoing mutability of nature is acknowledged, it is not futile to search for the general laws of its development, as Dewey suggests. The task is to uncover those laws that can provide the broadest and most profound formulation of the processes of change, embracing both being and becoming in their interconnections and convertibility.

Chemistry has not been content to discover and analyze the separate elements or even to arrange them in orderly sequence in a table of atomic weights. It has gone further and sought to understand and explain the interaction and transformation of atoms and molecules in their infinite diversity, as a guiding principle of its research.

Philosophy and mathematics have passed through analogous developments. The first mathematicians dealt with invariant relations of space in geometry and fixed numerical magnitudes in arithmetic. Turning points came in mathematics when magnitudes were treated as variable, and spatial relations as transformable. This made it possible to represent not only states but processes in mathematical terms. Neither the invention of the calculus nor the introduction of groups of transformations into geometry abolished the validity or applicability of more elementary branches of mathematics; these were included as special cases of broader principles.

Dialectical thinking stands in the same relation to formal and metaphysical thought as the lower branches of mathematics to the higher. It takes as its foundation motion and transformation, not static relations and states of rest, and draws out all the logical implications of this principle.

*   *   *

In summation: Dewey did not present a coherent interpretation of the "nature of nature," one of the central issues in philosophy. His account of the relations between experience and the external world, between matter and mind, between material conditions and actions, subordinated the objective to the subjective factors in human life under the guise of giving equivalent status to them both in the "inclusive integrity of experience." He deprived causality of its objective basis by defining it as a purely logical category and awarding primacy to contingency in nature.

He did not acknowledge the objective basis of scientific concepts and laws that makes them true as well as applicable and fruitful. He injected extraneous emotional reactions and mental functions like imagination into the physical world, thus blurring the boundary between what belongs to nature and what comes from human interactions with it.

Dewey's empirical naturalism did not peer deeper into the heart of nature than any rival philosophy, as he claimed; nor did his instrumentalist conceptions come abreast of the most advanced procedures of contemporary natural science. They fell short of the aspiration of harmonizing experience with reality that motivated his philosophizing.

8

Dewey's
Logical Method

Dewey several times remarked that "contemporary logical theory is the ground upon which all philosophical differences and disputes are gathered together and focused" (*Reconstruction in Philosophy*, p. 134). This is so. The mainspring of a philosophy resides in the reasoning procedures through which its specific conclusions are reached. The method of production is as decisive in the sphere of intellectual activity as in the economy. Just as technology is an essential determinant of social structures, so the techniques of thought shape the framework of conceptual systems.

The differences between pragmatism and Marxism are sharply manifested in the contrast between their respective logical methods. These are incompatible and should not be indiscriminately mixed together. It is necessary to understand the roots and the nature of the differences between the opposing logics of instrumentalism and materialist dialectics and choose between them in practice.

Dewey was primarily a logician. From his earliest writings to his *Logic*, published in 1938, he displayed unflagging interest in the theory of thought. He gave courses in formal and Hegelian logic at Michigan from 1884 to 1888 and later taught Hegel's logic at Chicago.

In pragmatism he and his associates claimed to have developed a superior mode of thought that took into account the experimental procedures of modern science and gave a more correct, comprehensive, and concrete explanation of the nature of knowledge and the function of ideas. He began to elaborate the principal propositions of his instrumentalist logic around the turn of the century. These were first outlined in *Studies in Logical Theory* published in 1903. The essays in that original volume were rewritten and reprinted with others in *Essays in Experimental Logic*, which appeared in 1916. His final conclusions were presented in the *Logic* of 1938. It contained the ripened fruit of a lifetime devoted to the study of the theory of knowledge.

This systematic exposition of his views was designed, he wrote in the preface, to further the aim of "bringing logical theory into accord with scientific practice" and "with all the best authenticated methods of attaining knowledge." A critical review of its main positions can tell us how well he succeeded in these aims.

Logical Form and Material Content

The problem of the relation between content and form is critical in logical theory. The science of the thought process concerns itself with a special kind of form: the forms that the operations of thought have produced in the course of their evolution. These forms range from the concept to various kinds of propositions and sets of judgments.

What is the content of concepts and the more complex forms of thought studied by logic? Do they have a purely mental content or do they necessarily reflect empirical data derived from the external world?

There are two opposing viewpoints on this issue. At one extreme stand the pure formalists who completely detach the forms of thought from all material content and historical conditioning. They construe logical forms as entities existing by and for themselves apart from any objective reference. Form is absolutely counterposed to substance.

The other school maintains that forms void of substance are not only empty but fictitious; every logical form possesses real content, although some are richer in connotation than others. Logical form and empirical data have an indissoluble connection. Between the two poles lies a broad spectrum of eclectic combinations and variant positions.

Dewey clearly grasped the importance for logical theory of the relation between form and content. He wrote in *Logic:* "This problem is so fundamental that the way in which it is dealt with constitutes the basic ground of difference among logical theories." This is certainly true of all conceptions of logic, his own included.

Dewey grappled with the problem of form and content in logic from the outset of his career as a professional philosopher. His views on this subject had an interesting evolution. In his apprenticeship he was a disciple of Hegel as that German thinker's ideas were reinterpreted by the Anglo-American idealists of the late nineteenth century. He acquired a repugnance to formalism from the transcendental logic of the neo-Hegelians, which held that form and content, subject and object, reason and reality not only existed in inseparable unity but, in the last analysis of reality, where the Absolute reigned, were even identical with one another.

So long as he adhered to this outlook, Dewey was a severe critic not only of formal logic but also of the inductive logic that empiricists such as Whewell and John Stuart Mill had developed in the first half of the nineteenth century. Before Dewey, Mill had been troubled by the gap between the traditional formal logic and the actual procedures of modern scientific investigation as he perceived them. He had sought to overcome this deficiency by devising a supplementary logic of induction that purported to analyze and codify the actual empirical procedures of the natural scientists.

Mill did not discard the deductive logic originating with Aristotle but kept it as a department of reasoning subsidiary to his newer inductive theory. He instituted a division of labor between the two. The deductive procedures of the older logic were supposed to take care of the formal aspects of the reasoning process, while the methods of induction that he enumerated, described, and classified were to cover inquiry into matters of fact.

This split the domain of logic into two opposed parts—one deductive and *a priori*, the other inductive and *a posteriori;* and thereby gave rise to two different kinds of logic, one pure, the other applied. Although the latter-day English empiricists considered the compromise a satisfactory working solution of the problem of form and content, it threw the science of logic into a state of disunity and disarray that Dewey, among others, deemed unacceptable.

In his revulsion against formal logic Dewey at one time swung to the extreme of denying that it had any value or validity whatsoever. "Formal thought, with its formulae for simply unfolding a given material, is of no use to science," he asserted (cited in *The Origin of Dewey's Instrumentalism* by Morton G. White, p. 90). This total rejection of formal logic was unwarranted. The formal canons stemming from Aristotle have been found inadequate as a logic for all purposes, and especially for the higher functions of thought dealing with complex processes and the essentially contradictory constitution of all things. Nonetheless, even today they are indispensable as an elementary tool of thought. Formal logic bears the same relation to dialectical logic as hand tools to machine tools. An ordinary hand drill is useful for many purposes, even though work requiring a high degree of precision can be better performed by an automatic turret lathe or a boring machine.

Humans thought in a syllogistic manner, proceeding from a major premise through a minor one to a conclusion, long before Aristotle and others singled out the successive steps that make up this chain of reasoning and named and analyzed the various kinds of syllogism. For better or worse, all of us continue to reason along this line, day in, day out. At the same time this primary type of reasoning is unsuited to the more developed operations of thought and has been supplanted and incorporated into a more elaborate and correct system of logic.

Even after molting his absolute idealism, Dewey retained his sweeping repudiation of formal logic and sharp criticisms of the shortcomings of Mill's inductive supplement. He likewise clung to the conviction, shared with Hegel, that the severance of the forms of thought from their objective content was an inadmissable distortion of reality.

As he moved along toward instrumentalism, however, he modified the categories of the Hegelian logic in a characteristic manner. For example, under the ideological influences of Darwinism and the psychology of William James, plus the impact of Progressivism, he substituted his own beveled, gradualist version of "conflict" for Hegel's keen-edged definition of contradiction. To Hegel everything contained within itself opposing poles. Their interactions generated the phases of the evolution of the entity until the eventual irreconcilable clash between the essential elements caused its transcendence to a new and higher stage through the destruction of the positive pole by the negative. This dialectical process of development found its perfected logical formulation in the law of the negation of the negation.

For Dewey the struggle between the contending sides of a single situation did not of necessity, by its very nature, lead to the destruction of the one by the other in an act of negation that lifted the entity to a higher form of its own being. The "unbalance" between the conflicting forces was to be resolved by the readjustment and reconciliation of the differences in a reconstructed situation. He thereby deleted the mainspring of the dialectic from his logic, making it revolve around the reformation of a "troubled situation" rather than its revolutionization.

Dewey's eventual solution of the relation between logical forms and content in his *Logic* was neither fully formalistic nor thoroughly materialistic, although his "naturalistic" theory came much closer to the materialist than the formalist standpoint. He categorically denied that logical forms could exist apart from their content. He agreed with such masters of logic as Aristotle and Hegel, as well as the materialists, that forms of any kind are inseparable from objective content. Moreover, he took an evolutionary approach to the genesis of logical forms.

Logical forms come into existence only under certain circumstances, when controlled inquiry is undertaken in order to actualize potential uses of things. "Logical forms accrue to subject-matter in virtue of subjection of the latter in inquiry to the conditions determined by its end—institution of a warranted conclusion" (*Logic*, p. 372).

Dewey's view that logical forms are created through historical processes of inquiry was correct. But he did not go deeply enough into the problem because he failed to divulge the ultimate roots of the science of logic in the interactions and interrelations of the physical world.

Logic and the Physical World

Inanimate nature stands at the opposite pole to logical thought. What are the connections of the one with the other?

Dewey seriously attempted to provide an empirical basis for the processes of thought and to account for the unity of logic with the rest of reality as experienced. A consistent materialism or evolutionism would hold that the fundamental "matrix of inquiry" (in which methods of inquiry are generated and operate and to which they refer) is the physical world. Humanity, an offspring of nature, occupies a particular place and plays a unique role in it. Its activities and intelligence function in unbreakable association with the physical environment. How, then, can it be overlooked that the underlying "natural foundation of inquiry" is the physical world?

Dewey says that "the final test" of the applicability of a proposition "resides in the *connections* that exist among things" (*Logic*, p. 55, emphasis in the original). Yet he does not view these existential conditions as the ultimate determinant of logical processes. There are two major kinds of involvement and interaction of existential conditions on earth: the interrelation of purely physical events with one another, and their interaction with human beings.

Even if we set aside the question of whether inanimate events exhibit any logical pattern and what this may be (the dialectic of nature), there remains the problem of the causal relation of the inorganic world to organic activities that eventually give rise to human procedures of inquiry. This problem is posed for logic by any case of conscious behavior.

I walk out of the house, notice that black clouds are gathering, return to the house, get an umbrella and come out again. What has determined my course of conduct and the thought pattern motivating it? I have learned from experience that as a rule in that locality rain descends when black clouds appear. The generalization derived from this repeatedly observed physical correlation in nature has guided both my reasoning and my action.

The core of my thought process takes the form of a syllogism: masses of black clouds portend rain; black clouds are gathering overhead; therefore it is likely to rain. From this reasoning I draw the practical conclusion of taking certain precautions to protect myself from a downpour.

The processes of nature that have been observed, understood, and generalized as laws underlie the "habits of action" that arise from my mode of thought. In the last analysis both my behavior and the concomitant reasoning depend upon the natural events I and others have experienced, noted, and reacted to. Yet this primary objective factor in the causation of my conduct and thought is absent from Dewey's explanation for the origin of logic. He neglects the first determinant of the thought process, the conditions of the physical matrix.

He points out that "although biological operations and structures are not sufficient conditions of inquiry, they are necessary conditions." This is correct. Why, then, are not the events and structures underlying the biological level also "necessary," though insufficient, preconditions? They too "prepare the way and foreshadow the pattern" of inquiry.

"If one denies the supernatural," Dewey writes, "then one has the intellectual responsibility of indicating how the logical may be connected with the biological in a process of continuous development" (*Logic,* p. 25). It is all the more obligatory for a consistent naturalist to show how the logical is connected with the inorganic world—and through what intermediate links. Dewey's failure to do this is the most glaring breach of continuity in his exposition of the real foundations of logic.

The Biological Basis of Logic

According to Dewey, logic is ultimately rooted not in the physical world at large, but in a special sector of it, the activities of organisms. The forms and content of logic have a biological basis. Its evolutionary beginnings can be traced back to the interactions between the organism and its environment and its corresponding motor adjustments. Habits that grew out of motor responses became the groundwork of learning. Habits of thought are the outgrowth of the repeated actions of animal behavior.

"Rational operations," he says, "grow out of organic activities" (*Logic,* p. 19). This is correct so far as it goes. But there is a step beyond this point. Genetically, organic activities grow out of preceding and surrounding inorganic conditions.

By locating an objective foundation for logic beyond the precinct of the thought process in which it is immediately manifested, Dewey opposed the formalists for whom logic has no earthly roots or material reference. The pure formalists believe that the forms and content of logic are self-centered, self-generated, and self-contained, amounting to a mere subjective pattern within the human mind. They are unable to explain how logical thought came into existence, takes the forms it does, and can be applied fruitfully to objective reality—except through some miraculous parallelism between the realm of reason and the external world. Indeed, some consistent adherents to this viewpoint deny that logic has, or needs to have, any intrinsic relation or reference whatsoever to society or nature.

Dewey rejected this idealist position and searched for the correlation between logic and the outside world. He pointed to biology, as exhibited first in animal and later in human behavior, as the source of logical thought. He saw it as an instrument, a set of ideas about ideas and instrumentalities, that originated in the efforts of living creatures to adapt themselves to their environment and get along better in the world.

It is true that habits of thought that produce patterns of logic are foreshadowed in animal struggles for survival and emerge out of the persistently repeated actions of human beings in their productive exchanges with nature. As Lenin observed: "Man's practice, repeating itself a thousand million times, becomes consolidated in man's consciousness by figures of logic. Precisely (and only) on account of this million-fold repetition, these figures have the stability of a prejudice, an axiomatic character" (*Philosophical Notebooks,* in *Collected Works,* vol. 38, p. 217).

The forms as well as the content of logic were prefigured and evidenced in animal behavior long before humans became conscious of them and scientifically analyzed them. The formation of intelligence in humans was preceded and prepared by the evolution of sagacity among the animals. The higher animals are capable of many of the elementary operations of inquiry, including induction, deduction, abstraction, analysis, synthesis, and experiment. Their learned actions are predicated on primitive steps of reasoning from simple premises to conclusions.

A cat is capable of reasoning on the basis of those limited generalizations learned from its experiences. When it stalks a mouse, it implicitly proceeds from the unstated syllogism: mice taste good; this is a mouse; it is edible. The mouse likewise acts in accord with its own generalized experience—cats are dangerous; this is a cat; therefore, it is dangerous—and scampers away.

Of course, neither the cat nor the mouse is capable of understanding that their behavior has a syllogistic pattern. Such an idea could never enter their heads, which do not reason about reasoning. That feat of intelligence required the capabilities of a civilized culture leading to the insights of an Aristotle.

While Dewey is essentially right in his view that there is a "community of factors in the respective patterns of logical and biological forms and procedures" (*Logic,* p. 41), that does not tell the whole story. Logic, like biological behavior itself, is anchored in the external environment.

Dewey went only part way in meeting the requirements of a materialist logic; he hesitated to develop the empirical side of his theory to its full logical conclusion. His refusal to admit that logic can be traced in its origins to the processes of nature, and that its content reflects these processes, coincides with the fundamental epistemological position of pragmatism—that thought in general, and ideas in particular, do not disclose any antecedent reality. To assert that thought reflects reality is, in Dewey's eyes, to revert to the false and outmoded "intellectualistic" tradition of Aristotle and Hegel, who taught that the real was rational and the rational had reality.

By removing the organic tie between reason and reality Dewey did not, as he claimed, progress beyond Spinoza and Hegel, who believed that the order and connection of ideas was the same as the order and connection of things. He moved backward even from Aristotle. These eminent thinkers held that logic and nature are interdependent, that the same content is expressed in different forms in the objective world and in mental procedures, and that a logic without correspondence with external reality would be meaningless and worthless.

In this respect the older logicians were closer to the truth than Dewey, who left a gap between logic and nature that could not be completely bridged by recognizing the role of biological functions in the making of logic. Animal behavior, which comes between nature at large and human thought, itself rests upon the physical habitat.

The Social and Historical Preconditions of Logic

Dewey next examines the social setting, or "cultural matrix," out of which logical properties evolved. He singles out language as the prime factor "in effecting the transformation of the biological into the intellectual and the potentially logical" (*Logic,* p. 45).

To make this explanation plausible, he stretches the definition of language to cover virtually all the activities and artifacts of human beings from the means of production to the media of communication. "A tool or machine, for example. is not simply a simple or complex physical object having its own physical properties and effects, but is also a mode of language. For it *says* something, to those who understand it, about operations of use and their consequences. To the members of a primitive community a loom operated by steam or electricity says nothing. It is composed in a foreign language, and so with most of the mechanical devices of modern civilization" (*Logic,* p. 46).

Dewey here invokes a literary metaphor to rub out the essential existential difference between instruments of labor and verbal expression. Because of its place and function in their economic activity, a tool indeed has significance and value to members of the community who make and use it. And a steam-driven loom producing textiles in a factory might at first sight appear magical to preindustrial peoples familiar with only hand weaving.

But while speech may accompany the fabrication and employment of tools, it is wrong to subsume the material instrument of production under the category of linguistic expression. This inverts both the order of their origination and their real relations in the social process.

Labor and language are two of the fundamental social and historical preconditions of logical thought. The first has a more inclusive character than the second and came into existence before it. Laboring activity was the novel and unique function that humanized our progenitors and elevated our species above the other primates. The use and making of tools and weapons to produce the means of subsistence, protection, and shelter preceded the development of articulate speech among our ancestors. Tools have been found in Africa that are from two to three million years old. It would be more correct to classify language as a tool than tools as forms of expression, as Dewey does.

Moreover, as Dewey's associate G. H. Mead recognized, gesture language, carried on with the hands and whole body, was a more rudimentary mode of expression and communication than talking in words and sentences. Even today not only primitive peoples but we ourselves resort to this form of "language without words" when we nod our heads in assent or shake them in dissent.

Laboring fostered the emergence of audible speech. Dewey himself writes that language arose as "a medium of communication in order to bring about deliberate cooperation and competition in conjoint activities, that has conferred upon existential things their signifying or evidential power" (*Logic,* p. 56). These "conjoint activities" were centered around procuring and producing the necessities of life. Articulate utterances were called forth by the cooperative behavior involved in working for a living. While the instruments of labor transmitted human energies to the materials worked upon, speech served as a medium of coordination among the laborers. The hominid that first learned to talk and think began by putting its hands to work both in producing and communicating, long before its tongue and brain became apt at verbal conversation.

Dewey does not view speech as an outgrowth and adjunct of productive activity but endows it with a prior and superior status. Language is the producer of "all that culture involves" and is the only means of transmitting its acquisitions from generation to generation. Like Vico, he believes that language constitutes the essence of the human species.

In actuality, the continuity of social development is based upon and assured by the transmission of the humanly created conditions of production, starting with the crudest stone, wood, or bone implements and the technical skills involved in their fabrication and use. The modification of the things of nature by collective work is the material matrix from which the earliest culture evolves.

Once language emerges, it becomes an integral and indispensable element of human activity of all kinds, and primarily of productive activity. Speech and thought grow in importance as labor progresses.

Dewey in his own way takes note of the primacy of work when he writes that "tools constitute a kind of language which is in more compelling connection with things of nature than are words . . ." (*Logic,* p. 94). It should be added that the instruments of labor have this "more compelling connection" because they enable humans to bring about changes in objects that turn them to useful account. Both tools and words, which can be likened to "sound-tools," serve and promote the purposes of labor. But without the interposition of the instruments of labor, words alone could not transform the materials of nature into useful objects.

Dewey explained that the Greek thinkers who created the science of logic exalted knowing above doing and making. They hypostatized Reason because of the class structure of their society, in which craftsmen, mechanics, and artisans were dominated and depreciated by the leisured aristocracy. But this insight did not inoculate Dewey against a touch of the same bias. He himself unwittingly made the head superior to the hand by giving priority to speech over work in the formation of humanity and the march of historical development.

Since labor is animated and directed by purpose in the brain before it is objectified through practice, its activities promote the development of consciousness beyond mere sensation and perception. The labor process generates ideas, which find expression in articulate utterances. Thus labor, language, and thought evolve in constant interaction with one another.

Logic is the science of the thought process. But since the results of thought are crystallized in language, the analysis of the forms of speech has provided the starting point and the raw materials for analyzing the patterns of thought. The connection between logic and language is based upon the union of language and thought.

Dewey traces the origin of logic as an autonomous branch of knowledge to reflection upon the structures of language. Logic emerged, he wrote, when the Greeks began to "reflect upon language, upon *logos*, in its syntactical structure and its wealth of meaning contents" (*Logic,* p. 58). The first analysis of logical forms proceeded from analysis of the forms of grammar.

This account of the genesis of logic conforms to Dewey's thesis that culture is primarily a product of language, which gives meaning to associated activities, and that language is the key to transforming the biological into the intelligible and the logical. But it is rather superficial to attribute the advent of logic to the analysis of language, although that study did play an important part in its making.

What impelled the Greeks to focus sustained and deep-going attention upon the elements of rational discourse? The way for logical theory was prepared not simply by examining the structure of language, but by the exceptional conditions assembled in the secular and rationalized atmosphere of the most highly developed Greek cities.

The science of logic is one of the many innovations of Greek culture, which range from the creation of philosophy, geometry, and rational medical practice to comedy and tragedy. The Greeks rather than other peoples of antiquity pioneered these developments by virtue of the special features of their urban life, which was based upon a merchant, craft, and slave economy engaged in elementary commodity production.

The citizens of the democratic states like Athens participated as equals in public affairs. Questions of policy were settled not by kings and nobles but by debate in the agora, where every male member of the polis could speak freely and follow the arguments of the contending sides. Skill in public speaking was the stock-in-trade of the advocate, the rhetorician, the sophistical teacher of wisdom, the statesman, the general, and even the ordinary active citizen.

Dialectics flourished in the adversary proceedings and disputations of the assembly and law tribunals. This art of discussion by way of antitheses, invented by Zeno, was brought to perfection in the Platonic dialogues, which proceeded by way of contradiction and its resolution. One of the two principals in the debate put forward a proposition, which was challenged and opposed by the other. The discussion unfolded until the original thesis was either rejected or modified and restated in a form acceptable to both parties.

Such practices gave an impetus to defining and classifying concepts, analyzing and naming the steps in the reasoning process, and discovering the rules that guided and governed them. These three aspects of dialectics were reflected in the threefold meaning of *logos*. This Greek term referred at the same time to the speech of orators in the assembly, reason (the capacity for arguing that distinguished humans from beasts), and the lawfulness in things.

The democratization of written language along with public speech-making led to the study of grammar together with logic. Alphabetic writing, which was widely known among the members of the Greek communities, promoted abstract thinking and enabled the parts of speech and the elements of thought to become distinct objects of cognition. The growth of mathematics and theoretical problems raised by the new science of geometry provided a model of rational procedure for the logicians.

Finally, logic was called upon to cope with the problems brought forward by the polemics of all the contending schools of philosophizing since the Milesians, such as the relation of the one and the many, the same and the different; the nature of contradiction; the status of the law of identity. Restless speculation about how the contradictory aspects of things could be rationally formulated and consistently defined preoccupied thinkers from Parmenides to Socrates. In such Platonic dialogues as the *Theatetus*, all the elements that Aristotle was to organize into a systematic exposition of the canons of logic are present as in an uncrystallized solution.

Such were the immediate preconditions that gave birth to the first system of logic, which was formulated by Aristotle and his school.

Appraising Aristotelean Logic

Dewey's appraisal of formal logic casts light upon some distinctive features of his own logical positions. Aristotle's logic rests, he noted, upon his theory of being and of knowledge. The same pattern of characteristics is reproduced on the ontological, epistemological, and logical levels of Aristotle's system.

In Aristotle's metaphysics nature consists of unchanging substances with inherent and fixed properties. Each one of these entities is energized by a form that directs it toward a prescribed end. All together they constitute an ordered hierarchy of qualitatively different kinds of things, each with its special essential nature and possessing various grades of being from mere potentiality to plenitude.

Aristotle teaches that the mode of cognizing objects differs according to the extent of their changefulness and variability. Sensation and perception, the lowest kinds of apprehension, deal with what is particular, partial, and unfinished; things that are disfigured by matter. Whatever is changing and tending to pass into its opposite, whatever is transient and perishable, can be sensed and perceived but is too indefinite to be rationally known. As an imperfect and unfulfilled entity, it belongs to the accidental, not the necessary and general.

Necessary forms of being can be held up to scrutiny in two ways: by definition and by classification. The first sets forth the essence that makes things what they truly are. The second ascertains what kind of unchanging species they belong to or are excluded from. The objects of genuinely scientific knowledge consist of self-sufficient, self-active substances, having different essential natures, occupying places of different value in the hierarchy of species, and controlled by their own innate ends.

The classical logic was molded by these presumptions. Each subject of a judgment is as self-contained and unchanging as each substance.

Propositions must take the form of attributing a predicate to a subject in accord with the scheme of nature in which everything is identified by inclusion in or exclusion from a substantial species. Universal propositions refer to these self-contained substantial entities.

The syllogism is a chain of propositions that proceeds from a general premise to a particular conclusion through three steps of deduction. It is the logical analog of subsuming every entity under the appropriate species with its eternal characteristics.

Dewey's delineation of Aristotle's ideas is accurate. The various segments of his philosophic system are all cut from the same cloth. Aristotle's doctrine that anything changeable is so imperfectly realized and unformed that it can only yield inferior knowledge goes with the view that only the permanent and imperishable, the perfected being, can be truly known by our reason and is thereby the proper province of logical thought.

The elementary logic of Aristotle, and even more its underlying metaphysics, have been outmoded by the progress of science, culture, and logic over the past 2,500 years. The theory of universal evolution has proved that there are no timeless and imperishable entities in the universe. The theory of organic evolution has demonstrated that species of plants and animals are not immutable but, like everything else, come into existence, develop, and die out. Historical evolution shows that social formations are not everlasting but can be modified and even revolutionized in accord with the growth of the social productive forces.

These revolutionary advances in the scientific and philosophical approach to reality have brought about a reversal in attitude toward change itself and the ways of dealing with it. For Aristotle change was the mark of matter, which could be empirically handled but was not, like form, susceptible to intellectual grasp and logical definition and classification. Becoming was contingent, not necessary; particular, not general; it belonged to the nonessential side of being.

Nowadays change, development, evolution are seen as the very essence of the material universe. Being is a phase of the never-ending processes of becoming. Meanwhile, physical science has done away with the teleological interpretation of motion and change as tending toward an inherent end.

Dewey's criticisms of the metaphysical, nonevolutionary, teleological traits of Aristotelean logic are well-founded. Yet he does not address himself to its fundamental defect—its incapacity to cope with the contradictory aspects of reality and thereby with the lawful changes of things into their own opposites.

Aristotle, like other Greek thinkers, was fully familiar with the existence of contradictions in things. But he could not see how change and contradiction could be comprehended, logically formalized, and rationally formulated because these were qualities of physical matter, not essential form. He thereby excluded these aspects of reality from his logic and relegated them to the prerational realm. The categories of his logic are motionless. They are limited to dealing with what is static and unvarying in quality. They are incapable of encompassing the processes through which one thing is transmuted into something else.

Dewey's instrumentalism prevented him from perceiving the core of truth in formal logic that was Aristotle's enduring achievement. This is made plain in his counterconception of the nature and function of the three basic principles of formal logic: identity, contradiction, and excluded middle.

Aristotle's logic should not be low-rated as merely an outdated relic of Greek culture and science, an ideological reflection of the class structure of the Greek city-states. It has more lasting substance than that. Its principles correctly formulate, if but in a partial and one-sided way, existing features of objective reality. These endow its laws with a degree of usefulness.

The law of identity—A equals A—expresses the relative stability of things that enables us to distinguish one from another and make them the subject of meaningful judgment. Things are equal—or sufficiently similar—to themselves despite their variations over limited spans of time so that they can be treated as constants.

The law of formal contradiction, which is the inseparable complement of the law of identity, sets forth the truth that, if a thing is equal to itself, it belongs to its own category and cannot be included in some other.

The law of excluded middle, which logically flows from the first two, says that something is either categorically affirmed or categorically denied. Either A is B or it is not B; no third is possible.

According to Dewey, Aristotle was wrong to regard these as ontological principles that reflect inherent relations of propositions. They are not properties of objects. They are merely stipulations that regulate the course of inquiry. If it is asked why such limiting goals have to be satisfied, Dewey answers that the findings of previous inquiries make the requirement reasonable.

Such an explanation does not step beyond the closed circle of the processes of inquiry themselves. Since Dewey's theory is not ultimately grounded on the relations, properties, and processes of objective reality, he denies that external conditions could impel inquiry along the particular lines expressed in these rules.

Aristotle's logic was more soundly and securely based than Dewey's purely functional logic in that one respect. The Greek genius correctly saw the necessity to base logic on the objective characteristics of being, whereas Dewey's logic rests on human habits. The foundation of the latter's logic is anthropological, not ontological.

Here is how Dewey presents his view of the first principles of formal logic: "According to one view, such principles represent ultimate invariant properties of the *objects* with which methods of inquiry are concerned, and to which inquiry must conform. According to the view here expressed, they represent conditions which have been ascertained during the conduct of continued inquiry to be involved in its own successful pursuit. The two statements may seem to *amount* to the same thing. Theoretically, there is a radical difference between them. For the second position implies . . . that the principles are generated in the very process of control of continued inquiry, while, according to the other view, they are *a priori* principles fixed antecedently to inquiry and conditioning it *ab extra*" (*Logic,* pp. 11-12).

The two conceptions of logic are radically different. One bases itself on organic habits and does not go beyond them; the other is more broadly and deeply based upon elements of objective reality that determine habitual actions and operations—and thus determine the inquiries and inferences of logic.

The adjectives "invariant" and *"a priori"* inserted by Dewey do point to certain weaknesses of Aristotle's logic. But they also obscure the source of its strength and longevity. Aristotle was the first to discern the central importance of the law of identity in the thought process and make it the keystone of logical theory. This law, which is alien to mythical and mystical modes of explanation, is indispensable for scientific inquiry and rational thought and discourse.

Aristotle went astray in two ways. He made the law of identity into an absolute rule that applied unconditionally to all things under all circumstances without exception. And he disjoined identity from difference, giving it a simple, homogeneous nature, whereas in concrete reality it has a dual composition. By ignoring the differences within identity, his idealized, oversimplified, abstract, and one-sided interpretation of this category had a metaphysical, not a dialectical, character.

Things are not only stable but unstable. They are subject to change to such a degree that they can be transformed into something quite different. Logical theory has to take this contradictory aspect of the constitution and development of things into account. But the very premises of Aristotelean logic— based upon the principle that A always equals A, that a thing is under any and all circumstances equal to itself and no other— preclude it from acknowledging this essential aspect of reality. This inherent and insuperable limitation of formal logic eventually led to its supplanting by a higher, more comprehensive, more concrete system of logical thought: the dialectic, based upon the recognition of ceaseless change and the contradictory character of reality.

That does not warrant the denial of the validity of the laws of formal logic within their limitations. Dewey falls into such a barren negation. He attributes no more objective content to the laws of logic than he does to the laws of nature or the laws of social development. For example, he writes that physical laws are "inherently conceptual in character. . . . they are *relations* which are thought not observed" (*Quest for Certainty,* pp. 206-07, emphasis in the original). He goes so far as to describe causal laws as a mere "figure of speech" (*Logic,* p. 445). As an indeterminist, he also considers that no laws arising from the regularities of historical phenomena are to be found in the processes of social development; these exhibit no causal necessity.

While Dewey accords a regulative value to the laws of logic, he fails to see that they can fulfill such a function only because they reflect certain features of the material world that exist prior to the processes of inquiry and in fact condition its conduct.

His Theory of Inquiry

Dewey's approach to logic is off the beaten track. So great were the differences from conventional conceptions that he himself questioned whether his general theory should be termed logic as it is commonly understood. He believed that his book by that name might better be described simply by its subtitle: *The Theory of Inquiry.*

Peirce described Dewey's enterprise as the "natural history of thought." While he, too, looked upon his pragmatism as part of a general theory of inquiry, Peirce developed his logic along very different and much more mathematical lines.

Dewey did not base his logic on a theory of being, like Aristotle, or upon a dialectic of becoming, like Hegel, or upon the evolution of material reality, like Marx. Nor did he conceive of logic as some kind of propositional calculus, as the formalists and mathematical logicians do.

His logic of experiment takes its point of departure not from the nature of things but from what human beings do when they are in trouble. Activities do not involve logic so long as life proceeds without serious friction or conflict. But as soon as they encounter some block, people embark on a special mode of activity called inquiry which is called upon to clear up questions and dispose of problems in theory and in practice.

Their methods and instruments of inquiry give a logical character to their conduct. The rules, procedures, and forms that enable the operations of inquiry to be successful, that is, to resolve doubts and remove difficulties, constitute the content of logic. Logical theory studies the ways and means of inquiry that have been successful in past practice and can be applied to direct further inquiries in all areas of human endeavor.

Dewey discriminates five steps in the pattern of inquiry. The process originates in a felt disturbance of the equilibrium between the living creature and its environment which causes difficulties, generates uncertainty, and demands a readjustment of customary responses. Dewey is not Descartes, for whom doubt was a subjective phenomenon to be dispelled by individual intuition. The doubtfulness, the conflict, the indeterminateness are not simply in the thinking subject; they are pervasive qualities of the objective situation. That is why they cannot be eliminated merely by thought but have to be transformed by appropriate practical intervention. Dewey's theory of inquiry, like his theory of knowledge, is also a theory of action.

After the situation is seen to be one calling for a readjustment of customary responses, the specific nature of the problem at hand must be ascertained. This is arrived at through analysis and observation of the circumstances of the case.

Observation of the factual conditions generates ideas about what the difficulty really is and suggests lines of activity that might lead to a solution.

Then comes the phase of reasoning out the implications of the various hypotheses or anticipating the possible consequences of the intended plan of action.

The last step is the experimental test; the hypothesis is put into practice to see whether it yields the expected results. It is either confirmed, invalidated, or found wanting. In the event that the operation works out, the originally indeterminate and uncontrolled situation becomes a controlled and determinate one. The problem is settled, at least for the time being; the ambiguity is cleared up; effective activity can be resumed without hindrance.

The following is Dewey's summary statement of this procedure of reflective thinking and intelligent experiment: "Inquiry is the controlled or directed transformation of an indeterminate situation into one that is so determinate in its constituent distinctions and relations as to convert the elements of the original situation into a unified whole" (*Logic,* pp. 104–05).

It may be remarked that Dewey does not as a rule draw a sharp and clear distinction between the objective and subjective factors in the given situation but often leaves the two confused. This can be misleading because a situation may be indeterminate in two different senses, objectively and subjectively. As an ongoing process, it may still be developing, unfinished, unconsummated, its conflicting elements calling for discordant responses. Or the participant may be confused or doubtful about its nature and outcome, not knowing what to do about it at all and seeking to clarify his or her mind on these matters. A situation that is objectively determinate may appear uncertain to the individual. This difference becomes especially important in regard to the issues of the class struggle under capitalism.

All the elements of traditional logic concerning the forms of inference and judgment and the types of propositions (quantitative, qualitative, particular, general, universal) are reinterpreted in accordance with this outline of inquiry, and their functions are fitted somewhere in the sequence. As Dewey wrote toward the end of his career: "I tried the experiment of transferring the old well-known figures from the stage of ontology to the stage of inquiry" (quoted in *John Dewey on Experience, Nature and Freedom,* edited by R.J. Bernstein, p. 148).

In Dewey's view, thought is not self-starting but is provoked by a specific disturbance. Inquiry proceeds from the initial state of interrupted activity, through ideation and experimentation, until it is consummated in a reconstituted situation that satisfies the need for continued functioning. A proposition is intermediary and a judgment is conclusive in the settlement of a situation. But "final judgment is attained through a series of partial judgments" (*Logic,* p. 133). A judgment itself is instrumental to the practical reconstruction that terminates the inquiry.

The goal of inquiry is not the discovery or confirmation of truth. It is the attainment of a settled belief, the assertion most warranted under the given conditions. This assertion contains no necessity; it only has a greater or lesser degree of probability and can be unsettled even at the next turn of events.

For most philosophers since Plato and Aristotle, truth is a statement about things as they really are and falsehood asserts what is not. For Dewey, truth as warranted assertion is a relation between the first stage of inquiry (a situation giving rise to a problem) and the final stage of judgment, which gets rid of the problem. A belief is warranted not by its causal conditions and objective correlates, but by the efficacy of its consequences. Any correspondence of statements or ideas to facts is not existential but operational. It is similar to the relation between a plan and its fulfillment or between a purpose and its realization.

Dewey's model of logical behavior does point to many significant features of intelligent activity of the kind involved in a child's learning, an adult's figuring out his or her everyday problems, and a scientist's work. It bears the impress of his lifelong interest in the processes of education.

Yet it deletes some basic factors of logical thought, misconstrues others, and is deficient in dealing with complex processes of a dialectical character. Its gravest fault, which flows from the pragmatic theory of knowledge, lies in the assertion that the principles of logic refer to no material content and have no objective foundation. Logical forms, as Dewey sees it, are constituted in and through the process of inquiry in order to carry it out. They are the result of prior inquiries in practical activities or scientific research that have proved effective in problem-solving. But they do not reflect any antecedent existence. The conversion of eventual functions into antecedent existence is the greatest of philosophic fallacies, Dewey insists (*Experience and Nature,* p. 35).

If a predicate is affirmed of a subject ("This rose is red"), this simple form of judgment does not correspond to any property of that particular thing. Nor does the form refer to any general relation of objects. The subject–predicate relation happens to have been useful in repeated inquiries on countless occasions and is therefore available for further inquiries. Yet it cannot claim to have any backing in the actual integration of redness with the rose itself.

The materialist holds that objective conditions in the structure of natural and social phenomena underlie the regular recurrence of the subject-predicate form of thought. According to Dewey, not such causes but only the practical consequences give this form validity. Logical and mathematical forms, he says, are intrinsically postulational. They are not "given and imposed from without" by any external causes but are created in the course of inquiry as the best means for carrying it to a successful conclusion.

This denial of the objective relationship of the forms of thought to reality breaks down in regard to the most elementary unit, the concept, which expresses what is essential, determinative, and general in objects. Concepts are derived from perceptual materials based upon our sensations of objects in the external world. They are not arbitrarily postulated; their content is determined by the natural and social environment.

The concept of humanity is an abstraction that comprises those essential characteristics that distinguish our species from all others: the capacity to make and work with tools, talk, reason, generate fire, etc. These attributes are common to all its members.

To be sure, there are concepts of a very different kind. The centaur, half man and half horse, is one of them. In their form the two kinds of concepts are similar; both are mental images of something formed by generalization from particulars. But they have a diametrically different content in relation to the external world. One expresses what really exists; the other does not.

This is not to say that centaurs have no mode of existence whatsoever. These creations of our imagination have a place in art, literature, mythology, and language. But they have no material existence.

Dewey's interpretation of the principles and forms of logic as postulational is more formal than material. It slides over the difference between a man and a centaur. For him reasoning takes the forms that it does, logic consists of the forms that it has, solely because of their successful usage in inquiry. They then become postulates for further inquiry.

Thus, if our reasoning is syllogistic, that does not reflect the relations of anything outside of us, according to Dewey. This particular pattern of inference from a premise to a conclusion, which everyone engages in without ever having read a treatise on logic, is nothing but a habit that humans have fallen into because it brings results.

But why has this mental habit been so persistent and why does this form of thought produce results? Is it not because it corresponds to something "given and imposed from without"?

Logical and other concepts give extremely simplified representations of the relations in objective reality and thereby inescapably distort them to a certain extent. The same is true of chains of concepts. The statement "The rose is red" formally dissociates two elements, the thing and its color, that are actually integrated. Thus the mode of linguistic expression can breed errors of abstraction and lead to metaphysical misunderstandings. It is like a snapshot that freezes a moving and changing reality into an immobile posture. Yet all this does not cancel out the objective relevance and truth of the proposition.

Indeed, a syllogism unites the singular, particular, and general aspects of things and their mutual interconnections in a chain of reasoning. All men are mortal (general); Socrates is a man (singular); therefore, Socrates is mortal (particular). The process of organic evolution that Darwin disclosed exhibited this logical pattern. It is initiated by a deviation from the norm (singular); this variant is multiplied (particular); and eventually becomes the rule (general). That is one aspect of the logic of the origin of species.

Peirce, who also grappled with the problem of the nature of general ideas within the framework of pragmatism, did so in a less shallow way than Dewey. What does a statement like "this is hard" mean, he asked. He answered that whoever tries to scratch or dent the object will find its surface extremely resistant compared to softer substances.

But Peirce did not stop at operational consequences; he took two steps beyond that pragmatic point. This experimental evidence indicated, he said, that hardness was an inherent power, a disposition in the thing itself. Moreover, this universal was actually embodied in the thing like the universals *in re* of the scholastic realists. Although Peirce went wrong in ascribing material reality and causal efficacy to general ideas, which are mental abstractions, he did at least try to view them as connected with objective reality, as Dewey did not.

Having deprived logical principles of any material foundation,

Dewey was irresistibly driven to ascribe a purely ideational and nonexistential content to them. This violated the empirical method and was a lapse into a position belonging to the very rationalism and idealism he spent so much time combating.

Such a deviation is a recurrent phenomenon in the tradition of empiricism. When it gets into difficulties, the empirical school has sought to make up for its limitations by appealing to the crudest form of rationalism. Thus, in defiance of empiricism's mandate that all knowledge comes from sensation, its founder, Locke, resorted to self-evidence and intuition to establish the truth of mathematics and morality; in the case of religion he invoked revelation.

This aberration is unavoidable because empiricism, the particularist and individualist philosophy par excellence, is weakest in dealing with the relation of the general and the universal to the particular, and especially in explaining the dialectical development of the concrete case, the given instance, from the singular to the particular (species) and eventually to the general, the universal, and the necessary.

Dewey's solution was to drain all the reality and objectivity from the general. Thus he writes: "According to present logic . . . universal and necessary propositions in their logical content are *non*-existential, while all *existential* propositions are singular or several. I am not objecting to the latter conception. It is the only view possible from the standpoint of present science" (*Logic,* p. 95).

He expounds the nominalistic view, popular among pragmatists and positivists, that singularity and plurality have a greater reality than generality and universality. However, the general is no less a feature of the nature of things than the individual or the particular, and is so treated by science. Take the theory of the evolution of species. This is as necessary and universal a proposition as modern science has produced. While any single entity or collection of things exemplifies its operation over time, the totality of things also substantiates its truth. Evolution is both a universal truth (no exception to its operation is known) and a necessary one (because of the nature of reality as matter in continual motion). This keystone of modern scientific knowledge is one of the most incontrovertible refutations of the instrumentalist view that all propositions without exception must be partial and probable.

It might be added that even in terms of formal reasoning the pragmatic position is untenable. For it is a fallacy to say in one breath that no proposition can be necessary and universal, and then to say in another that all of them must be partial and probable. This endows probability with the very necessity and universality that has been proclaimed impossible.

The Problem of Contradiction

The touchstone of any system of logic is the way it handles the problem of contradiction. This question is so decisive because the universe in its endless movement and transmutation is inherently and irremediably contradictory. This trait is reflected in the process of conceptualization.

Dewey discussed his views on this subject in *Logic* in the chapter on "Affirmation and Negation." His own affirmations and negations can be summarized in the following propositions.

1. Affirmation and negation are conjoint relations; one does not exist without its converse.

2. These correlative categories are not ontological but purely instrumental.

3. Contradictions do not objectively exist; they are conceptually formulated and applied to promote the conduct of inquiry.

4. Negation does not logically eventuate in the suppression of one pole of a contradiction by its other; their relations are readjusted without any necessary qualitative change.

Affirmation, the assertion that something exists, and negation, which denies it is so, are clearly correlative, as Dewey holds. The one is the antithesis of the other in the same sense as yes and no, plus and minus, debits and credits.

The existence or nonexistence of the determinate qualities of things finds expression in the judgments we make about the real world. These range in extremes from the categorical affirmative to the categorical negative.

In Aristotle's logic these two types of propositions are mutually exclusive. What is affirmative is not negative and what is negative is not affirmative, and that's that. This dichotomy accords with the basic laws of formal logic and is indeed dictated by its principle of noncontradiction. John Locke believed that the propositions "What is, is" and "It is impossible for the same thing to be and not to be" were self-evident, necessary, and irrefutable truths, the axioms of all reasoning.

However, these principles had been rejected by Heraclitus

before Aristotle made them the prime postulates of his system. The former asserted that everything both is and is not, is itself and its other, and that this unity of opposites is the source of all movement and change. Coming into being and going out of being are possible only through the continuous transition from one contrary to another.

This dialectical conception of contradiction as an interpenetration and struggle of essential opposites which characterizes all things was the nerve center of Hegel's logical theory. Affirmative and negative determinations of the same thing or the same concept, which are ruled out of existence and considered irrational by the formal logicians, are deemed fully warranted by the contradictory nature of all phenomena, processes, and ideas. In concrete reality these opposed determinations are at once the same and different; each is both its identical self and its other. A not only equals A but equals non-A—and the second equation is more profound and true than the first.

In formal logic if some proposition is affirmed it can only be true or false; it cannot be both true and false at the same time. There is no mediation between the two contradictory judgments. In dialectical logic the opposed determinations of positive and negative are differential moments or aspects of the same thing and can be both true and false at the same time, though not in the same measure.

This generalization applies to the rules of formal logic itself. The assertion that A equals A is true insofar as it applies to something relatively stable. But it becomes less and less true as the object under consideration changes in its characteristics, and the assertion eventually turns into untruth as the object is transformed into its opposite. The leading principle of this elementary logic is therefore relatively true but quite false if taken as an absolute.

Dewey denies that identity-within-difference and difference-within-identity, the key concepts of dialectical logic, express any concrete objective realities. Similarity and dissimilarity, the basis of contrast and comparison, are the products, he says, of the selection or rejection of data required for the operations of inquiry leading to the reconstruction of a given situation. The contrast between two things, or two features of the same thing, does not denote objective difference or identity but only different values in inference, reasoning, and reconstruction.

The correlative concepts of affirmation and negation, in his opinion, have a purely regulative function. Positive propositions do not assert what is—or negative ones what really is not—as Aristotle taught. They merely perform the office of defining what is to be included or excluded, what is relevant or irrelevant, in the conduct of an inquiry. "From the standpoint of the functional connection of positing and negating with determination of unsettled or indeterminate situations, they are means, through the operations of selection and elimination they respectively prescribe, of *re*qualifying the original indeterminate situation" (*Logic,* p. 183).

For Dewey, the functional efficacy of a positive or negative proposition does not depend upon whether its content corresponds to the facts of the case, but only upon whether it assists the inquiry to a successful conclusion—something' that can be known or determined only after the event.

This purely functional definition of affirmative and negative judgments removes them from the domain of knowledge. They are not true or false but only more or less useful. Although Dewey contends that this conception of the nature of propositions is thoroughly scientific, it takes into account only one side of the activity of science.

Science is a process of unfinished investigation and endless discovery of the nature of things disclosed by experimental research and creative thought. It is open-ended; whatever has been earlier affirmed is subject to later revision, correction, and concretization.

The greatest uncertainty pervades the growing edge of science. The hypothesis is one of its means of development. As science advances, the hypothesis itself can develop from a suggestion or surmise into a verified fact or law. This aspect of scientific knowledge is scanted in Dewey's account of its method.

Science is not only a method of exploration of the unknown; it is also a solid body of knowledge about the laws, properties, and relations of the world. The totality of scientific truth grows as more accurate and penetrating theories and more comprehensive laws replace less precise and more restricted ones. These positive and negative conclusions about reality are the product of all the previous activity of science as well as the basis of its current procedures. These ideas are so useful in theorizing and in practice because they are true, not false. The law of gravitation discovered by Newton is no longer a hypothesis but the formulation of a fact that has been tested—among other ways, by sending vehicles to the moon and bringing them safely back to earth.

Dewey writes that affirmative and negative propositions do not have a one-to-one correspondence with objects as they are (*Logic*, p. 198). However, if they are to be effectual in actually resolving an unsettled situation, they must have a certain measure of correspondence or else they would lead inquiry and action astray. This correspondence distinguishes them from purely speculative or fantastic assertions.

By emphasizing that the sole meaning of a proposition is in the acts that have been or are to be performed, Dewey neglects the question of what does or does not actually exist. By divorcing his logic of action from the logic of being he deprives logic of its most decisive dimension.

This immateriality can be seen in his definition of what contradiction is—and is not. Dewey believed that contradictions have no more than a subjective character. They exist in the mind but not in the outside world. His disciple, Sidney Hook, has vehemently argued against Marxism that, while judgment, affirmation, and proof can be contradictory, it is nonsense to attribute contradiction to things and phenomena. "Since the time of Aristotle it has been a commonplace of logical theory that *propositions* or *judgments* or *statements* are contradictory, not things or events" (*Reason, Social Myths and Democracy*, p. 202).

Marxism has a much broader and much more correct conception of the nature and scope of contradictoriness than the formalist, positivist, and pragmatic schools. Contradictions not only exist objectively but are universally operative since everything moves and changes by the necessities of its inner nature as well as its external connections. Motion, a state in which an entity both is and is not in the same place in the same time bracket, is inherently contradictory.

There are both objective and subjective contradictions. Dewey mentions the phenomenon of light, which has a dual nature. This discovery has an instructive import for logic.

The old controversy over whether light was made up of waves or particles has been answered in a dialectical manner. According to the experimental data, neither of these contrary propositions is completely true or false. Certain tests show light to be radiant energy and others show it to be discrete units of matter. That is the concrete truth about this contradictory phenomenon.

Dewey notes that this contradiction is present or presents itself in the case of light. But he is unwilling to acknowledge that light is actually, in itself, physically contradictory. It is only construed as such for the purposes of inquiry. The duality has a heuristic value, that is, it leads a person to investigate light along those lines.

In fact, the conclusion about the contradictory nature of light is more than an assumption that is useful in carrying on further inquiry; it is a true affirmation about its essential properties.

In a footnote Dewey takes pains to refute the notion that this step in the progress of scientific knowledge can be interpreted by a dialectical formula. The scientific problem has been solved, he says, not by the manipulation of the triadic concepts of thesis, antithesis, and synthesis but by analysis of specific conditions and experimental results.

To be sure, no one but an arrant idealist would believe that a logical formula could determine the course of scientific discovery. A concrete understanding of the contradictory aspects of light was gained only through experimental evidence.

But beyond its empirical and practical side, what was the significance of this process of discovery for logic? Since light turns out to possess antithetical features, these features can be viewed dialectically. If the wavelike nature of light is taken as the thesis, and its particulate nature as the antithesis, then it can be said that thesis and antithesis underwent negation and the valid elements of both these exclusive assertions became integrated into a new and higher synthetic theory of the nature of light.

Contradiction exists in social no less than in physical relations. The capitalist system is so contradictory because capitalists and wage workers are opposing social realities as well as economic categories. The antithesis is embodied in the single person of the petty capitalist who continues to work alongside his hired hands in the shop or in the fields. This transitional figure is a living contradiction, an aspiring boss who has not yet shed all the characteristics of his original status as one laborer among others and who may fail in his bid to join the exploiters.

Debt is intrinsically contradictory. This sum of borrowed money is negative to the debtor but a positive asset to the creditor. On a broad scale, in the course of the business cycle the invigorating (positive) effects of borrowing are most evident during the boom, while its debilitating (negative) side is violently demonstrated in times of downturn and crisis. Such is the inner logic of capitalism.

The objectively contradictory characteristics of phenomena acquire subjective expression when they are reflected in our thought about them. Formal thinking fastens upon only one side of a contradictory phenomenon and fails to see (or denies) the existence of its correlative.

For example, the Soviet Union under Stalinist domination is one of the most contradictory countries of the twentieth century. Thanks to the 1917 socialist revolution, it has the most advanced relations of production and forms of property. Yet, as a result of its bureaucratic degeneration, its postcapitalist economic foundation is saddled with a totalitarian political structure in which the masses of workers and peasants, in whose name the revolution was won, have few democratic rights and no decision-making powers.

After the 1920s Dewey could see nothing but the tyranny of the bureaucratic overlords in this complex social formation. He dismissed as unimportant and irrelevant its most decisive determinant: the nature of the social economy.

Contradictions in the mind belong to two different types. There are real contradictions and purely logical ones. The former are reflections of many-sided processes and phenomena themselves. The latter exist only as inconsistencies in our thinking; they have no analog in reality.

If it is asserted that the economy of the Soviet Union is progressive and socialist in tendency while its existing method of rulership is reactionary and antisocialist, these formally antithetical statements reflect the contradictory constitution of the degenerated workers' state at this stage of its development. However inconsistent they appear when taken separately, both propositions are true because they correspond with the contradictory social reality they define.

However, when certain pseudo-Marxists say that the nationalization of the means of production is essential to socialism but that the collectivization of property in the Soviet Union has nothing socialist about it, this specimen of false reasoning is a subjective contradiction. It has neither formal logical consistency nor objective validity.

Dewey does try to go beyond his functionalism and reach out toward the objectivity of contradictoriness by linking affirmation and negation with physical and biological processes. He points to conjunction and separation in nature, and selection and rejection among the animals, as prototypes of affirmation and negation in logical inquiry.

The existence of comparable processes on the physical, organic, and intellectual levels would seem to indicate the universality of contradictoriness. Dewey, however, is disinclined to adopt so bold a generalization.

Conjunction and separation provide a particular instance of the dialectic of the one and the many; the one is differentiated and divided into the many and, conversely, the many are fused into one. But Dewey's theory of logic has no room for either the unity of opposites or their conversion into one another. Although he acknowledges that all determination involves both negation and affirmation, he does not develop the consequences for logic of their interplay.

The logic of the transition of one phenomenon into another is formulated in the law of the transformation of quantity into quality. By ignoring this law Dewey remains imprisoned in formalism. For him contingency can never pass over into necessity or hypothesis into law. These opposing categories stay outside one another and do not come together at any point.

For example, he contends (*Logic,* p. 474) that there is "no logical necessity" for an eclipse of the moon to take place at a certain time and place. There is only "a very high order" of probability of the occurrence. But it can be argued against this view that given "the nature of the existential conditions"—the continued existence and relations of the earth and the moon—an order of probability so high as to preclude the possibility of nonoccurrence acquires the character of necessity. And the necessity of such an event is not only physical but logical.

Dewey is aware of the significance of contradiction. "Nothing is more important in inquiry than institution of contradictory propositions," he notes (*Logic,* p. 197). But he has a very special conception of the role of such propositions. On the one hand, they are not descriptive of reality. On the other hand, they are not strictly conceptual. They are regulatory expedients that serve to mark out the limits of an inquiry. To assert an "either-or" is to set the stage properly for carrying out an experiment.

Without contesting the value of this function of contrary propositions in scientific work or in everyday affairs, we must ask: What logic is exhibited in the resolution of any real contradiction? Here the limitations and narrowness of Dewey's instrumentalism become very visible.

"In no case of controlled inquiry is a flat negation of a generalization taken to be final," he asserts (*Logic,* pp. 196–97). Whereas, according to the law of contradiction in formal logic, the negative of an assertion is unconditional, Dewey holds to the contrary: that no negation is ever final. Both of these categorical positions are one-sided. A negation can be partial or total, provisional or terminal, depending upon specific circumstances.

Dewey's denial of finality deprives negation of its full meaning and power. Negation is more than a partial and provisional exclusion of one thing by another. Carried to its culmination in reality, it involves the destruction of one pole of an antithesis by its other and the transformation of the entity into something fundamentally new and different.

One example of a finalized resolution of a generalization, both pro and con, concerns the problem of God's existence, which has troubled humans for thousands of years. The religious-minded fervently believed that He existed; the atheists declared that the deity was a fiction. Scientific inquiry has arrived at the conclusion that the flat negative is true, whatever obscurantists and agnostics say. This definitive generalization provides the basis of a consistent materialist world outlook.

Dewey's definition that all judgment, provisional or final, is the requalification of a given situation through its reconstruction holds good only until a situation undergoes radical change. At that point the revision of a generalization in thought, or the change in a political and social system, passes beyond quantitative modification and gives way to a qualitative transformation. The characteristics of a species can undergo diverse modifications. But if these become extensive enough, they involve transmutation into a new species. There is an essential difference between these species even though one has given rise to the other.

This critical changeover at the extreme end of a development is slurred over in Dewey's thought. In reality contradictions do not remain static; their terms keep changing. Their interrelations can unfold in very different ways, depending upon circumstances. They can be readjusted in accord with shifts in the balance of contending forces. In that case the original contradiction subsists and is reinstituted and reproduced in a variant and more highly developed form. Although its components are reciprocally modified, both endure. Negation is partial, not thoroughgoing.

However, sooner or later, at some point along the way, the accumulated changes so alter the relationship to the advantage of one side or the detriment of the other that their polarization is driven to the extreme and their unity disrupted. At the climactic point of their conflict one of the opposing forces shatters the existing setup and eliminates the other. This disposes of the contradiction in a decisive and conclusive manner. In the totally new formation that results from this radical negation, the unviable attributes belonging to the old components of the opposition are eradicated while their positive elements are preserved, although in a transfigured form.

Dewey's interpretation of negation fits the conditions of that part of the process of change in which the affirmative and negative poles of a contradiction readjust their respective relation without fundamentally challenging each other's continued existence. But it fails to encompass and explain the ultimate stage in the evolution of negation where the contradiction is permanently disposed of in a revolutionary manner through the destruction of one side by the other.

The contraposed methods of dialectical and instrumentalist logic in dealing with the meaning of negation may be illuminated by two cases, one from the history of physics and the other from American history.

Is the supplanting of Newton's laws by Einstein's theory a revolutionary event in physics? Dewey argues that this development disproves the contention that any valid scientific generalization is flatly and finally negated; the prior one is simply modified and revised.

This observation is valid insofar as it is directed against formal logicians who would hold that the one was completely true and the other totally false, with no continuity or identity between them. In fact, both are true, although the relativity theory contains far more truth than its predecessor. The Newtonian laws have turned out to be a special case of the more general principles of relativity.

Classical mechanics holds true only for certain definite domains of reality; its generalizations best reflect the movements of macroscopic bodies. It loses its validity in the micro-world, the sphere of quantum mechanics, and at very high speeds and at very great distances in the universe that are covered by the relativity theory.

Whatever is correct in Newton's propositions has been

reaffirmed and even corroborated at a more fundamental level while the sweeping forms in which its key concepts were originally presented (absolute space, time, simultaneity, etc.) have been disproved and discarded. The limits of their applicability have been charted and their absoluteness relativized.

In what ways did Einstein revolutionize physics as Newton had done before him? Up to the twentieth century Newton's laws went unchallenged. Physics kept adding new data and spreading into new branches without controverting the theoretical foundations of the Newtonian system.

Dewey pictures the transition of physics onto an Einsteinian basis as though no more was involved than a reformation of Newton's ideas. In actuality the break in continuity effected a thoroughgoing reorganization of the structure and content of physical knowledge.

The concepts of absolute space, time, and simultaneity were negated and replaced by relative coordinates; the concepts of mass and energy were retained but shown to be interconvertible. The conservation of mass and the conservation of energy were two absolutely separate principles in nineteenth-century physics and chemistry. This extreme dualism was overcome by combining mass and energy into a single formula, $E=mc^2$. The sum total of their power is conserved in all physical processes, and in appropriate circumstances energy can be transformed into mass or vice versa. Moreover, new concepts were introduced to explain the behavior and properties of elementary particles.

Relativity physics is as revolutionary compared to Newton's laws as nuclear weapons are in relation to conventional weapons. In both cases there is not a simple continuation or extension of the old but a qualitative change in content and consequences. Although the new laws of nature incorporated whatever had been experimentally confirmed and found valid in the old ideas, these were renounced without compromise in a decisive break with the past.

This continuity in discontinuity is characteristic of all progressive development. Its fruitful negation is the opposite of the barren negation of formal logic. While Dewey recognized the affirmative aspect of this process of negation, he did not do justice to its negative side.

It is true, as Dewey says, that "new evidential evidence" led to the revision and overthrow of the classical theory. But the testimony of these new facts, verified by experiment, necessitated the creation of a more comprehensive conception, which negated Newton's principles. From the standpoint of logic, the rupture in these successive stages of progress in physics was more consequential than the residual elements of continuity between them.

The worth of Dewey's logical procedure can also be checked by applying its postulates to the history of Southern slavery. From the colonial era this institution was an extremely troublesome factor in American life. It flagrantly contradicted the principles of liberty, equality, and democracy proclaimed during the first American revolution.

Nonetheless the representatives of the Northern commercial bourgeoisie and Southern planters who together headed the War of Independence and set up the republic managed to keep this anomaly under control. With certain restrictions they incorporated slavery into the new nation and even gave it constitutional sanction. Their differences over this question were adjusted by compromise.

This part of the process met the specifications of Dewey's logic. A troubled situation presented itself; the source and nature of the difficulty was recognized; various ways and means of resolving the problem were brought forward and weighed; finally a scheme was devised and put into effect that took care of the original disturbance. The indeterminate, unsettled situation was converted into a determinate and settled one by the white rulers of the land.

And so it went for the next seventy years. The solution to the contradiction between slaveholding and other forms of private ownership of the means of production more or less worked from 1789 to 1861. The conflicts that arose between the planters and Northerners were settled by negotiation between the contending sides within the framework of the Union (the Missouri Compromise of 1820, the Nullification Controversy of 1833, the Great Compromise of 1850).

Then, in 1860, when Lincoln's election sharply shifted the balance of forces in the federal administration against the slave power, the antagonism reached a point where compromise was no longer feasible. Having seen the reins of national government snatched from their hands, the planters found further coexistence with the Northern camp intolerable and launched their proslave rebellion under the banner of the Confederacy.

In logical terms this signified that the components of the unity of opposites constituting the contradiction that had plagued the country from its birth had diverged to the point where one pole had to completely negate the other. This was accomplished by the victory of the North, resulting in the destruction of the slave power and the abolition of slave ownership.

The compromises from 1820 to 1860, terminated by the slaveholders' rebellion, demonstrate that Deweyan logic holds only for those situations where the antagonisms between contending social forces remain so undeveloped that they can be arbitrated by mutual accommodation. But the method breaks down in theory and in practice once their differences reach the breaking point. Dewey's logic of conciliation, readjustment, and reform, based on the premise that no generalization is ever flatly refuted, is applicable only to periods in which the class struggle has not attained the maximum intensity.

On the other hand, the logic of Marxism, which corresponds to the real dynamics of the class struggle, can explain all its successive stages, from the evolutionary periods when relative class harmony and compromise prevail, to the revolutionary outbreaks when open class war is on the agenda.

The dialectical law of the transformation of quantity into quality explains how the one period passes over into its opposite as the underlying class differences pile up and come to a head. It is a logic based on difference-within-identity which takes into account contradiction in all phases of its unfolding, from unity through increasing differentiation up to the revolutionary climax of qualitative change.

Within the confines of Dewey's linear logic, it is incomprehensible why revolution, which overturns the old order rather than modifying it, is a rational occurrence. The dialectic not only forecasts the necessity of such an upset but prepares people for its advent.

Logic and Social Problems

Dewey envisaged his theory of inquiry as a tool that was not only in accord with scientific practice but could be used to investigate social problems and to direct political activity. If, as he believed, philosophy "should terminate in an art of social control" (*Experience and Nature,* p. 127), then logic should serve to make it feasible. He therefore rounded out his treatment of logic with an analysis of the procedures of social inquiry and recommended his philosophy as a means for helping resolve fundamental conflicts within society.

Unlike most traditional logicians, who set their logic apart from everyday life and scorn to put their doctrines to work on practical problems, Dewey aspired to go beyond the classroom and the author's study and show that his ideas and procedures could be applied in the arena of social forces. He was one of the few American philosophers to do so.

Most academicians believe that any demand upon a logic to demonstrate its usefulness in social affairs is irrelevant and absurd. The absurdity and irrelevance is all on their side. A general logic, apart from specialized branches like mathematical logic, that cannot help clarify social processes and guide politics would be a trifling and sterile set of ideas not worth the attention of people seriously concerned about the problems and destiny of humanity.

Today the very survival of civilization depends upon understanding the structure and dynamics of the system in which we live. A theory of thought that offered no aid or enlightenment to the supreme task of social change and betterment would be not merely diversionary but harmful, since it would block the acquisition of a logic that could fulfill that function.

Any logical theory that claims to give a correct account of the forms and functions of thought should be obliged to prove its value in public affairs as well as in the departments of science. Indeed, social questions and political issues offer fields that severely test the strength or weakness, truth or falsity, depth or shallowness of any logical doctrine.

The limitations of Dewey's method, already discussed in connection with one crucial conflict in America's past, are equally evident in relation to the current class struggle. The central historical problem of our epoch revolves around the struggle between capitalism and socialism. This is being fought out as well as thought out on a world scale. What is the origin, nature, and evolution of the relations between the two major contending forces, the capitalist rulers and the wage workers?

The capitalist mode of production and its special forms of property issued from the disintegration of feudalism in Western Europe. It was the first system to be based upon a world market and generalized commodity relations in which all elements of the economy, above all labor power, are bought and sold.

Capitalism is rooted in the exploitation of the wage workers by the private owners of the means of production. These two classes are as interlocked as slaveholders and slaves. They constitute an organic unity; the one cannot exist without the other. But theirs is a contradictory unity of opposites.

This opposition is asserted in the struggles over the division of the wealth produced by the working class in the form of value. This is the material mainspring of the movement of capitalist society and the source of the class conflicts within it. The mutual antagonisms of the exploiters and exploited pass through a protracted process of development in which their differences are regulated within the framework of the existing capitalist organization of labor.

But they finally reach the point where reconciliation on this basis is no longer possible. The evolution of capital-labor relations inexorably culminates in a showdown struggle for supremacy. If the proletarian revolution is victorious, the capitalist owners are dispossessed of their property and ousted from power by the workers and their allies and cease to exist as a class. Since the Russian revolution of 1917 this has happened in fourteen countries in one way or another.

What is the dialectical logic of this historical process? Out of precapitalist formations, economic development brings into being a new social formation with its own specific contradictions. In this unity of opposites the capitalists constitute the positive, the workers the negative pole. For a prolonged period and up to a certain critical point their class differences ripen within the undivided whole. Then their accumulated antagonisms undergo a qualitative change: they become so sharp that evolution passes over into revolution.

The negative social force that has been subordinate raises itself to predominance by its own action and suppresses the old positive force. The capitalist class that once dispossessed, dislodged, and destroyed its precapitalist predecessors is negated in turn.

Dewey's logic as applied to the evolution and outcome of class relations under capitalism takes issue with this Marxist analysis of twentieth-century history. According to his line of reasoning, the nature of capitalism has not been fundamentally and permanently determined by its essential relations of production. While its economy may have exploitative features and its social structure may be marked by class distinctions, the system is not rigidly fixed. It has enough flexibility to remedy its evils without revolutionary upheaval by reshaping its economic and political institutions along equalitarian lines.

Dewey does not deny that capitalism breeds many grievous conflicts. Indeed, these maladjustments provoke a "felt need" and pose problems that call for rectification. The steps leading toward the solution are indicated by his method. First, locate the cause of the difficulty in order to define the nature of the problem; second, devise a means or a number of alternative measures for correcting the situation; third, try them out one after the other, modifying the original plan, rejecting this or that optional hypothesis and substituting another until one is found that works. In this way the difficulty can be removed and the situation pragmatically reconstituted.

This sounds like common-sense procedure. And, in logical terms, that is what it is. That is how a burglar operates when he wants to pick a lock or a mechanic proceeds when he tries to find the source of engine trouble so as to be able to repair it.

According to liberal reformists like Dewey, capitalism is not working for the benefit of all the people and stands in need of repair. So let all men and women of good will and good hope get together in the common cause of locating the trouble and drafting plans to improve the machine. Soon it will be running better than ever down the road of progress.

What's wrong with this logic? In the first place, it fails to direct attention to the real source of the trouble. The cause is not the maladjustment of this or that part; the entire mechanism, which operates for the profit of the few, not the needs of the many, is outmoded. It no longer works. It is ready for the junkyard.

Since the pragmatists' diagnosis is so far off the mark, their prescriptions for a cure are bound to fail. The methodological source of Dewey's error can be traced back to his definition of the aim of logic as the controlled transformation of an indeterminate situation "into one that is so determinate in its constituent distinctions and relations as to convert the elements of the original situation into a unified whole" (*Logic,* pp. 104-05).

This procedure might be applicable and effective if the situation that caused the trouble were actually indeterminate. But that is not the case with capitalism, especially at this late stage of its career. Its constituent distinctions and relations are so determinate that they irrevocably define its nature and predetermine the main course of its further development and ultimate destiny. The problems besetting working people cannot be resolved by patching up the system or rearranging its component parts.

However, according to the pragmatic view, nothing can be so categorically determined and fixed in advance. The specific degree of determination of anything can be ascertained only after indefinite experimentation, not before. It is dogmatism to think otherwise. This supreme article of faith finds its sociological application in regard to the conflict between the capitalists and the workers.

According to Dewey's logic, the exploiting mechanism inherent in the relations of the polar classes is not to be regarded as an unalterable feature of the capitalist structure, which can be eliminated only by its overthrow and replacement by a new order. The evils it breeds are subsidiary factors, excrescences that can be chipped away by gradual reforms. Capitalism retains elasticity enough to be transformed by intelligent people of good will with the right plan of therapy. It can become a classless society free of exploitation, inequality, and oppression.

Marxist logic says: This liberal perspective is a pipedream! Capitalism in its monopolist, militarist decadence has less and less resilience; its foundation and framework forbid its conversion into a progressive, nonexploitative, equalitarian society. Its drives go in the opposite direction and they cannot be turned around by liberalistic exhortation and doses of reform.

Capitalism is already a "unified whole" consisting of antagonistic and irreconcilable forces. The only way to replace it with a harmonious social whole is to abolish the private ownership of the monopolized means of production, which is at the root of the trouble. And that requires revolutionary action by the working masses.

Dewey correctly remarked: "The first distinguishing characteristic of thinking . . . is facing the facts" (*Reconstruction in Philosophy,* p. 118). His logic suffers from the fatal flaw that it prevented him—and others who think like him—from facing the fundamental facts about the nature of American capitalism.

The Reform of Logic and the Logic of Reform

How does Dewey's logic stand in relation to that of his predecessors and contemporaries in this field? Just as he proposed his instrumentalist theory of knowledge as the most reliable guide to diagnosing the ills of capitalism and reorganizing its institutions, so he intended to renovate logic along fully scientific lines. This same task was undertaken in the preceding century by John Stuart Mill. Dewey was no more successful in fulfilling that aim than his English precursor.

Dewey did take a big stride in the right direction by making practice an integral constituent of his logical method. He thereby sought to overcome the disjunction between pure and applied logic, with the application of logical propositions to empirical material coming as only an afterthought to the completed system. But he halted midway in unifying theory and practice by keeping his logic of purposive action at an unbridgeable distance from objective reality.

Kant maintained that logic had not progressed beyond Aristotle's system, the principles of which were as unchallengeable as the axioms of Euclid's geometry. He was wrong on both counts. Dewey correctly observed that logic had advanced considerably since the Greeks; its principles have evolved as science has developed increasingly complex methods of inquiry.

Dewey saw the motive force of logical progress in the growth of mathematical and physical science. "As the methods of the sciences improve, corresponding changes take place in logic," he wrote (*Logic,* p. 14). It might be added that advances in philosophy and the social sciences, including history, have also contributed important elements to the development of logic.

The science of logic as an independent branch of knowledge has passed through three main stages of development. These are represented by the formal logic of Aristotle, the idealist dialectical logic of Hegel, and the materialist dialectic of Marx. Dewey's logical treatise is largely directed against formalism and the vices of the idealists, although he does not once mention Hegel by name. And he adverts to the views of dialectical materialism only in one or two casual paragraphs.

Logic has evolved and its categories have become more extensive, precise, and flexible as our knowledge of nature, history, and the processes of thought has expanded. The immense improvement in this instrument of reasoning has enabled thinkers to probe more deeply into the essence of things and of thought and their modes of development.

Dewey, however, did not believe that the advances in logic enabled us to arrive at a greater degree of truth and insight into reality. As an instrumentalist, he regarded the norms of logic as essentially postulational, hypothetical, and tentative.

This kind of logical theory flouts the basic principles and practices of science, which aims to explore and explain objective reality by proceeding from hypotheses through theories to laws verified by empirical evidence and experiment. If exceptions to the rule occur, these are either more complex manifestations of the same laws or become the starting points for the discovery and development of new and wider laws of phenomena.

Dewey concluded his exposition by explaining that every logic, whether related to the theories of knowledge of empiricism, rationalism, realism, or idealism, is a selective extract from some of the conditions and factors of "constituted inquiry." His instrumentalist conception certainly lifts certain prominent features out of the total process of scientific investigation and our total knowledge of the world, but it exaggerates their role and slights others that are more fundamental and decisive.

Those features of his logic, from indeterminacy to the purely postulational character of its principles, that he singles out as the leading elements are well adapted to supply a methodological rationale for the outlook and practices of liberal reformism. The congruence between his theory of inquiry and his sociological and political views is no more fortuitous than in the case of Aristotle. Both the ancient Greek and the modern American thinker elaborated a logic inspired by their specific class situation and appropriate to its needs.

This is plain to see in Dewey's attitude toward the class struggle. He objected to the Marxist theory of the class struggle as the chief characteristic of civilized societies and the motive force of their development on the ground that it prejudices "the characteristic traits and the kinds of actual phenomena that the proposed plans of action are to deal with" (*Logic,* p. 506). This statement that the doctrine of class struggle is a prejudice gives a clue to the defects of his logical method and its role in the contemporary class struggle.

A prejudice is a preconceived opinion adopted without adequate grounds or prior to actual knowledge. The theory of class relations developed by historical materialism is, on the contrary, a judgment grounded in the sciences of sociology, history, and politics.

Both induction and deduction—which are, as Dewey says, correlative logical procedures—have entered into the elaboration of the laws of the class struggle. The theory was first of all derived from a comprehensive examination of the course and characteristics of social processes analyzed by rigorously scientific methods. Its conclusions are based upon voluminous data extending over several thousands of years. They are empirical generalizations drawn from the facts presented by the history of civilization, including American history.

This inductive result from a massive array of representative particular cases is buttressed by a systematic insight into the origins, nature, and functioning of class society and the lines of its evolution taken from the study of political economy, history, and sociology. Historical materialism explains how classes emerged through the growth of the productive forces that broke up primitive collectivist formations, created new divisions of social labor, and promoted a sizable surplus of products which became the stake of class contention. The class struggle has revolved around the appropriation of this expanding surplus of wealth in various ways by successive possessing and ruling classes from slaveholders to capitalists. Just as natural selection is the cardinal proposition of the theory of organic evolution, so this truth about the relations and behavior of civilized human beings is the basis for a scientific approach to social phenomena and offers the most profound understanding of historical progress.

After this generalization about the central role of the class struggle in past history had been formulated and confirmed, it could be applied in the same deductive manner as any other scientific law. It could be used to anticipate, predict, and prepare for particular future occurrences and thus serve as a reliable guide to social and political activity.

While it must be justified by the facts, like other scientific laws, the centrality of the class struggle is not a speculative proposition. It has been put to the test of experience in contemporary life over and over again. Where this law has been consistently taken by movements, parties, and individuals as a guide to dealing with social and political problems in theory and practice, it has yielded the most fruitful results for the working class and the cause of socialism. Negative experiences with class collaboration (Indonesia in 1965 and Chile in 1973), contrasted with the positive outcome of revolutions from Russia in 1917 to Cuba in 1959, have confirmed the validity of unyielding class struggle—the application of this historical law in social and political practice.

Dewey's logic conflicts with the materialist and dialectical method in all decisive aspects of social relations. For him the class struggle is not a verified law expressing the most fundamental factor in economic, social, and political life. It is at most a postulate that may or may not be warranted or applicable to this or that moment of social development in general, and capitalist society in particular.

Using his premises this generalization can never lose its provisional status. No matter how many times it has been shown to be justified by the facts or by the consequences of its use or abuse, it can acquire no necessary or coercive character.

This presumption that theories must always remain hypotheses and can never be transformed into certainties, regardless of the course and results of social and scientific development, runs counter to the progress of science itself. Numerous concepts and theories have begun as surmises and ended up as validated truths, as objective knowledge of the external world. The atomic theory of matter is one of the most conspicuous instances in physics and chemistry; verification of the concept of the gene is a more recent conquest of biology.

From his congenitally postulational and hypothetical definition of all general ideas, Dewey concludes that they can have no necessity or certainty. They are once and for all indeterminate and inconclusive. Therefore the class struggle is only one possible variant of capitalist development; other options are equally likely.

This impartial attitude toward the alternatives of class conflict and class collaboration is only a facade. Though the alternatives are supposed to be equally balanced, that is only the appearance, not the reality. Behind the formal impartiality a hidden finger has tipped the scales in favor of a policy of conciliation. In practice, which after all is the supreme test of truth for a pragmatist, Dewey rejected the method of class struggle and justified the use of class collaboration.

Dewey's criteria for what is the most reasonable interpretation of history and the best course of conduct in relation to class antagonisms conform to the preconceptions of liberalism. The less radical means are not only to be preferred and tried first but repeated indefinitely, because they would disrupt established relations less. Extreme action should be resorted to only as a last desperate expedient and without much hope of a happy outcome. It goes against the grain of the liberal compromiser for whom contradiction is never final.

When it comes to confronting and judging the realities of the class struggle, the doctrinairism and prejudice is on the side of the liberal rationalizer. According to his logic, the relations between capitalists and workers are fundamentally indeterminate and variable. No categorical generalization about them is solidly founded. These relations need not be overthrown or abolished; it would be better for all concerned if they were equitably reformed through agreed-upon changes of a nonrevolutionary kind.

On the plane of logic and scientific method, this accords with the proposition that a hypothesis always remains itself (A equals A) and cannot be converted into its opposite, into a verified law that is something essentially different from its original state. Nor can a possibility be transformed into a certainty; at most it can acquire a high degree of probability. Thus there is no objective basis in the realities of the capitalist system for choosing in advance class struggle rather than class collaboration as the most effective way to eliminate its evils.

This line of reasoning, this set of inferences from premise to conclusion, leaves the field wide open for the means of social and political action to be chosen arbitrarily according to the inclinations of the individual. In reality, the decision is not made so capriciously and uncausally but in obedience to the class position one occupies and interests one defends, as happened with Dewey himself.

Dewey's logic in social affairs did not formulate the best procedures of science. It departed from them to the extent prescribed by the requirements of middle-class liberalism. Although he urged logic to come down to earth and occupy itself with everyday problems, this opponent of the class struggle would not believe that in the last analysis logic could itself become an instrumentality of the class struggle. Nevertheless, the stipulations of his own teachings provided an ironic demonstration of this dialectical outcome.

9

The Instrumentalist
Theory of Knowledge

The answer to the question, What is the basis of knowledge? goes far to determine the real position of a thinker and distinguish one school of philosophy from another. This is especially the case with philosophers in the tradition of empiricism who, from Locke on, have hinged their method upon their approach to knowledge rather than upon a conception of being.

Dewey's theory of knowledge is regarded as his capital contribution to American thought and is certainly central to his instrumentalism. In common with other empiricists, Dewey held that all knowledge depends on experience. However, "experience" is a tricky term, one which allows differing interpretations and inferences. It can become the starting point for arriving at positions as far apart as materialism and pure idealism.

That is because experience is a complex phenomenon, having, as Dewey said, a "double-barrelled" character. Experience is the active interrelationship between the external world and the individual; between the thing and its sensation, perception, image and idea; between the objective and subjective aspects of human life. The history of thought demonstrates that philosophers can deduce diametrically different conclusions from this category, depending upon which side they view as primordial. It is therefore imperative to find out just how a particular philosopher uses, or abuses, the term to see where his thought is heading and likely to end up.

Berkeley made experience identical with its subjective elements and thereby used it as a ladder for ascending to spiritual idealism. Hobbes, on the other hand, brought forward the objective side of experience as the bedrock of his mechanical materialism. Dewey's version of experience is very different from the experience described in Hegel's *Phenomenology* or the experience of the existentialists, fraught with anguished emotions.

The nub of the problem lies in how the relations between experience and nature are conceived. Is experience considered to depend on nature, or nature on experience? Does the material world come first and experience later—or the other way around? Is nature experienced—or does experience give rise to nature?

Materialism gives a plain, unequivocal answer. It says nature existed long before experience, which depends wholly upon the external world. Experience is connected with such higher forms of material organization as living, feeling, reacting, reasoning beings. It is a special phenomenon bound up with the interactions of living organisms with their environment.

What is Dewey's viewpoint? It must be understood that he did not maintain any definitive position or adhere to a consistent line on this all-important issue. He wobbled all over the lot, unable to stay permanently in a single place.

His evasiveness exasperated his colleagues, as Martin Gardner, a student of Morris Cohen's, testified: "The question was whether Dewey believed that there was an actual external world, with some sort of structure, so that there could be a meaning to the correspondence theory of truth. Cohen, of course, like Russell, was a 'realist' in his acceptance of a correspondence theory; and this was one of his principal disagreements with Dewey. I recall Cohen speaking, with sadness in his voice, of various attempts he had made to find out exactly what Dewey thought about this, and of his inability to pin Dewey down to an answer. He had finally written Dewey a careful letter, explicitly asking him for light on this point, but had received only a polite, but still evasive reply" (*Portrait of a Philosopher: Morris R. Cohen in Life and Letters*, by Leonora Cohen Rosenfield, p. 171).

Mead, Dewey's cothinker at Chicago, was no less equivocal on this prime question. T.V. Smith writes: "Long after I had become a colleague of Mead, I asked him one day at lunch, for instance, whether he thought that there was anything existing before life came upon the scene. This seemed to me a question to be answered plainly Yes or No, depending upon one's drift toward

Realism or Idealism. Mead answered the question at great length. Or at least he seemed to think he did. I repeated the question for a Yes-or-No answer. He answered it at greater length. I then asked him plaintively to answer it so that I could understand his answer. He seemed as puzzled at my perturbation as I at his 'equivocation.' I never did understand; and, naturally enough, I came to doubt whether he did.

"I took it that he was confused, having left Idealism (Hegelianism) and not having arrived firmly at anything else. This type of confusion, between the knower, or the knowing, and the known, seemed so to dog the steps of the Pragmatists that I decided that they were all what I came to call 'basement-Idealists' rather than, with Hegel, the 'attic' kind. They all seemed to me to doubt—what I could not doubt—that anything existed apart from some experience, and yet they seemed unwilling to face the consequences of such a position. They wanted to be Idealists without giving up the fruits of Realism. It made them unhappy to be thus accused, but so they seemed to me" (*A Non-Existent Man,* p. 48).

At various times Dewey gave four different answers to this question of the relation between experience and nature. (1.) The external world doesn't exist independently of experience. (2.) It does—and he has never denied it. (3.) It does—and then, on the other hand, it really does not. (4.) The very question is meaningless: "There is no problem, logically speaking, of the existence of an external world" (*Essays in Experimental Logic,* p. 281).

At least two things are evident from this careening about. Either he couldn't conclusively settle the matter in his own mind, and therefore couldn't give a clear and consistent response to others. Or he couldn't accept or tolerate the foursquare position of materialism.

Certain passages in Dewey's writings appear to approach the realist standpoint. For example, "Never in any actual procedure of inquiry do we throw the existence of the world into doubt, nor can we do so without self-contradiction" (ibid., p. 302). But this statement does not really come to grips with the substantive issue, which is not whether the world exists (even Berkeley did not deny that), but whether the world exists prior to and independent of the experiencing subject.

In 1909 Dewey wrote to James that his "instrumental theory of knowledge is clearly self-contradictory unless there are independ-

ent existences of which ideas take account and for the transformation of which they function." And he added: "I have repeated
ad nauseam that there are existences prior to and subsequent to
cognitive states and purposes, and that *the whole meaning of the
latter* is the way they intervene in the control and revaluations of
the independent existences" (quoted in *The Thought and
Character of William James,* by R. B. Perry, vol. 2, p. 532).

This, too, sounds as though Dewey admits the independent
existence of the objective world. But what he really means
amounts to this: there are non-cognitive aspects of experience
that both precede and succeed cognitive ones. Throughout he
remains within the closed circle of subjective experience and does
not decisively step beyond it.

He does not deny nature's existence. But he makes its existence
depend upon experience, and not the other way around. For him
"the world of fact" and the course of ideas are "two correspondent
objective statements of the active process itself." That is, the
ongoing process of experience transcends either of its two
objectified forms, nature and the thought process. This is not far
from Hegel's idealism, except that Dewey substitutes the activity
of experience for the dialectical process of the Absolute Idea and
ends up close to a biological, or what T. V. Smith calls a
'basement,' idealism in place of a logical one.

Unresolved ambiguity on the basic question of the relation of
experience to nature is built into the inner structure of the
instrumental theory of knowledge. Thus the contemporary
opposition between instrumentalism and Marxism in epistemology continues the older division between empiricism and
materialism on this score. Locke was unclear on the connection
between material causes and ideas in the mind, although he
stated that "what in sensation is *heat,* in the object is nothing but
motion." Dewey's position is more elusive than Locke's, though
there was far less excuse for his lack of clarity since two and half
centuries of advance in epistemology had elapsed since *An Essay
Concerning Human Understanding* was written.

But more is involved than a perpetuation of the traditional
vagueness or duplicity of empiricism on the interconnection
between the objective world and sense impressions or ideas.
Dewey's evasiveness is not the outcome of ignorance or
indifference since it was many times called to his attention. He
clung to ambiguity on this key issue because it was vitally
necessary for the construction of his pattern of thought and the

conclusions derived from it. He even converted his shilly-shallying into a supreme merit of his theory.

By refusing to take a firmly fixed position on the priority of nature over experience, the pragmatists could run with the idealists or hunt with the realists, without being committed to either. They claimed that they had risen above the one-sidednesses of idealism and materialism; in fact, they fell below both in consistency. Idealism is at least coherent within itself, even though it contradicts reality. Materialism is consistent both in itself and with the facts. The epistemology of pragmatism is neither.

Historical Development of the Category of Experience

Although Dewey rejected many assumptions of traditional philosophy, he was very conversant with the history of its ideas. This was evidenced in his historical approach to the concept of experience.

In a perceptive article called "An Empirical Survey of Empiricisms" he singled out three main stages in its development. The first originated in classical Greek philosophy and was predominant until the seventeenth century; the second was British empiricism. His own instrumentalism sought to give adequate expression to the third, which emerged from nineteenth-century science and was still in the process of formation.

The Greek thinkers regarded experience as the store of information and skills garnered from everyday activities, transmitted from past generations, and incorporated in custom and habit. Empirical knowledge was exemplified in the procedures of physicians, the matter-of-fact know-how of craftsmen, and predictions about the weather. It had both a social and a practical character. Experience was bound up with sense perception and acquaintance with particulars. Its elementary conclusions were useful and indispensable in ordinary affairs. But the limited generalizations of common sense, though tested and confirmed by experience, remained on the level of opinion and did not rise to the height of genuine science.

Plato and Aristotle sharply demarcated this inferior kind of knowledge from true science, although Aristotle held that empirical knowledge was the prerequisite for arriving at scientific insight. Science depended upon reason which, in searching for the causes of things, went beyond the individual, particular, and contingent to the universal and necessary, thus disclosing the eternal nature of reality. Mathematics, which proceeded from indisputable axioms to necessary conclusions, furnished the model for such demonstrative knowledge of the universe.

According to Dewey, this ancient interpretation of experience had three flaws. It depreciated empirical knowledge by exalting the findings of pure reason. Practice was construed as narrow, unintelligent, and merely utilitarian in contrast to the free and unbounded character of abstract theorizing. The senses and bodily activity were consigned to the lower realm of phenomena, while reason was the high road to knowing ultimate reality.

This rationalistic theory of experience, stemming from idealism, had socioeconomic roots, he went on. It reflected the division between the manual worker and the upper orders; it accorded with the aristocratic structures of slave and feudal societies and with the level of science in antiquity and the middle ages.

This derogation of experience was challenged and overthrown under the impact of the scientific and political revolutions of the seventeenth century. The principles of the new outlook were set forth in Locke's philosophy. Just as the British bourgeoisie made the monarchy subservient to parliament, so Locke's empiricism dethroned reason along with intuition as faculties by which the inner nature of reality was grasped. It made reason into the servant of sensation. Empiricism reversed the priorities of rationalism by setting aside innate ideas and first principles, sustained by prejudice, custom, and tradition, in favor of firsthand contact with nature.

Sensation was put forward as the source of all knowledge. Material conditions took precedence over the ideal; isolated sense data over the logical; induction over deduction; the individual over the social; the relative and probable over the dogmatically certain. Except for religion, mathematics, and morality, there was no such thing as absolute knowledge, only partial and probable truths. In this account of experience, mental association was the sole cement that bound together passively received sensations and disconnected impressions.

Dewey paid tribute to the innovations of the classical empiricists from Locke to the Enlightenment. Their ideas provided invaluable weapons of criticism against outworn ecclesiastical and political institutions. The most liberal and democratic among them affirmed the rights of the individual and promoted belief in the progress and perfectibility of humanity through education and improvements in social circumstances.

However, the critical role that empiricism played in throwing off the dead weight of the past had more importance than its constructive achievements in Dewey's eyes. Its inclusion of experimentation in the formation of knowledge was nullified by its insistence on the passivity of the experiencer. It suffered from excessive individualism and a fall into skepticism, phenomenalism, and sensationalism, along with a false associationalist psychology and an inability to explain the formal features of mathematics.

The results of nineteenth-century science and especially the new psychology based on biology necessitated, he believed, a different concept of experience, one that viewed its content as primarily biological, practical, and social rather than sensory, theoretical, and private. The active orientation of people coping with difficulties replaced the passive observation and reflection of individuals. This new version of experience turned attention from the causes and generation of ideas to their consequences in action. In science it brought about a change from the method of induction based on particulars to the imaginative creation of hypotheses to be validated in practice.

That is the path Dewey took to repair the breach between practice and theory, overcome the disjunction of experience from reason, and fuse these opposing aspects of human life into intelligent practice. His treatment of the evolution of the successive theories of experience since the Greeks was full of insight and displayed an acutely dialectical spirit. The Greek idealists had brought out the social and practical features of experience but went wrong in counterposing it so sharply to the rational and scientific faculties and in degrading experience to the purely phenomenal and particular. While the British empiricists reinstated the worth of the sensory, the practical, the probable, and the individual in the process of knowledge, they had neglected the biological, social, and historical aspects of human experience.

Dewey's reconstruction of the content of experience aimed to salvage the enduring elements of the earlier theories, eliminate their defects, and overcome their one-sidedness by integrating their valid contributions into a more comprehensive conception. Experience of all kinds was not merely subjective but objective, not purely individual and private but collective and public; it was not only a mental reflection but also involved active inquiry. He aspired to raise the Aristotelean ideal of intelligent practice to a higher level by making experience experimental, practical, and reasonable. This endeavor to work out a fully rounded empirical account of experience gave his special version of that category a central place in his philosophy.

The Pragmatic Conception of Experience

In his review of the category's evolution Dewey did not discuss the opposing interpretations of experience presented by idealism and dialectical materialism, although the peculiarities of his own instrumentalist version would have been easier to grasp in contrast with them.

In *Phenomenology of Mind* Hegel considered experience to consist in the conscious interpenetration of subject and object. Their changing relations in the dialectical process of development give rise to successive types of experience ranging from sensation to scientific and philosophical knowledge. In the lowest form of experience, its sensory mode, the subject is least realized and most dominated by the object. The two constituents of experience become fully identical only in the highest mode, where the subject, rather than substance, expresses and embodies the reality of the Absolute Spirit.

Two features of this opinion are relevant to the problem of the relations between object and subject. (1.) Experience embraces the whole of reality; nothing falls outside its purview. The self-development of reality coincides with the entire process of experience. (2.) To be is to be experienced; there is no object without a subject.

The view that experience is the primordial, all-inclusive reality is the common premise of many idealist philosophies. The idealist principle that reality is identical with the subject–object relation directly conflicts with the materialist position that experience comprises only that historically restricted and specific area of reality in which the higher animals, and humanity above all, interact with nature.

For Marxists, experience is the totality of the practical activity of the human collective throughout history. While its objective and subjective components are in continual dialectical interaction in all aspects of social life, the two factors do not stand on the same level or have equal weight. The material conditions of development not only exist prior to the subjective actions and reactions of the collectivity and the individual through which they operate, but also have the determining influence over them. Whereas for idealism the subject in the form of self-conscious mind determines the nature of experience, dialectical materialism recognizes that the objective is ultimately determinative, however powerful the subjective may become as society gains command over nature.

The pragmatic manner of interpreting the interrelations of the objective and subjective elements of experience is closer to idealism than to materialism. The essential quality of experience, Dewey says, is that it contains subject and object "in an unanalyzed totality."

James gave a phenomenological backing to this conception when he remarked in his *Psychology* that the world originally presents itself to the individual as a "buzzing, blooming confusion." This observation does not go very far in analyzing the inner nature of experience and its connections with the rest of reality.

A tiny baby may have the kind of experience in which everything else is confused with itself. It took many hundreds of thousands of years before primeval humanity clearly and regularly demarcated their own kind from other animal species and surrounding nature. In dreaming, the subject is usually mixed up with the object.

But the infant comes to learn what early humanity found out when it labored and what the dreamer knows upon awakening— that there is an essential existential difference between the sensation and sensed, the knowing and the known, the internal response and the external stimulus, the reflection and the reality. From that point on, experience is no longer "an unanalyzed totality" but is disclosed as made up of distinctly different, though interactive, objective and subjective components. The progress of knowledge and science disentangles them and clarifies their relations of dependence and independence.

The spontaneous materialism of humanity takes it for granted that an external world comes before sensation, perception, or thought about it. Although Dewey is a stickler for the data of direct experience, he discounts this testimony of everyday life. It is important to understand why.

The conception of the indivisible integrity of experience is the keystone of the pragmatic theory of being and the most distinctive feature of its theory of knowledge. It enabled its adherents to obscure and even invert the actual relations between the objective and subjective.

Under the guise of transcending the opposition between the two, the objective determinants of existence are deprived of their priority and subordinated to the subjective factors. Instead of being posterior to the external world and derived from its interactions with the social subject, experience engulfs them both in an indiscriminate embrace. Experience thereby serves as a misty term in which object and subject become dissolved in a formless unity.

James accentuated this all-inclusiveness of the pragmatic interpretation in his definition of "pure experience." He wrote: "Though one part of our experience may lean upon another part to make it what it is in any one of its several aspects in which it may be considered, experience as a whole is self-containing and leans upon nothing" (*Essays in Radical Empiricism*, p. 193). He thus assigned to experience a status that belongs only to nature. Nature alone is self-contained and self-containing; experience, which is an outgrowth of nature on this planet, is not.

James explained the antimaterialist service performed by this notion of the absolute autonomy of experience. It "gets rid, for example, of the whole agnostic controversy, by refusing to entertain the hypothesis of trans-empirical reality at all" (p. 195). He disposed of the independent existence of the world apart from experience by the easy expedient of dismissing it as a "pseudo-problem."

Dewey was not so offhand as James in dealing with "trans-empirical reality." As a representative of the left wing of the pragmatic school, he took a much more naturalistic approach to the relations between the objective and subjective. But he shared with James the notion that experience was the all-inclusive entity, merging the objective and subjective, that absorbed the external world.

He defined experience on a biological basis, as the transaction between an organism and its environment, of which the interaction between humans and their conditions of life is a special case. Unlike the idealists, he did not construe experience as a form of thought; it was a process of action. But he made the monism of experience "in an unanalyzed integrity" transcend the real dualism of the subject and object.

By focusing on the integration of the objective and subjective and slurring over their opposition, pragmatism fails to point out that experience is a unified whole only within those limits where human beings are involved. It masks the fact that pristine nature exists entirely independently of experience and is separable from it both in reality and in thought.

Dewey furthermore denied that experience is in any sense a mode of knowing. This accorded with his refusal to attribute any cognitive function to sensation, the elementary grade of experience.

The Role of Sensation in Knowledge

Sensation is the primary source of knowledge. All our information about the objects in the outside world comes to us in the first place through the channels of the senses. The acknowledgment that the direct perception of things and their properties is the first step in the acquisition of knowledge and also its elementary form was the common premise of both materialism and classical empiricism.

Dewey's sharpest break with the traditional empirical theory of knowledge was on this key point. Indeed he turned it inside out. Whereas Locke regarded sensation as the origin and basis of cognition, Dewey maintained that it was completely noncognitive. "Sentiency in itself is anoetic," he stated in *Experience and Nature* (p. 259). "Things in their immediacy are unknown and unknowable, not because they are remote or behind some impenetrable veil of sensation or ideas, but because knowledge has no concern with them," he argued (p. 86). Sensations are not cases of knowledge, however rudimentary. They are "natural events having, in themselves . . . , no more knowledge status or worth than, say, a shower or a fever" (*Essays in Experimental Logic,* pp. 253–54). They are simply "had," suffered, or enjoyed.

This degradation of sensation to just another natural event, void of intrinsic significance and without cognitive reference to the external world, is gainsaid by the evolution of the sense organs themselves. Taste, smell, sight, sound, touch, and the visceral senses originated and developed because they enabled creatures to receive vital information about their environment and react effectively to changes in it. Moreover, living beings evolved only those sensory organs and capacities that were necessary and useful to promote the survival of the species. If sensations did not reflect the properties of things, if taste and smell gave no clues to the chemistry of the animal's habitat, the senses would not have such tremendous importance in the economy of life.

For Dewey, sensations were merely stimuli to action, not the crudest mode of knowledge. They are "urgent not cognitive in quality. . . . The discussion of sensations belongs under the head of immediate stimulus and response, not under the head of knowledge" (*Reconstruction in Philosophy,* p. 84).

Dewey thereby reduced sensation to irritability or excitability, which is the precondition for sensation in living matter. In fact, sentiency is a superior type of reciprocal action between the organism and its surroundings, bound up with the physiology of the central nervous system in higher organisms. The sensations that convey information about the properties of objective reality and enable animals to orient themselves to external nature are both urgent and cognitive. The sight, scent, or sound of a predator registered in the brain of the beast tells it to move out of danger.

The question is: Do sensations make sense? Dewey insists that sensations do not provide any significant immediate acquaintance with the features of things. They acquire meaning only through an act of inference whereby the sense datum is taken as a sign for something else. Knowledge is always mediated by such signs. "Sensory qualities . . . acquire cognitive function when they are employed in specific situations as signs of something beyond themselves" (*Logic,* p. 147).

If sensations bear no *prima facie* significance, how can the given sensory quality serve as a sign for anything except through a purely arbitrary connection? In fact, the representative capacity of the sensation is tied up with the characteristics it presents that have an organic connection with their source.

Dewey explicitly rejected any realistic theory of knowledge that says sensations reflect the properties of things. He claimed, for example, that a toothache is at first felt as nothing more than a blank pain without the slightest indication of its intrinsic nature or origin. This does not jibe with either experience or dental science.

The location of the pain in the mouth points to its specific character as the sensitivity of a tooth, leads us to classify it as a toothache rather than a headache, and sends us to a dentist instead of a physician. Sensation can be vague and ambiguous, misleading as well as leading, since it is no more than the beginning and basis of knowledge. Yet this indefiniteness does not denude it of informative character. If a sensation's full qualities and connections were self-evident, further investigation would be superfluous. All the same, its specific qualities impart a certain degree of evidence in regard to its context. The sensory, motivational and cognitive processes of pain simultaneously interact.

The inferences that are subsequently deduced from sensory data are guided by its clues and predicated on its genetic connection with its causal conditions. However, according to Dewey, the pain as such has no ontological property. It can take on the logical function of signifying a toothache only by an act of inference on our part. Although it is not a representation of anything except itself, it thus becomes representative of something else.

However, its representative capacity does not come out of thin air. That depends upon its organic relation with the objective conditions of its occurrence. Its ontological unity with the rotting tooth invests the pain with its evidential capacity and logical potential. The sensation was aroused by the pathological state of the object and is inseparable from it.

Indeed, the experience of a toothache can exemplify the transformation of a sensation into verified knowledge. The excruciating sensitivity is immediately interpreted as a dental problem; the dentist tracks down its cause in the decay of a particular tooth; the pain disappears after he fills or extracts the tooth and does not recur. In this case all the successive phases and degrees of knowledge have been brought into play. It starts from sensation, goes through perception and hypothesis (ideation), and culminates in practical alteration that removes the cause of the problem and is verified by the desired result. Yet the whole cycle hinges on the symptomatic character of the original sensation as the subjective manifestation of the diseased state of the real object, the tooth.

Pain is nature's signal that warns the organism of danger. When a finger touches a red-hot stove, the painful sensation not only imparts a powerful stimulus to withdraw contact but conveys a meaningful message about the temperature of the stove. Although instrumentation is required to ascertain its exact degree, the pain at once categorizes the stove as not cool but intolerably hot. This is not a matter of inference but of direct experience. The information-bearing character of sensory data is negatively demonstrated by the perilous situation of persons whose nerve endings have lost the ability to feel.

All sensation has a dual character; it is both immediate and mediatory. What it discloses about itself also permits us to infer something about something else.

A plant is immediately seen as green, not red or blue. This color is not subsequently attributed to it by inference, although our understanding of the complex physical-physiological process by which light is transferred from the object to the human eye and the nerve impulses travel to the brain, making possible the perception of different colors, is a product of inferential knowledge resulting from prolonged scientific investigation. The particular color sensation is a trustworthy enough clue to the properties of objective reality to direct our inquiry and guide our action, as spectrum analysis proves.

The sensation is a messenger that brings a report of something or other that is not identical with itself but has caused it to come into being. The ache is not a bare sensation but an "ache-of-a-tooth." However incomplete, fragmentary, vague, and confusing the sense datum may be, its presence denotes the existence of an external entity with which it is causally linked.

Any theory of sensation must recognize both the presentative and representative features of a phenomenon. Although the sensation is not identical with the object sensed, its qualities reveal their inseparability. Dewey deprived sensation of its objectivity by dispossessing it of any immediate informational character. In *Logic*, he denied the existence of any immediate knowledge. The representational function he assigned to it thus becomes inexplicable except through a tieup inferred in the mind after the phenomenon appears.

In breaking with empiricism on the cognitive quality of sensation Dewey perforce moved toward the viewpoint of rationalistic idealism, which likewise did not regard sense experience as a genuine degree in the development of knowledge. Leibniz, for example, believed that the soul contains in itself the principles of the different ideas and theories; external objects only provide the occasion for their appearance, serving as a triggering mechanism to bring them to light. Dewey's reduction of sensation to a bare stimulus is a biological variant of this approach. This is an eccentric view for a behaviorist like Dewey, since the conditioning of reflexes in the organism, which is the crudest form of experience, is the biological basis of knowledge.

Truth and Error

Aristotle defined truth and falsehood as follows: "To say of what is that it is not, or of what is not that it is, is false; while to say of what is that it is, or of what is not that it is not, is true" (*Metaphysics*, 1011b.26). This conception of truth and error is fundamentally sound and supplies the basis for understanding what they are. The content of knowledge depends upon the representation of objective reality in conceptual terms. What is known or not known, what is asserted or denied, is intrinsically linked with what is and what is not.

Aristotle's formulation, though correct, is inadequate. This first approximation to the truth about truth is too simple to cover the complexity of the problem. Though it provides the indispensable starting point for comprehending the nature of truth and error, it has had to be amplified through several thousand years of philosophizing by a more comprehensive and many-sided definition.

Aristotle himself refers in the same passage to certain difficulties about this conception that were brought forward by previous thinkers. Heraclitus pointed out that all things both are and are not. Anaxagoras maintained that there must be an intermediary between the opposing terms of a contradiction. But Aristotle could not see how there could be mediation between contraries in logic, nor how something could really be and not be at one and the same time.

According to his logic, we must either affirm or deny any one predicate of any one subject. That is, a thing must either be or not be; a predicate must either be so or not so. Aristotle's scheme of things awarded primacy to being—and unchangeable being to boot!—in our knowledge of it. His logic subordinated becoming to being and thereby dialectics to formalism.

Two thousand years later Hegel most fundamentally exposed the shortcomings in the Aristotelean approach to truth and error and indicated how to overcome them. Truth and error, he agreed, had to conform to what is and what is not. But what is the intrinsic nature of everything? It both is and is not at one and the same time. To one degree or another every special state of being is involved in a continual process of becoming something else.

This contradictory essence of being, which is in an unceasing process of development, has to be expressed in logical terms. Just as everything is in motion and changing from what it is toward what it is not, so statements made about anything at any given time contain elements of falsehood along with truth. A statement about some of a thing's aspects and relations may not apply to others, and a statement that is valid under certain conditions may be contrary to fact when the conditions change. Therefore truth and error cannot be conceived or applied in a static and fixed fashion. The one can pass over into the other, depending upon the given circumstances and their changes.

Hegel reversed Aristotle's priorities by subordinating being to becoming and formal logic, the science of fixed relations, to dialectics, the logic of development. This dialectical approach to truth and error was taken over and recast along historical materialist lines by Marxism.

Since Aristotle, the correspondence theory of truth has been upheld by diverse philosophical schools (the Stoics, Aquinas, Spinoza, most materialists). Its most serious rival is the coherence theory propounded by the idealists. This makes internal consistency the hallmark of truth; the more systematic our beliefs, the truer they are. This doctrine is wrecked by the fact that what is formally consistent may utterly contradict reality and collapse when put to the test of social practice. The absence of essential relevance to objective reality makes this theory untenable.

Dewey's instrumentalist conception of truth and error differs from both the correspondence and coherence theories. He discarded internal consistency as the criterion of truth after he gave up neo-Hegelian idealism. On the other hand he rejected outright the principle that truth and error depend upon the correspondence, or lack of it, of the idea or belief with the facts of the case. He repeatedly stated that knowledge does not disclose or depend upon objective reality. "The assumption that the true and valid object of knowledge is that which has being prior to and independent of the operation of knowing" is a basic error. Known objects exist as "the consequence of directed operations," not because of conformity of thought or observation with something antecedent (*Quest for Certainty*, p. 196).

It is true that objects come to be known as the consequence of directed operations, but it is not true that what is thereby known did not exist before and apart from the processes of inquiry. The double helix structure of DNA, which was discovered as the result of a complex series of directed investigations, existed within the molecules aeons before its configuration was disclosed and verified

Because of the historical limitations of knowledge, truth has a subjective component. But it is essentially, fundamentally, objective. It is that part of the content of human ideas that does not depend upon the subject. Truth is inseparable from what exists in reality. Once truth is pulled away from that secure anchorage, it is cast adrift on the waters of subjectivism. That was the case with Dewey. He detached truth and error from their roots in antecedent reality and attached these qualities of ideas exclusively to the results of human action.

For the instrumentalist, truth is not derived from conformity with what exists in the world around us but is created by and dependent on people's practical activities. Truth accrues to an idea or a hypothesis when it proves effective in disposing of a problem.

While the settlement of a problem may testify to the truth of an idea, the practical activities of human beings do not create the correlation between things and our statements, beliefs, or ideas about them, whether true or false. They serve to disclose and verify this relation, i.e. substantiate it.

According to Dewey, "verification and truth completely coincide" (*Essays in Experimental Logic,* p. 346). This identity is false. The two may coincide in ongoing situations where personal intervention is the decisive factor, as when I say I shall visit someone's home at three o'clock and then keep the appointment. In such cases I cause something to happen and make the assertion true. But where humans are not causally determinative of the facts, the truth about anything is not created but only validated by our practical activity. It was true that electrons existed before anyone suspected that fact, and it will remain so even if humankind should be wiped out.

The pragmatists set up two criteria of truth other than correspondence with the real state of affairs. One is what people come to believe; the other is the advantages such beliefs bring. Both are subjective standards.

James assigned truth to whatever ideas satisfied the wants and promoted the interests of the individual. Peirce and Dewey shared a more collective, though no less subjective, conception. For

Peirce "the opinion which is fated to be ultimately agreed to by all who investigate, is what we mean by the truth, and the object represented in this opinion is the real" ("How To Make Our Ideas Clear" in *Collected Papers of Charles Sanders Peirce,* vol. 5, p. 268).

The essence of truth was to be found in the same psychological criterion, according to Dewey. He was extremely ill at ease with the terms "truth" and "error." The index to his *Logic* contains no reference to error and only one to truth. He inclined to put these troublesome categories on the shelf because they are so indissolubly tied up with reality.

Dewey therefore proceeded to redefine truth as "warranted assertibility." This cumbersome circumlocution was designed to get around the substantive issue of what ultimately determines truth and error. It makes the truth hinge not upon correspondence with objective facts, but upon "a decent respect for the opinions of mankind."

Dewey's agreement with Peirce that the opinions of people in the long run are "what we mean by the truth" is a new version of an old error. Numerous philosophers and theologians have appealed to the common consent of humankind (the *consensus gentium*) to justify moral precepts or religious doctrines such as the existence of God and immortality. Thus the French royalist reactionary de Maistre asserted: "Truth, whose name men pronounce so boldly, is nothing else, at least for us, than that which appears true to the conscience of the greatest number of people" (quoted in *The Rise of Anthropological Theory,* by Marvin Harris, p. 55).

The revival of the consensus theory by the pragmatists transposed the general assent from the past and present to the far future. But that temporal shift does not eliminate the subjectivist core of this position. The universality of a belief is no proof of its validity. Unless and until the basis of such unanimity is securely established in the conditions of objective reality as tested by social practice, it can be as wrong as the once common belief that the earth is flat.

The extent to which pragmatism has deviated from its philosophical progenitor can be measured by its reversion to consensus as the standard of what truth is and means. Classical empiricism was launched with Locke's argument in the first chapter of his *Essay Concerning Human Understanding* that, because of the immense variability of beliefs, the existence of innate ideas could not be demonstrated by reference to common consent. Moreover, Locke regarded ideas (sense data), generated by the influence of objects in the surrounding world upon the sense organs, as the basis of knowledge.

For James an idea is workable and therefore true if it supports the beliefs of a person in an indeterminate situation. For Dewey the truth of an idea is equated not with the benefits it brings to the individual, but with its verification in practice. It is meaningless, Dewey says, to ask whether propositions are either true or false. He criticizes "popular positivism" for being "in some respects the heir of an older metaphysical view which attributed to ideas inherent truth-falsity properties" (*Logic,* p. 520). For him propositions have no such qualities. They are either effective or ineffective in resolving difficulties. And if they yield successful or satisfactory results in practice, they are true or "warranted."

It might be asked: Why do the most qualified observers come to agree upon a certain content as true rather than alternatives that are rejected as unwarranted? And what gives this content reliability in practice? The instrumentalist has no adequate answer.

The correspondence theorists have a ready answer to such questions. Knowledge is both true and useful insofar as its content harmonizes with the facts of objective reality. Instrumentalism leaves this decisive aspect of the problem of truth and error in the dark.

Dewey says: "That which guides us truly is true—demonstrated capacity for such guidance is precisely what is meant by truth" (*Reconstruction in Philosophy,* p. 128). But workability is a function of the conformity of ideas with the facts. Unless a map accurately delineates the features of an area it will not guide the traveler to his or her destination. Its usefulness depends upon prior existing conditions. Just as a rear-view mirror would be useless and dangerous if it did not convey a reliable image of what was behind the vehicle, so sensations, perceptions, and the conceptions based on them would be misleading and worthless unless they indicated to some extent what is and, conversely, what is not.

The defects of Dewey's instrumentalist theory may be illustrated by the following example of genuine knowledge tested by practical experiment. What is a particular fragrance made of?

To solve this problem, the oderiferous gas is sent through an analyzer and all its constituent molecules are identified. When for commercial purposes it is desired not only to know about its constituents but to produce the fragrance, the essential molecules are assembled and synthesized into an artificial replica of the natural odor.

The natural and artificial fragrances have the same physical content and produce the same olfactory result; the two are interchangeable. Thus the original analysis and the synthetic reconstitution reciprocally confirm the validity of the conceptual reflection of the thing in chemical terms.

Dewey's one-sided version of knowledge and truth focuses on the practical result but omits the antecedent molecular reality that makes it possible and determines it. This conforms to the pragmatic disposition to concentrate on the consequences of things, ignoring their causes and the links between them.

Bertrand Russell noted that Dewey pays little attention to the problem of error even though it is inseparable from the existence of truth. An explanation of the nature of error would be a good test of the validity of his conception. But error is simply equated with unworkability. That brings us back to the question of what makes something work or not work.

What makes a statement or theory unworkable, unwarranted, and not useful is the discordance of its content with what exists. The convergence as well as divergence of truth and usefulness is exemplified by the question of the shape of the earth. The assumption that the surface of the earth is flat is useful within very short distances and for all those purposes where its curvature can be practically disregarded. But it is not warranted, workable, or true for the earth as a whole.

The fundamental falsity of the first statement and the truth of its contrary are determined not by the criterion of usefulness, which depends upon human needs and aims, but by the geological structure of the earth, which antedated humanity and exists apart from us. Dewey's instrumentalist definition of truth and error is wrong and "unwarranted" because it conflicts with reality.

Relative and Absolute Truth

Dewey persistently polemicized against the existence of absolutes in any field, from mathematics to morality. He wrote an entire book, *The Quest for Certainty,* to disqualify the fruitless search for cognitive certitude of reality that had captivated idealists and materialists alike since the time of the Greeks.

He himself was an unrestricted relativist. This viewpoint molded his theory of knowledge and his conception of the nature of truth. He regarded truth as relative through and through; it did not possess any objective quality.

It is correct to say that all specific truths are, like the aspects of reality they reflect, variable, changeable, partial. That is one side of their content. But it is not the whole of their nature; it is not the most important truth about truth.

Truth is a more or less adequate reflection in our minds of the world around us. But our knowledge at any given time presents only a rough approximation of that objective reality. It cannot be a complete or definitive representation of what is.

The process of learning about reality is endless, since the universe has infinite aspects and is continually changing. Our knowledge proceeds from very partial truths to more and more comprehensive and profound ones. The body of verified information about the world grows along with the power of humanity over its operations.

The succession of new scientific hypotheses and invalidation of old ones can give rise to the notion that truth has no objectivity whatsoever. But the process of development of our knowledge testifies only that truth is historically relative, not that it is purely subjective. Dialectical thinkers can agree with Dewey that there are no absolute truths established once and for all. Nothing is that eternal. But he confused the impossibility of eternal truth with the non-existence of objective truth.

It has been demonstrated that Newton's laws of mechanics are not unconditional but relate only to certain domains of physical phenomena. They do not apply without qualification to the subatomic and cosmic realms. The recognition of this relative applicability does not deprive Newton's laws of their objective truth; they are valid and trustworthy insofar as they reflect relevant features of the mechanical movements of the world.

Dewey's argument, against certain idealists, that the truth is not handed down to us ready-made but is the product of humanity's historical activity and continued experimentation, is acceptable. The search for truth, along with the exposure and eradication of error, is a never-ending process.

Dewey does not, however, give a correct interpretation even of the relative aspect of truth. He makes it depend upon the incapacity of any single generalization to untangle problematic situations. But the relativity of truth issues from more objective sources—from the changeability and diversity of reality on the one side and the historical limitations of our experience and knowledge on the other. The totality of our correct knowledge to date equals that which our ideas have in common with the facts. This unity is not created by our activities, as Dewey holds; it is only disclosed and demonstrated by them.

Like the dialecticians, Dewey recognized the perpetual perishing of all things. From the acknowledgment of this fact he slid over into an oversimplified relativism that left no room for absolute truth. Since every single truth about the world is relative, he reasoned, there is no such thing as absolute truth. He failed to grasp the dialectical connection between relative and absolute truth.

It is true that at every stage of its development our knowledge of reality is restricted by the level achieved in science, technology, and production. There is always infinitely more to be known. It is not possible to attain an exhaustive knowledge of any one thing, and still less of everything, not only because of the historical boundaries of human thought but also because of the mutability and endless variety of things.

But relativeness is only one side of the matter. Every relatively true conception of an object discloses some absolute knowledge about it, however incomplete and approximate. Every relative truth contains a particle of absolute truth and is a step, however small, toward the acquisition of the totality of truth about the universe. Absolute truth is made up of the sum of the relative truths in our possession.

The relativity of cognition is itself limited by the existence of objective truth, which grows in volume and precision with the progress of knowledge. Our fund of knowledge keeps approaching absolute truth without ever reaching that asymptotic ideal. It is absolutely true that bodies consist of atoms. From Leucippus and Democritus to Bohr, science has learned more and more about the atom, its internal structure, its transmutations, etc. This knowledge, resulting from deeper insight and experimentation into the recesses of matter, is objective, enduring, correct, and absolute. Even though no truth can exist apart from the mind, since it is a property of ideas, the content of truth does not depend upon thought but is derived from the surrounding world.

But for Dewey knowledge is essentially subjective, not

objective; truth is purely relative, without any absolute character
to it. One hypothesis replaces another not because it comes closer
to objective knowledge and thereby absolute truth, but simply
because it is more useful for given purposes.

The Nature of Ideas

Dewey presented a singular notion of the nature of ideas: they do
not have their source in objective reality; they do not disclose
antecedent existences; and they can never be more than
hypothetical. These three negations define the specific character
of the instrumentalist theory of knowledge and set it apart from
realist or materialist theories, which hold that concepts derive
their content and meaning from correspondence with the facts,
that ideas turn into truths and theories into verified laws when
this objective relationship is substantiated.

According to Dewey's operational "conception of conceptions,"
ideas have three important traits. (1.) They are instruments of
intentional regulation leading to acts to be performed. (2.) They
are purely prospective and reconstructive, not retrospective or
reflective. They do not refer to what exists, nor even to what has
previously been achieved, but exclusively to what is to be done.
"Ideas are anticipatory plans and designs which take effect in
concrete *re*constructions of antecedent conditions of existence"
(*Quest for Certainty,* pp. 166-67). (3.) They are utterly conditional.
"Ideas and idealisms are in themselves hypotheses not finalities.
Being connected with operations to be performed, they are tested
by the consequences of these operations, not by what exists prior
to them" (ibid.).

This one-sided view blanks out the most decisive characteristic
of ideas, their intrinsic connection with objective reality. Ideas
are intermediary and have regulative functions; they do have an
intentional character directed toward the future; and they often
do lack certainty. Instrumentalism goes astray not in recognizing
these features and functions of ideas, but in taking them for the
whole story. The real thing and its mental image have a common
content but different forms, like the original text and a
translation. What is objectively real has been transposed into the
human brain and processed into the subjective form of concepts,
categories, and logical laws. Dewey dismisses the unity of content
between the conceptual reflection and its substantial reference,
although this is the determinative factor that enables us to orient

ourselves correctly in any given situation and change conditions effectively.

The assertion at the base of the instrumentalist epistemology, that truth does not consist in the agreement of our ideas with a prior and independent reality, is contrary to fact and even to common sense. While false ideas distort reality, the specific essence of true ones, which constitute the substance of our knowledge, is to disclose and reflect the features of objective reality.

The concept of "two" is prospectively useful in many kinds of contexts and operations. Does this idea of a given quantity disclose nothing about antecedent existences before it is applied in practice? In fact, it refers to a definite quality of objective reality, duality, which is the primordial form of plurality. As a member of an infinite series of cardinal numbers, "two" is amenable to many levels of abstraction. Yet the content of this elementary mathematical conception in our minds corresponds to a specific aspect of independent material existence. Otherwise it would not so firmly have impressed itself upon the awareness of primitive people and even subhuman creatures.

If ideas are purely instrumental to human purposes and directed toward something to be experienced in the future, as Dewey contends, it might be supposed that those ideas that have proved effective as guides in action—not once but over and over again—would thereby have demonstrated their correspondence with the objective reality they were derived from and led to. Dewey refuses to accept this conclusion. While we may rely more upon them, the nature of ideas is not substantially affected no matter how often or how fully they have demonstrated their serviceability. From the beginning to end they retain a provisional character.

Genuine knowledge and definite truth thus become extremely elusive—almost illusive. They are something that "never is but always is to be" possessed. At most our knowledge can attain a very high degree of probability, but it can never pass into certainty. "Even the best established theories retain hypothetical status," he wrote in his last work (*Knowing and the Known,* p. 328).

This doctrinaire probabilism, embraced by positivists and pragmatists alike, cannot withstand the test of experience. It is absolutely certain that because of their biological makeup all people now inhabiting this planet will die within an ascertainable period as their predecessors have done. This certainty is not grasped by animals and its truth only gradually dawned upon primitive humanity. Whoever believes that this is no more than a probability, so they may be immortal, will sooner or later succumb to this categorical law of life.

The purposive and reconstructive functions of ideas cannot be separated from their representative content. These two aspects are integrated in the acquisition and usage of scientific knowledge. Dewey said: "Everywhere an idea, in its intellectual content, is a projection of what something existing may come to be" (*Quest for Certainty*, pp. 299-300). But it is even more a reproduction of what something has been and is. An idea not only indicates a possibility to be realized but summarizes a reality that may be possibilized—and the extent of its possible realization is given by the structural content of the concept as well as by the conditions of its development.

The idea of flying to the moon was an impossibility until contemporary science and technology, plus the resources of two giant powers, made it possible. The plan was able to be put into effect because the ideas guiding the intricate acts to be performed were in conformity with the objective realities involved in the mission. Among these ideas was Kepler's discovery of the moon's elliptical path.

It is not true that an idea's object can only be in the empirically attainable future (as Dewey puts it, that "ideas are statements, not of what is or has been, but of acts to be performed"). Thoughts arise from reflecting upon antecedent objects and events before they project plans for human action. Our judgments about what lies ahead are based upon a growing fund of prejudgments derived from the historical experience of humanity in its dealings with reality. While these contain a measure of uncertainty, they are useful because they have been removed from the realm of speculation and become part of authenticated knowledge.

To establish that the essence of knowing lies in practical reliability alone, and not the conformity of concepts with the objects reflected by thinking, Dewey gives the example of a man lost in a wood. He has some notion of the way out and, acting on that map in his mind, finds his way home (*Essays in Experimental Logic*, chapter 8). A materialist would conclude that he did so because his mental picture corresponded with the geography of the wood. Dewey would object to attributing the successful outcome to any such "archetypical antecedent reality." The objective determinants that made the plan of action useful in achieving the man's purpose are ignored. What Dewey sees as nothing more than coincidence between a plan and its execution, materialists more correctly and comprehensively view as correspondence between a proposition and the objective facts.

If ideas had no objectively determined content, as Dewey believes, then one would be as good as another until tested. In actuality, they are far from being all on an equal footing. Some are better than others *before* the problem is tackled and the situation is reconstructed. They are more useful in directing activity and fulfilling our aims not only because of their consequences after the event, but because of their derivation and content before being put into effect: they reflect the essential features of the real world more precisely, deeply, and comprehensively. The relation to objective reality also finds corroboration in the failure of predictions. If a hypothesis is disproved by the results of experiment, this negative outcome casts an indirect light on the real nature of things.

Knowledge goes through different stages of development, starting with fragmentary sensory knowledge and narrow empirical inductions and culminating in rational truths and theoretical knowledge.

Dewey does not admit the full range of degrees in the progress of knowledge. He cuts away the modes of knowing at both ends of the spectrum: on the one side the crudest form of sensory apprehension, which humans share with animals, and on the other the height of conceptual abstraction occupied by physical laws like the conservation of energy and universal generalizations like the theory of evolution.

We have previously discussed his denial that sensations in themselves have cognitive quality. "Sensations count only as stimuli and registers of motor activity expended in doing things," he states in *The Quest for Certainty* (p. 156). He also denies that natural and social laws formulate the inner essence of objective realities; to him they are simply helpful expedients for directing us to desirable objectives.

He does say that "ideas . . . have to meet the conditions set by the need of the problem inducing the active inquiry" (p. 86). This appears to be a concession to the materialist outlook. But for him these conditions hardly affect the content of the ideas themselves.

In the advance of scientific knowledge, ideas change their

content in accord with the discovery of new facts. Consider the conception of the solar system. The revolutionary innovations of Copernicus retained as the basis of cosmic order the idea of circular planetary orbits, which dated back to the Greeks. Kepler corrected this error by proving that the orbits were elliptical. This idea was truer than the one it superseded—and more useful for further observations and later operations—because it more precisely fitted the structure of the solar system. That fact was decisive in its adoption by scientists. Dewey could not adequately explain the objective reasons for such changes in ideas, or why one should be chosen over the other, because he considered only their practical usefulness and not their material basis.

Dewey persistently polemicized against the view of the idealist metaphysicians that genuinely valid ideas must conform to some eternal and unchangeable Reality. This criticism was justified; reality is ever-changing and the concepts that reflect it cannot be frozen. But the mutability of all things does not warrant canceling out the objectivity of the ideas referring to them. It means rather that our thought must take these changes into account by keeping ideas flexible, correcting and concretizing them, or resorting, where necessary, to new and more precise ones.

Despite his evolutionary attitudes, ideas maintain a static quality in Dewey's epistemology. They are permitted to vary only within a narrow compass, and must under all circumstances occupy a middle location between the extremes of impossibility and certainty. Through thick or thin, conceptual generalizations cling to their provisional character. They can be highly probable but never necessarily or categorically certain.

He wrote: "Here it is enough to note that notions, theories, systems, no matter how elaborate and self-consistent they are, must be regarded as hypotheses. They are to be accepted as bases of actions which test them, not as finalities. . . . As in the case of all tools, their value resides not in themselves but in their capacity to work shown in the consequences of their use" (*Reconstruction in Philosophy,* p. 121).

Dewey's logic is at fault for this incapacity to see that ideas, like everything else, begin in one status and may evolve into an opposite one. A notion that starts out as merely possible becomes probable and can end up as certain and lawful—provided it is not revealed as false. All depends upon the material circumstances that shape its content and course of development. The conversion of an idea from a sheer guess into a truth exemplifies the operation of the law of the transformation of sufficient quantity into a new quality. After enough evidence has been accumulated and the causes of the recurrences have been disclosed and understood, the generalization sheds its indeterminacy. Its contingency has been reduced to the point where its necessity is overwhelming and conclusive. This happened with the theory of evolution.

Dewey argued that contemporary science had deprived ideas of all certitude. "Theory in fact—that is, in the conduct of scientific inquiry—has lost ultimacy. Theories have passed into hypotheses," he wrote in the 1948 introduction to *Reconstruction in Philosophy* (p. 28). However, if such theoretical constructions as phlogiston, caloric, and the ether have become dead hypotheses, other once-speculative theories have graduated into verified truths. Nineteenth-century science converted the conservation of energy from a hypothesis into a fundamental law of physical change—and this has been expanded by the twentieth-century discovery that mass and energy are equivalent and interconvertible. This is no longer a tentative speculation but a confirmed law which has become the bedrock of present-day physics. The gene went through the same process of verification in twentieth-century molecular biology.

It is still uncertain whether the quark exists as an elementary subunit of the proton. The fate of this hypothesis will be decided on the basis of further experimental evidence proving or disproving its actual existence, its truth or falsity. This will likewise determine its degree of usefulness in microphysics.

Dewey's theory of knowledge dovetailed with his theory of being. He insisted that ideas are inherently suppositional and purely conditional and can never change into certainties, regardless of the findings of physical, social, and scientific development. This stemmed from the pragmatic assumption that reality is so indeterminate, contingent, and precarious that no conceptual generalizations can be definitively proven, and that natural, social, and mental processes are not lawful. These errors make his epistemology and his ontology equally defective.

The Object and the Object of Knowledge

The theory of knowing has had to be revised as knowledge has been amplified under the quickening pace of social and scientific advances in the modern world and as the means of gathering information have been radically improved. Kant, for example, based his epistemology on the premise that plane geometry represented the sole system of spatial relations. The non-Euclidian geometries elaborated in the next century overthrew one of the principal props of his theory of *a priori* forms.

In earlier periods knowledge relied almost wholly upon the data of observation. This led materialists and empiricists alike to regard consciousness as the product of passive perception and to neglect the function of practical activity in the promotion of knowledge.

As science, technology, and engineering developed in the nineteenth and twentieth centuries, the contemplative attitude toward phenomena was increasingly superseded by the experimental approach of deliberately intervening to change them. Today experimental practices play an ever-greater part in extending and verifying what we know.

Dewey called attention to this qualitatively distinct stage in the modes of understanding the world and sought to draw out its implications for philosophy. His effort to incorporate the role of experiment and the use of instruments into the theory of knowledge was a very positive feature of his outlook.

However his special theory not only discarded certain defects of the old epistemology but rejected some of its valid positions as well. In order to make room for the practical and reconstructive side of knowing, he felt impelled to crowd out the materiality of the object.

Dewey employed a deceptive technique of argumentation. He would start by exposing some metaphysical error of idealism, such as Aristotle's belief that substance was immutable, and convincingly demonstrate that everything was changeable. From this launching pad he would proceed to attack the materialist view that things have a substantial reality before and apart from their involvement in experience. In this way he aimed the initial polemic against idealism at the more important target of materialism.

His criticism of metaphysical errors, however, does not invalidate the materialist outlook.

In rejecting absolute time and absolute space, relativity physics does not deny that time and space remain objectively real forms of the universe. Nor does the recognition that all objects are changeable imply that they are no longer material entities.

Dewey himself was, as the materialist professor Roy Wood Sellars observed, "a half-reformed idealist" (*The Philosophy of Physical Realism*, p. 9). Idealistically inclined thinkers of all degrees and descriptions must devise a formula for expunging the materiality of things and hinging their existence on one or another subjective factor such as sensation, perception, intuition, or thought. The pragmatic Dewey assigned this function to a process of inquiry culminating in reconstructive activity.

The idealist substructure of his theory of knowledge was manifest in his version of what an object is and how it is related to an "object of knowledge" or a "scientific object." In ordinary language an object is a concrete entity that exists independently of our perceiving, knowing, using, or changing it. It becomes an object of knowledge upon being observed and investigated, and a scientific object insofar as its essential characteristics have been rationally explained.

Dewey gave quite different meanings to "object," "object of knowledge," and "scientific object" by depriving the object of any substantial character or ontological status. It was dissolved into the sequence of changes a thing passes through, the sum of the relations it enters into, and the meanings it acquires. Its quality of objectivity was not regarded as intrinsic but rather as derived from its ingression into human experience. The object does not exist in its own right, with all the wealth of its specific determinations, apart from the subject. It becomes a determinate object only as the result of inquiry, as part of experience; it thus has a purely conceptual and instrumental character.

For Dewey, objects remain enclosed within the charmed circle of inquiry and are not permitted to step beyond it. The dematerialized objects are replaced by products of knowledge in the form of "objects of knowledge" or "scientific objects."

Pluto, the smallest and remotest planet in the solar system, is invisible to the naked eye and was unknown until it was discovered after decades of search in 1930. When it became an object of knowledge to astronomy, this heavenly body did not change as a result. What happened was that a new theoretical and practical relationship was established between ourselves and the object. Dewey's theory confused this "existential transformation" between ourselves and the external object with the transformation of the object itself.

The basic errors of rival theories of knowledge, he wrote, come from "the assumption that the true and valid object of knowledge is that which has being prior to and independent of the operations of knowing. They spring from the doctrine that knowledge is a grasp or beholding of reality without anything being done to modify its antecedent state—the doctrine which is the source of the separation of knowledge from practical activity. . . . the true object of knowledge resides in the consequences of directed action. . . . an archetypal antecedent reality is not a model to which the conclusions of inquiry must conform" (*Quest for Certainty*, pp. 196-97).

This sacrifice of the antecedent and autonomous being of objects equated them with the ideas we have of them or the uses we make of them. Their actuality was made to consist in whatever potential or prospective purposes they serve. As Dewey's cothinker Donald A. Piatt stated in expounding his logical theory: "An object and an object of knowledge are basically the same thing, for an object arises as an existential state of affairs gets settled in and by inquiry" (*The Philosophy of John Dewey*, p. 130).

In defending this view Mead argued that the appearance of an organism capable of digesting brings grass into existence as food. This reasoning stealthily substituted the biological function or social utility of a thing for its physical reality. Eating does not bring grass into existence but only adds another functional relation to it. Dewey makes this participation in experience the basis and source of objectivity. To be an object is to be connected with the inquiring subject in some way.

By making the existence of objects contingent upon their construction and reconstruction in the course of inquiry, Dewey nullified the all-important distinction between what is known and the means of knowing it, between the objective and subjective conditions in the process and content of our knowledge. The material object was sublimated into what is known about it, what is done with it, or what is made of it.

It is as misleading to identify the object as a material reality with the object of knowledge, its concept, as to confuse history itself—which comprises the activities and achievements of our species from the beginning of humanization—with historical knowledge and theory, even though the same term "history" is used for both the objective process and our understanding of it.

Before it was processed into paper, the material of the page on which these words are printed was a tree growing in a forest. To be sure, it has been "existentially reconstructed" by active, intelligent individuals—but from one kind of object into another.

When Dewey was an absolute idealist, he affirmed that "all existence . . . must be known existence," thus identifying objects as elements in individual consciousness. As an instrumentalist, he shifted the locus of existence from consciousness to an all-encompassing stream of experience. Berkeley maintained that "to be is to be perceived." In Dewey's epistemology the perceiving, knowing subject is displaced by the active experimenter—"to be is to be experienced," and things are as they are experienced. He is aligned with Berkeley in opposition to the materialist view that being as such precedes perception and experience. The knowing and doing of the subject depends upon the object and is derived from it, not the other way around.

Practice and Theory

The relationship between theory and practice is the hub of any scientific theory of knowledge. Instrumentalism's approach to this problem differs from idealism and rationalism on the one hand and dialectical materialism on the other. Pragmatism upholds the unity of theory and action and gives primacy to practice in their interaction—as its baptismal name, taken from the Greek word *pragma* (action), indicates. Dewey himself designated his standpoint as "experimental empiricism" to distinguish it from the passive reception of sensations in the older empirical epistemology and align it with the method of natural science.

As a partisan of reconstructive activity, Dewey campaigned against the separation of knowledge from action upheld by the classical tradition, and he condemned its metaphysics which made practice inferior to theory. In accord with their disparagement of labor and the primitive level of their science, Greek philosophers, especially the idealists, disregarded the role of experimentation, of doing, in the acquisition and testing of knowledge. Most of their successors up to Bacon's time followed suit. The principal tendency in Western philosophy, accentuated by Christian theology, has been to exalt reason above experience on the ground that theory gives access to absolute and perfect Being, to the properties of Ultimate Reality, whereas practice merely has commerce with imperfect, changing material things.

The tenacity of these rationalist values can be seen in the fact that *The Encyclopedia of Philosophy,* republished in four volumes by Macmillan in 1972, contains no entry on "practice." Apparently this category does not deserve philosophical consideration, although the editor claims in the introduction that "no philosophical concept or theory of any importance is not identified and discussed in the work" (p. x).

Dewey had far more respect for the worth of practical activity. He disdained any glorification of ideas for their own sake. He assigned philosophy the task of overcoming the division between routine practice and experimental intelligence in fields ranging from the sciences and logic to morality and politics. Knowing had to serve doing by helping to change troubled situations and remove roadblocks to progress. Theory's divorce from practice was the cardinal sin of idealism, while the lack of a correct theory of inquiry was the source of thoughtless and misdirected activity in everyday affairs.

William James had construed the practical in highly individual terms. Dewey, following Peirce, gave a broader scope to the concept, identifying it with social habits and the repeatable experimental procedure of the community of scientists. Nonetheless he continued to regard the will of the individual, rather than the practice of the collective or the class, as the ultimate agency of social change.

Practice is the work that people do in changing nature and social life. Long the Cinderella of philosophy, it was taken out of the scullery and put in the center of the household by the Marxist theory of cognition.

Practical activity has four functions in the promotion of knowledge. It is the starting point, the constant basis and impelling force, and the aim of learning about the world. It is also the decisive test of the validity of ideas.

The formation of humankind testifies to the historical priority of practice over theorizing. When the hominids emerged from the primate state, they had a negligible understanding of the world around them. Their intelligence expanded and deepened as they engaged in a novel and distinctive type of activity, cooperative labor. In procuring and producing their means of livelihood through purposive and regulated interchange with nature, they gradually accumulated insights into the forces of nature and the properties of the objects they fashioned and used.

The interplay between practical experience and rational comprehension is exemplified by fire, the first chemical process humans learned to generate and control. It provided warmth, light, and protection, and gave greater digestibility to food. The methods devised for kindling fire, feeding and dampening the flames, maintaining and transporting it, and the uses to which the power of heat were put, demanded intent observation and led to comparison of experiences and rudimentary generalizations about the nature of this phenomenon. In the course of time the empirical data derived from the technical practices connected with the applications of fire in cooking, heating, metallurgy, pottery-making, and other productive activities laid the basis for the theoretical science of combustion. Half a million years of social practice preceded the knowledge that heat was a mode of the kinetic energy of molecules.

Practice is also the progenitor of the social sciences. The science of politics began with Aristotle, when the new practices issuing from the convulsive changes in the class alignments and methods of rulership of the more advanced city-states of ancient Greece had to be accounted for, justified, and criticized. In the fourteenth century Ibn Khaldun set forth the first elements of sociology under the impetus of the transformation of Arab life brought about by the transition from nomadry to settled urban conditions. The science of statistics and the theory of probability were developed out of the needs of insurance, state finance, and commerce.

The cognitive capacities of humanity have kept growing in extent and depth as their practical abilities and control of the environment have progressed. The requirements of social practice have been the main spur to the advancement of knowledge. These have not only set the specific tasks to be solved by inquiry but accelerated the pace of cognition by discovering ways to solve problems and devising instruments and equipment, such as scales and retorts, the telescope and microscope, that open new pathways to knowledge.

Geometry and writing, two of the most valuable acquisitions of knowledge, are means of scientific inquiry. Both came into existence at the dawn of urban civilization as a result of practical needs. Elementary geometry, which deals with such properties of space as lines, angles, triangles, circles, and other figures lying entirely on one plane, originated in Babylon and Egypt with a few empirically arrived at statements involved in the problems of surveying and measuring land. It was subsequently systematized into formal and logical shape by Euclid around 300 B.C.

The development of writing shows graphically how practical interests prepare and promote theoretical ones. Preagricultural and uncivilized peoples are illiterate; they have no need for writing and have not invented any such system. Writing had a practical economic origin; it was used by priestly and military administrators in the cities of Mesopotamia, India, and Egypt to keep accounts. This innovation was to revolutionize the transmission of human knowledge and become the characteristic mode of expression of theoreticians, scientists, and the intellectual elite, from the ancient scribe to the modern author and journalist.

Practice is the major purpose of cognition. People study the world and investigate its properties and laws in order to apply this understanding to satisfy their social needs, create useful things for the betterment of human living, or—in class societies—to advance their class interests. However gratifying the pursuit of greater theoretical comprehension is to the individual, however indispensable pure research is to the advancement of science, theory by itself cannot change reality any more than emotion can. It would be pointless and sterile apart from implementation in social action; it would not advance without the prod of practical necessity.

This holds true for both the natural and social sciences. Even though the practical uses and social ends may not be immediately and clearly in view, they are the ultimate justification for theorizing about any subject. Becquerel's discovery of radioactivity was at first a purely scientific piece of knowledge. Before long it was put to use in medicine (X rays) and later in nuclear fission. The secular democratic ideology that conflicted with the divine and absolute right of the monarchy found fruition and vindication in the revolutionary movements of the popular masses that actually overthrew royal power.

Finally, practice is the supreme and definitive test of the validity and objectivity of ideas. The existence—or nonexistence—of truth, the correlation between ideas and facts, is proven by the results of practice. If people deliberately act upon their knowledge of reality and attain the ends they aim at, the successful results certify the correctness of the ideas—their correspondence with the nature of the things perceived or thought about. Conversely, failure signalizes falseness or insufficiency. The unity between truthfulness and usefulness was finely expressed by Francis Bacon: "There is a most intimate connexion and almost an identity between ways of human power and human knowledge. . . . That which is most useful in practice is most correct in theory" (*Novum Organum,* II, lv).

Dewey saw the highest expression of the fusion of practice with theory in the experimental methods of natural science heralded by Bacon. It provided the best model of inquiry in all other areas of human life and thought, and he sought to convince others to apply its procedures, as he interpreted them, in the solution of political, ideological, and cultural problems.

Notwithstanding his exceptional appreciation of the place of practice, Dewey's conception of this key philosophical category had serious shortcomings. He inflated the voluntary and subjective side of practical activity and minimized the fact that the initiatives taken in human action are invoked, circumscribed, and decided by the objective material conditions of life.

He did not consistently observe that the activities of production and the relations issuing from them have been the prime determinants of both practice and theory at all stages of historical progress. Indeed the key to the bifurcation of mental and physical labor that so concerned him was to be found at that momentous economic turning point when the accumulation of a social surplus product led to new divisions of labor that endowed the possessing and appropriating classes with the privilege of monopolizing theoretical knowledge. This grave deformation, whereby a small minority had the leisure and means to occupy itself with the problems of thought and the higher levels of culture while the mass of wealth producers were kept in ignorance with their noses to the grindstone, has marked all forms of class society.

Dewey did account for the past opposition of theory and practice through a class analysis. He pointed out that different social strata not only engaged in different kinds of activities but evaluated them according to different standards. That was evidenced in the disesteem of labor and experimental science in Greco-Roman and feudal times. Yet he expected the American people as a whole, from the ruling elite to the poor, to set aside their class positions in a joint effort to apply scientific method to social reform.

Practice embraces endeavors in all domains of social life from science and industrial techniques to politics and artistic creation. Through its association with the evolution of class relations, practice can acquire a revolutionary character when the popular masses move to overthrow established institutions.

Dewey's outlook reduced this extremely important outgrowth of practice to insignificance. In his view, practical intervention should remodel bad conditions only up to the point of agreed-upon reform but not beyond. Although he was reluctantly willing to opt for radical action against fascism or military dictatorship, he believed that the practice of revolution, or any preparation for it, should be avoided at almost any price.

In the extended reproduction of social life through history, the practical and the theoretical keep spurring one another in a spiraling ascent. The demands of practice stimulate theoretical elaborations which enrich, correct, and redirect further practice. More intelligent and effective practice fosters new advances in theoretical understanding. The reciprocal action of these two poles of human endeavor in the dialectical process of knowledge is manifest in all branches of science.

Thus the practical need in advanced technology for more powerful sources of energy than the electrical, chemical, and physical sources hitherto available has propelled nuclear physics into the forefront of contemporary research, providing deeper insights into the structure of matter and the processes of microcosmic phenomena.

Dewey situated theory in a broader context of doing than any other thinker of the democratic school. In his theory of inquiry, felt difficulties call for ideation in the form of hypotheses which are acted upon to see whether they can dispose of the problem. However valuable it may be in its own right, theorizing is intermediary and auxiliary to the practical reconstruction of the situation.

However, in his zeal to pull down the idealist fetish of pure reason, Dewey did not give theoretical cognition its rightful due in the total process of learning about reality. His definition of the most intelligent action fell short of the highest aims and achievements of science, which seeks to gain knowledge of the laws that govern the development of all things in the universe. Since Dewey denied the objective existence of lawfulness, of cause and effect, he stopped short of illuminating the crowning form and result of theory. The goal of scientific inquiry and the highest grade of knowledge is not, as Dewey taught, probable hypotheses, but the logical generalizations contained in verified knowledge of the comprehensive laws of nature, society, and thought.

Through reasoning about the chemical data at his disposal, Avogadro in 1811 enunciated his famous hypothesis that equal volumes of all gases at the same temperature and pressure have equal numbers of molecules. This proposition remained in dispute until the turn of the century when it was confirmed by overwhelming experimental evidence. Today his hypothesis has become a law, a demonstrable truth. Such a synthesis of logical generalization with the results of observation and experiment, each buttressing the other, is the epitome of scientific knowledge.

In highlighting the role of experiment, Dewey slighted the importance of general theoretical conclusions in natural and social science. His method pivoted, in the last analysis, more on the trial-and-error procedures it rationalized than on tested principles that formulated the essential relations, characteristics, and causes of the phenomena under consideration. Thus instrumentalism improved upon but did not transcend the inherent limitations of traditional empiricism, which was crippled by distrust of the general, lawful, necessary, and universal features of reality and tended to become bogged down in the particular, partial, and more superficial aspects of experience. As numerous critics pointed out, he focused more attention on the foreground of experience than on the causal background of events.

*   *   *

Dewey was deeply concerned over the gap between theory and practice in contemporary life. He attributed this discrepancy to the miseducation of the people; they had to be taught how to apply the methods that had accomplished such wonders in natural science, technology, and industry to "men's fundamental acts and attitudes in social matters."

He was uncertain whether the division between scientific procedures and everyday affairs was maintained by old intellectual habits or by deeper social causes. "What stands in the way," he wrote, in a muddled manner, "is a lot of outworn traditions, moth-eaten slogans and catchwords, that do substitute duty for thought, as well as our entrenched predatory self-interest" ("Science and Society," in *Philosophy and Civilization,* p. 328).

At the bottom of the Great Depression he stuck to the belief that the breach between science and labor could be mended, and social planning and controls instituted for the benefit of all, without going beyond the capitalist system. "We shall only make a real beginning in intelligent thought when we cease mouthing platitudes; stop confining our ideas to antitheses of individualism and socialism, capitalism and communism, and realize that the issue is between chaos and order, chance and control: the haphazard use and the planned use of scientific techniques" (ibid.). These platitudes of liberal rhetoric soared high above the concrete realities of property and power, poverty and powerlessness, that lay beneath the problems to be solved.

Dewey expected much more from twentieth-century American capitalism than it could possibly give. When the bourgeoisie set forth to conquer the world from the seventeenth century on, its demands, clashing with medieval scholasticism and feudal routine, had effected a fruitful marriage between renovated theory and enlightened practice through the rebirth of physical science and the extension of similar ideas to social phenomena. In its most progressive period the economic, political, ideological, and cultural imperatives of ascending capitalism profoundly transformed theory and practice alike in the Western world.

Capitalism, however, by its very class structure and reasons for existence cannot carry through the kind of fusion of scientific theory with social practice on the highest level that is needed for the further progress of science and society. Its process of production detaches science from labor and makes it into an independent force of production which is conscripted to serve the interests of the monopolists and their militarized state, as the development of nuclear weapons and other ghastly means of destruction testifies. With few exceptions workers—on the job or off—are not encouraged either to absorb or apply the methods of science, least of all in relation to social and political issues. Scientists and workers are kept apart under the rule of the profiteers.

In order to cooperate for the common good these layers of the people would have to begin by basing their actions upon the very antithesis between capitalism and socialism that Dewey dismissed as a diversion. The only practical way to overcome the evil effects of the separation of theory from practice, which is rooted in the constitution of class society, would be to imbue revolutionary action with the teachings of scientific socialism in a militant mass movement to abolish capitalist property and power.

Dewey's recommendations foreclosed this. That is why his instrumental theory of knowledge is an inadequate and ineffective instrument both for the scientific understanding of society and its practical reorganization.

10

History, Society,
and Politics

Proposed methods for resolving social conflicts formed the center of gravity of Dewey's philosophy. Colleagues like Russell and Santayana chided him for being far more concerned with humanity's prospects in society than its place in the universe at large. "He manifests no sense of the dark and unfathomable seas of being, wherein the world of human conduct occupies but an infinitesimal portion of time and space," observed Morris Cohen in *American Thought* (p. 293).

Dewey insisted that philosophy must serve to clarify social, political, and moral problems; any philosophy that sidestepped the treatment of such disputed issues, or subordinated them to loftier considerations, was otiose and harmful.

Dewey's preoccupation with the social side of philosophizing sprang from his active participation in public affairs through the Progressive movement as well as from his conception of the origins and functions of intelligence. Intelligence had been engendered, he taught, in order to aid the adjustment of organisms to their environment. It had undergone further development into conscious thought through the medium of language, which enabled humankind to share experience and thus to anticipate the consequences of current processes.

Philosophy, as the generalized method of inquiry, was for Dewey the highest form of intelligence. Just as intelligence intervened to reintegrate the disrupted relations between the creature and its surroundings, so philosophy had been born in social conflicts and sought to provide solutions for them. The mission of contemporary philosophy, he said, was to undertake in the most conscious manner the office of detecting and removing social maladjustments, which earlier philosophers had touched upon without fully comprehending what they were doing.

Dewey demanded that philosophers turn away from pretentious and futile "dealings with Ultimate and Absolute Reality" and apply themselves to the pressing problems of social life. "When it is acknowledged that under disguise of dealing with ultimate reality, philosophy has been occupied with the precious values embedded in social traditions, that it has sprung from a clash of social ends and from a conflict of inherited institutions with incompatible contemporary tendencies, it will be seen that the task of future philosophy is to clarify men's ideas as to the social and moral strifes of their own day. Its aim is to become so far as is humanly possible an organ for dealing with these conflicts," he wrote in *Reconstruction in Philosophy* (p. 45).

While emphasizing the social role of philosophy, Dewey disqualified its scientific character. Marxism affirms that philosophy can have a scientific foundation based upon a true knowledge of reality and its general laws of development. Dewey declared to the contrary that the main cause for the split between philosophy and science "is that philosophy has assumed for its function a knowledge of reality." Instead of searching for the truth about things, it brings out "values to be secured and shared by all. . . . It is a liaison officer between the conclusions of science and the modes of social and personal action through which attainable possibilities are projected and striven for" (*Quest for Certainty,* pp. 309, 311). That is, philosophy, unlike science, concerns itself with possibilities and values rather than realities and truths.

Dewey's Philosophy of History

A philosophy that is to cope with present-day "social and moral strifes" should be equipped with a correct conception of the course and causes of history. However, Dewey's unrestricted relativism and particularism inhibited him from elaborating a comprehensive and consistent theory of its development. Under cover of rejecting the historical absolutes of idealism, he denied that any general theory of the processes of social evolution had validity or value. Theories that discuss "*the* state, *the* individual; the nature of institutions as such, society in general," are worthless and even harmful, he asserted, because "they do not assist inquiry. They close it" (*Reconstruction in Philosophy,* p. 149). Historical, sociological, and political propositions acquire usefulness and meaning only in connection with concrete situations.

This distrust of generalizations about the nature of historical development gave an eclectic character to Dewey's explanations of social processes. His penchant for oscillating between near-materialist and idealist points of view was observable in his interpretation of the development of mentality from savage society through the ancient thinkers to his own philosophy.

In an article on the "Interpretation of the Savage Mind," republished in *Philosophy and Civilization,* Dewey undertakes to explain the peculiar mental structure of primitive humans along more or less materialist lines. "Occupations determine the fundamental modes of activity, and hence control the formation and use of habits," he tells us (p. 175). The pattern of habits arising from the hunting life shapes the rest of culture: art, ceremonials, marriage, customs, etc. Dewey likewise applies this criterion to later stages of social development arising from agricultural, pastoral, military, trading, craft, and commercial pursuits. He even traces our present basic mental structure to the original responses conditioned by hunting as modified by all these subsequent occupational activities.

Dewey extends the same sociological mode of interpretation to the history of ancient philosophy. The predominant features of the classical idealist systems from cosmology to psychology reflected the class structure of Greek society. Here is one citation out of many: "The old distinction between vegetative, animal and rational souls was, when applied to men, a formulation and justification of class divisions in Greek society. Slaves and mechanical artisans living on the nutritional, appetitive level were for practical purposes symbolized by the body—as obstructions to ideal ends and as solicitations to acts contrary to reason. The good citizen in peace and war was symbolized by the soul proper, amenable to reason, employing thought, but confining its operation after all to mundane matters, infected with matter. Scientific inquirers and philosophers alone exemplified pure reason, operating with ideal forms for the sake of the latter. The claim of this class for inherent superiority was symbolized by *nous,* pure immaterial mind" (*Experience and Nature,* p. 251).

He went on to point out that this class-conditioned pattern of thought, perfected by Plato and Aristotle, was taken over by Christian theology, entered into the dualism of Descartes, and persists up to the present time. "In Hellenistic thought, the three-fold distinction became that of body, mind or soul and spirit; spirit being elevated above all world affairs and acts, even moral concerns, having purely 'spiritual' (immaterial) and religious objects. This doctrine fell in with the sharp separation made in Christianity for practical moral purposes, between flesh and spirit, sin and salvation, rebellion and obedience. Thus the abstract and technical Cartesian dualism found prepared for it a rich empirical field with which to blend, and one which afforded its otherwise empty formalism concrete meaning and substance" (ibid., pp. 251–52).

Contemporary philosophy, concluded Dewey, must purge itself of these metaphysical preconceptions carried over from the dualisms of traditional class thinking.

Up to this point he recognizes that cultural phenomena and the movement and modes of thought have been determined, or at least heavily conditioned, by the economic activities and class relations of the given social formation. But when he confronts the democratic America of his own time, Dewey suddenly leaves solid ground, soars into the clouds, and suspends the rule that occupational activities, social structure, and class outlook shape intellectual traits. The liberal constituency of his generation and the ideas of his own philosophy are not animated or contaminated, he claims, by the material realities of bourgeois society. They have risen above gross class considerations and fly on the wings of a pure scientific intelligence. Henceforth the public-spirited procedures and democratic ideas of the instrumentalists will direct the development of American society and politics in an unbiased way regardless of its class structure.

The more astute adherents of Progressivism are quite capable of analyzing the past, or at least certain aspects of it, in a materialist manner. But the closer they come to their immediate environment and their own governing interests, the less realistic and more ethereal does their method of thought become. Dewey's detaching of his own philosophy from capitalist reality, and his innocent illusion that he is concerned only with constructing the most just and reasonable social order free from the stigmas of any particular class grouping, illustrates that tendency.

"Social" versus Class

Pragmatism claims to be the most concrete mode of thought, one which sticks to the facts given by experience, whereas other philosophies from idealism to Marxism are metaphysical and doctrinaire. Yet when Dewey analyzes civilized society, he falls into the vice of idealistic abstraction.

He asserts that "the social" is the most inclusive and important of all the categories of thought and makes it the pivot of his whole philosophy. (See "Social as a Category," *Monist,* April 1928.) Is this a warranted assertion?

The term "social" designates human association in general, living and working together in a body, as an integrated unit. It suitably covers those types of social organization where the means of production are collectively owned and the means of existence more or less equitably shared, as in tribal life or as it would be in a future form of communism. But it is inadequate and misleading when taken as the key to understanding the intervening forms of social structure, such as slavery, feudalism, and capitalism, where private property prevails. Such societies function as integrated units—but they are made up of antagonistic elements. Where society is split into owners of the means of production and propertyless laborers, into exploiters and exploited, rich and poor, rulers and ruled, the concept of "class" is more concrete, central, and applicable than the broader term "social."

Under such economic conditions class formations are the actual way in which the social is realized, the specific form in which social ties are expressed. The particular class relations of production and the special type of property ownership not only define but supersede the more general relation of common participation in a single social order. The connections between its components resemble the relation between the horse and its rider, not that between equal partners. The members of slave, feudal, and capitalist societies, which are built upon antagonistic relations, are governed by different laws of development and animated by different motives than those living under collectively owned economies.

Dewey's unconditional elevation of the social over the class concept obliterates the fundamentally different historical and economic factors which actually determine all the other manifest-ations of social activity in class formations. At the same time it illicitly introduces the notion of the harmony of social forces into a situation where conflict really predominates.

This presupposition serves as a pedestal for Dewey's contention that class interests, ties, and conflicts are not the dominant type of social relation under capitalism, and more particularly in democratic America. Whatever influence class considerations exert, they are not necessarily decisive, he believes, in any domain from politics to philosophy. The shared universal human relations summarized in the category "social" are, should be, or will be (his tenses are not always clearly defined) predominant over narrow class factors—provided the scientific method of instrumentalism is brought to bear.

Dewey derives his conceptions of society and the state from this false assumption that the bare fact of belonging to the human race or inhabiting the same country counts for more than any other relation.

Society and the State

Dewey presents a pluralistic theory of the structure of society and a conception of the state as a public servant.

The social order is composed of "societies, associations, groups of an immense number of kinds, having different ties and instituting different interests. They may be gangs, criminal bands; clubs for sport, sociability and eating; scientific and professional organizations; political parties and unions within them; families; religious denominations, business partnerships and corporations; and so on in an endless list. The associations may be local, nation-wide, and trans-national" (*Intelligence in the Modern World*, p. 382).

This picture of society as a loosely woven tissue of diverse groups without organic relation to one another is superficial and misleading. Society is not the sum of separately functioning groups overlapping and interacting in a haphazard manner. Each historical type of society forms a definite whole in which its component members have a specific connection with one another. The basic relations of its structure are constituted by the positions the respective layers occupy in the social economy.

In civilized societies the forces of production (which include both the means of production and living labor), the economic system corresponding to the level of these forces, along with the state structure and the cultural superstructure, are all interdependent elements of a single concrete social formation having its own laws of development.

Dewey brushes aside this organic unity, which marks each of the successive stages of social development, and breaks up the determinate social organization into disconnected bits and pieces of activity. This conception of society as a mosaic of external associations does not provide any criterion for determining the comparative rank and specific gravity of any given relation. It is thoroughly indiscriminate. In principle, it allows for one kind of association to be as significant as any other.

In reality, the economic relations of people are decisive in determining the nature of the social organization. The slave status of the Blacks, for example, determined not only their individual existence but the essential nature of the entire social system of the Southern states before the Civil War.

The differences and conflicts arising from inherently antagonistic economic relations manifest themselves directly or indirectly throughout the range of subsidiary social relations. The ownership of corporate bonds and stocks largely determines what the associations, attitudes, and outlook of the big capitalist will be. The fact that a person without property has to work for wages for this very capitalist corporation, and thereby belongs to the proletariat, means far more to him or her and to the rest of society than, say, church affiliation. Membership in a union has far greater social consequences than induction into a fraternal order or joining a bowling team.

Dewey, however, flattens out these qualitatively different types of association, throws them into a grab bag, and ties them together under the heading of "the public." Such a theory of free-floating and equally graded publics might have had a certain semblance of plausibility in reference to a small trading and farming community of the nineteenth century like Burlington, Vermont, where property was more or less evenly distributed and distinctions of wealth and social standing were not too glaring. But it ignores the fundamental facts of life in the highly centralized monopoly capitalism today.

"No family is as directly powerful in national affairs as any major corporation; no church is as directly powerful in the external biographies of young men in America today as the military establishment; no college is as powerful in the shaping of momentous events as the National Security Council," correctly observed C. Wright Mills, professor of sociology at Dewey's Columbia University. "Religious, educational and family institutions are not autonomous centers of national power; on the contrary, these decentralized areas are increasingly shaped by the big three [the military, political, and corporate elites], in which developments of decisive and immediate consequence now occur. Families and churches and schools adapt to modern life; governments and armies and corporations shape it; and, as they do so, they turn these lesser institutions into means for their ends" (*The Power Elite,* p. 6).

Dewey's pluralistic theory of society is almost as groundless as a pluralistic physiology would be that viewed the organs of the body as disconnected units, placing the heart and lungs on a par with the earlobes and eyelashes.

*   *   *

His theory of the state follows logically from this conception of society. The government has been set up by the various publics to serve public interests. The state is "a public articulated and operating through representative officers" (*Intelligence in the Modern World,* p. 379). This is a version of the social contract legend which has formed the starting point for all the theoreticians of bourgeois democracy and parliamentary rule since the seventeenth century. The people or their representatives were supposed to have come together at some point and decided to hand over their rights and powers to a sovereign body ministering to their common welfare.

The trouble is that none of the states known to history came into existence that way or conformed to those specifications. They arose at a certain point in the economic evolution of civilization, not simply to carry out socially useful functions, but even more to protect the privileged positions and advance the special interests of exploiting and ruling classes. That is what the government apparatus—the legislatures and assemblies, the law courts, the armies, the police, the tax gatherers—primarily were for. The state has been the product of irreconcilable class divisions in society—from the theocratic kingdoms of the ancient Middle East to the democratic republic of George Washington, Abraham Lincoln, and Franklin Roosevelt.

Dewey denied that the state is an agency of any particular

class, an instrument of repression, or even a product of class society. To him it is an indispensable servant of a people as a whole, which is composed of diverse publics. Class characteristics are a deformation of the state's fundamental purpose, especially in a democratic republic. He believed literally in Lincoln's words, that the government was "of, for, and by the people," and not the executive arm of the economically most powerful class. Insofar as the state was subjected to the influence of favored classes, it deviated from its true nature.

The free-trade liberals of the earlier generation of the bourgeois-democratic era had opposed a powerful centralized government, teaching, like Jefferson and Paine, that the best government was that which governed least. Dewey was a liberal of a much later time, when the capitalist state, instead of seeking merely to release the economy from precapitalist restrictions and then swim along with its automatic working, had to interfere with one sector of society after another and directly regulate the relations between contending classes in order to keep its system from capsizing.

He could not agree with the laissez-faire gospel of bourgeois liberalism or with the "rugged individualism" of "free enterprise" which masked the depredations of the monopolists. On the other hand, he could not wholeheartedly embrace the "collectivism," the total ownership of the main means of production by the state, which expressed the anticapitalist aspirations of the masses to secure control over their means of livelihood. The one, he believed, led to big business tyranny; the other to totalitarian enslavement.

So this middle-class democrat deliberately laid out a course between these two extremes. The state was to undertake specific measures to protect the public welfare or meet the legitimate claims of any particular portion of the public. But it should refrain from substituting itself for the private initiative of the people—or of business.

The government had to remain the servant, and not become the master, of the various voluntary groupings with diversified interests. Its office was to regulate their relations only to the degree required to prevent any one from dominating or crushing the others. The government was the Great Mediator, standing above all special groupings, arbitrating their conflicts of interest, keeping the nation in balance.

This is the rationale for the welfare state. The government acts

as impartial umpire over a mixed capitalist-collectivist economy
wherein competing units all work for the national good and no
one is granted special privileges.

C. Wright Mills has shown how far such a theory of the
balancing of interest groups diverges from the actual wielding of
power in American society. "The American government today is
not merely a framework within which contending pressures
jockey for position and make politics. Although there is of course
some of that, this government now has such interests vested
within its own hierarchical structure, and some of these are
higher and more ascendant than others. There is no effective
countervailing power against the coalition of the big
businessmen—who, as political outsiders, now occupy the
command posts—and the ascendant military men—who with
such grave voices now speak so frequently in the higher councils.
Those having real power in the American state today are not
merely brokers of power, resolvers of conflict, or compromisers of
varied and clashing interest—they represent and indeed embody
quite specific national interests and policies" (*The Power Elite,* p.
267).

Mills further points out that "the romantic pluralists of the
Jeffersonian school" (among whom Dewey belongs) are not
merely upholding an antiquated notion of American politics, but
unwittingly lending cover to the dictatorship of the elite of power
and wealth. The image of countervailing powers spread by the
instrumentalists is so well adapted to the rule of the rich that up
to now the plutocracy hasn't had to evolve defensive ideologies of
its own!

Cultural Lag versus Class Struggle

The progressive thinkers of the eighteenth century regarded
abstract reason in one form or another as the ruler of world
history; they reduced social conflicts in the last analysis to
conflicts between ideas. Ignorance and superstition impeded
historical advance; the spread of knowledge was its principal
accelerator. Further enlightenment would induce people to bring
about the reconstruction of social relations in the most reasonable manner.

Although Dewey criticized their ineffectual rationalism, his
philosophy of history did not go much beyond theirs. He saw
civilization proceeding from routinism to science, from brute force

to intelligence—a process best embodied in American democracy and expressed in his own instrumentalism.

Humankind has reached this point not through class struggle but through the solidarity of social forces, not by conflict but by cooperation. "To say that all past historic social progress has been the result of cooperation and not of conflict would be also an exaggeration. But exaggeration against exaggeration, it is the more reasonable of the two " (*Intelligence in the Modern World,* p. 445).

Dewey minimizes the importance of the fact that in an exploiters' economy, cooperation takes place on the basis of antagonistic class interests. The operation of slave society depended not only upon the collaboration of the slaves in the process of production, but also upon their enforced "cooperation" with the slave driver intent on extorting the maximum work from them. The socialization of labor which unites large bodies of workers under capitalism is accompanied by the increasing centralization of capital and its oppressive power. Cooperation under such conditions inevitably leads to intensified class conflicts extending from the place of production to all other spheres of social activity.

The conception that the main source of conflict in our time comes from the antagonistic material interests of the capitalists and workers Dewey finds as repugnant as the more general thesis that the class struggle was the prime mover of historical development in the past. Instead of opposing classes, the fundamental conflict today is between "institutions and habits originating in the pre-scientific and pre-technological age" and the new forces and ideas generated by modern science and technology. Antiquated institutions and ideas are blocking progress.

Among these reactionary ideas Dewey includes the ideas and practices of the class struggle. As a democrat, he believed that all class divisions and distinctions should be removed. Hitherto this has often been done through the mechanism of class struggle eventuating in revolution. But it would be false to deduce from these precedents that current social evils will, or should, be rectified in the same way. People who think so are enslaved by tradition or hypnotized by the apparent efficacy of force.

Humankind at last has within its grasp the possibility of using a better method of directing social change. This is the cooperative experimentalism that does not throw everything out all at once in a violent spasm but proceeds by small steps, checking the results constantly to make sure that the right road is being followed. Friendly cooperation between all social elements for the attainment of common ends on the basis of scientifically guided action will displace conflict or coercion.

To the causal force of the class struggle Dewey counterposes "the causal force exercised by this embodiment of intelligence." The dynamic factor in our society is not the independent activity of the masses headed by the industrial workers; it is something more disembodied. "The rise of scientific method and of technology based upon this is the genuinely active force. . . ." This liberal method of "inventive and cooperative intelligence" is inherently progressive, democratic, and creative—whereas the class-struggle methods advocated by Marxism are obscurantist, despotic, and destructive.

"It is no exaggeration to say that the measure of civilization is the degree in which the method of cooperative intelligence replaces the method of brute conflict." Thus Dewey substitutes the theory of "the cultural lag" for the laws of the class struggle. The road to the future is being blocked not so much by the resistance of vested class interests as by the inability of people of all classes to adjust their obsolete habits and ideas to the needs of the scientific age. The problem is primarily due to a failure of intelligence and education.

Certainly the institutions and ideas of class society are relics of a barbarous, prescientific past—but they have extremely powerful material reinforcement in the present. The conflict between the old order and the new does not originate, nor is it being primarily fought out, upon the plane of ideas and methods. The antiquated relations are incorporated in the capitalist regime, which does not intend to surrender its privileges without battle, as experience has shown.

How, then, are the tremendous productive forces generated by scientific and technical advance to be released for the good of humankind? Marxism has explained in theory, and the world socialist movement proved in practice, that the conquest of power by the industrial working class and its allies is the only way to eliminate the obstruction of the capitalist rulers.

Despite lamentations about their harmfulness, the conflicts between capital and labor continue and even intensify. What is to be done if they threaten to acquire a revolutionary character? Here Dewey invokes two supplementary arguments against the revolutionary implications of working-class struggle.

He warns that the entrenched power of the dominant economic class is too strong to be overcome by counterforce. This argument has been used by opponents of revolutionary movements from the Tories and moderates of the eighteenth century to the liberals of the twentieth. Yet they have not succeeded in holding back peoples and classes from engaging in revolutionary action when they felt obliged to do so. Jefferson, who knew something about the birth of revolutions, wrote: "Nor will any degree of power in the hands of government prevent insurrections." In the 1950s the fates of Rakosi of Hungary and Batista of Cuba could have added footnotes to this observation.

The British crown and the Southern slaveholders appeared as formidable in their own time as the monopoly capitalists today. Neither proved to be invulnerable against the aroused and organized movement of the American people.

Even so, Dewey has a last trump to play. If revolution is tried and turns out to be triumphant, it will only breed counterforce—a dictatorship in which our present freedom will be sacrificed. This pessimistic conclusion has no basis for support in our nation's history. The victories of the earlier American revolutions produced "a new birth of freedom" and a larger measure of democracy. Why, then, should a popular movement against the reactionary forces of our own time lead to less beneficial results? It is not from any empirical analysis of the conditions and forces of such an eventuality that Dewey draws his frightful forecast, but rather from his liberal prejudice against the ultimate consequences of the fight for progress under capitalism.

Classless Democracy

Dewey's conception of democracy crowns his pluralistic theory of society and his public service notion of the state. It is the crux of his entire philosophy.

In accord with his view that economic conditions and class relations do not determine the essence of political phenomena, he does not approach democracy as a historically produced and materially conditioned mode of government. He is the champion of a pure democracy "which never was on land or sea."

"The keynote of democracy," he wrote, is ". . . the necessity for the participation of every mature human being in formation of the values that regulate the living of men together. . . . all those who are affected by social institutions must have a share in producing and managing them" (*John Dewey's Philosophy,* pp. 400–401).

Dewey is here painting the portrait of an ideal democracy, not the features of any real one. None of the political democracies from ancient Greece to modern America meets these specifications. Each has been based upon relations of exploitation, exalted the rich over the poor, and restricted the participation of its people in the control of public affairs.

The Greek city-state republics were rooted in slavery, denied political rights to foreigners, slaves, and women, and were dominated by aristocrats. The democracies of the bourgeois era have been established on the inequalities of private property and the exploitation of wage labor by the capitalists. Their major policies have been formulated and executed by representatives of the wealthy classes. Many categories of citizens, including workers, women, Blacks, and young people, have been disenfranchised by various means. Even where all could vote, the power apparently vested in the electorate was actually exercised by the strongest and solidest section of the ruling class. American democracy has coexisted with chattel slavery, wage slavery, and imperialism.

Dewey believed that, while all this might have been true of other countries and perhaps even the American past, such perversions of democracy no longer needed persist in the United States. Here all the conditions had ripened for the creation of an unrestricted and classless democracy. Only tradition, lack of scientific method, and inadequate education stood in the way.

However, something much more substantial than ignorance thwarts the expansion of democracy for the American people. That is the social, economic, political, and military supremacy of the monopoly capitalists. This "power elite," as the liberal sociologists call it, has no permanent attachment to democracy. It will tolerate the forms of democracy so long as these can be manipulated to its advantage and as long as the workers do not seriously challenge its rulership. But the leaders of this elite will not hesitate to discard such forms and turn to a "strong state" of a military, Bonapartist, or fascist character when the present system runs into a blind alley and they fear the loss of their privileged position.

The dollar democracy of the United States has been based upon the revolutionary achievements of the eighteenth and nineteenth centuries and upon an expanding, progressive capitalist economy which enabled the ruling classes to obtain the support, or at least the tolerance, of the middle and working classes. Jefferson believed that democracy could not be secure unless it rested upon an extensive class of small landed proprietors. He coupled the decentralization of political power with the wide dispersal of property ownership.

Today both ownership and power have become highly centralized. How is democracy to be saved and strengthened under such circumstances? Dewey relied upon 'men and women of good will, drawn from every calling" who will unite to establish a classless society and a purified democracy. No single class will lead the way.

But a better democracy can be built only on the basis of a new and higher economic foundation. And this can be brought into being only by taking the means of production out of monopolist hands by nationalizing them. The organized working class is the only force in American society with the capacities to carry through such an assignment.

The creation of the "classless democracy" envisaged by Dewey is a historical impossibility and a theoretical absurdity. All the political democracies known to history have been based upon and backed by some class or combination of classes. And when the classless communist society of the future is attained, there will be no place for any form of state, democratic or dictatorial.

Meanwhile, the most pressing problem of political life today is not to effect a transition from class rule to a classless democracy, but to go from the decaying and narrowing democracy of the bourgeois order to a workers' democracy based on a nationalized and planned economy. The main agency for accomplishing this changeover is the independent organization and revolutionary action of the working class. A motley coalition of good-hearted and liberal-minded individuals drawn from all classes cannot do the job. The socialist rule of the working class can provide the only durable safeguard for democracy.

Dewey explicitly rejected this Marxist way of defending and developing democracy; he counterposed to it his liberal program of gradual reform along nonpartisan, nonclass lines. He and his followers put forward such views on democracy as though they were the highest product of scientific thought on the subject. In reality they were an anachronism reflecting the immaturity of American political life.

War and Revolution

Revolutions and wars are the most decisive events in the life of nations. They lay bare the contradictions at work in their social, economic, and political relations. They tear aside the pretenses of governments, classes, parties, and leaders and reveal their real positions and aims. The facts of overwhelming force uppermost in wars and revolutions confront ideas with the overwhelming force of facts. They pose issues with the utmost sharpness and leave little leeway for evasion or equivocation. That is why they provide the severest tests for all theories of the social structure, the role of the state, and the nature of class relations.

If, as Dewey taught, thinking is called forth by interruptions in the smooth flow of experience, then wars and revolutions, the most profound breaks in the continuity of everyday existence, should have commanded the utmost exercise of intelligence by the pragmatists. Yet their thinking on these mighty events had meager and disastrous results.

Dewey had much more direct experience of wars than revolutions. As an adult he lived through four wars: the Spanish-American war, the First and Second World Wars, and in his final years the Korean "police action." Despite the pretensions of their artificers and the illusions of the American people, all of these wars were primarily waged to promote the imperialist aims of the United States. Except for the first of this series, Dewey did not see it that way—at least while the war was on.

Although Dewey was pacifistically disposed, he was not an absolute pacifist. He admitted in the 1930s that force was sometimes necessary and could be intelligently and progressively used, though he cautioned against it except under extreme provocation. Time and again he declared that militarism was "the world's present greatest evil" (*Intelligence in the Modern World,* p. 514). He urged that conflicts of national interest be settled not by lawless violence but by the peaceful arbitration of law and courts.

However, he did not abide by this injunction once the United States entered a war. Then his patriotic devotion proved stronger than his pacifist scruples and judicial proposals. Only between wars was he ardently and vigorously opposed to military force.

Woodrow Wilson had been Dewey's fellow student at Johns Hopkins during the 1880s. He put faith in that Democratic president when Wilson proclaimed that the United States was going into the First World War to end war forever and make the world safe for democracy. After indulging in patriotism to the point of intoxication, he and his fellow liberals woke up to find reaction in the saddle at home and the threat of war as menacing as before.

During the 1920s Dewey actively supported the movement launched by S. O. Levinson to outlaw war. "For the reader and student of Dewey's philosophy, the Plan to Outlaw War has special significance," says his editor, Joseph Ratner, "because not just Dewey the man but Dewey's philosophy worked for Outlawry and had an influential hand in shaping its basic formulation." It "admirably and completely exemplifies his conception of *the method of intelligence* in social affairs" (ibid., pp. 528–29).

How intelligent and effective was his judicial substitute for war? This plan proposed that governments refer their disputes for settlement to a world court administering agreed-upon statutes. Even though the Hague Tribunal hadn't prevented the First World War, Dewey expected that, by mobilizing educated public opinion behind this plan, bellicose governments could be made to submit to the sovereignty of international law.

Those satiated capitalist governments which were not at that time contemplating new territorial conquests found it helpful to parade such paper pacts for a while. The French, British, American, and other governments signed the Kellogg-Briand Pact in 1928. This was supposed to ban war as an instrument of national policy, although the diplomats involved took care to insert escape clauses in their agreement.

This renunciation of war on parchment did not of course prevent Japan's invasion of Manchuria, Mussolini's annexation of Ethiopia, or Hitler's military ventures during the 1930s. Nor did it hold back the United States from going to war when the time came in 1941. The very Secretary of State Stimson who, under the Republican Hoover, pressed the Assembly of the League of Nations to officially endorse the World Court, served as Secretary of War under the Democrat Roosevelt!

Dewey himself, who in 1922 demanded that war "be made a

public crime by international law," approved that crime when it became national law twenty years later. In the 1920s he said that the militarists, not the pacifists, should be sent to jail during wartime. But in the 1940s the war-makers again held the highest and most profitable posts while the pacifist and revolutionary opponents of the war entered federal prisons as in the previous war. To his honor, Dewey at least defended the rights of these dissenters.

Dewey and his disciple Ratner attributed the failure of the Plan to Outlaw War to the fact that, whereas they intended to have the plan implemented and enforced by the people, their brainchild had fallen into the hands of untrustworthy statesmen (as indeed it did!) who exploited it for their own demagogic purposes. But they failed to explain why the capitalist diplomats had so easily duped and swindled the people—including the liberal proponents of the plan. To them this appeared to be an accidental outcome, an unforeseeable error.

However, the Marxists had forecast that any plan for permanent peace which relied upon the peace-loving and law-abiding qualities of the capitalist regimes was bound to be "unintelligent" and ineffectual and end in disillusion. The executives of such governments used the power of their offices not to maintain peace at any price, but to maintain the positions of the capitalist rulers, for whom militarism is an indispensable instrument of national policy and a bountiful fount of easy profits.

However praiseworthy Dewey's desire to abolish war was, his proposals were unrealistic. He used the wrong agencies and the wrong methods to arrive at his objective. He appealed to the power of an amorphous "public opinion" composed of all people of good will, leaving the politicians of the plutocracy in command of state power. The first grouping was far too nebulous and disorganized to be any match for the centralized command of the second. Instead of relying upon abstract arguments and moral appeals, the only available counteragent to the imperialist war-makers would have been an antiwar movement built around independent action by the working class and its supporters.

Dewey's remedy was as illusory and misleading as that of the idealist philosopher Josiah Royce who proposed a mutual insurance scheme to end war. Ironically for a pragmatist, Dewey's suggested solution to "the world's greatest evil" turned out to be thoroughly impractical, a pious hope rather than an effective means for accomplishing the desired end. What could be more Platonic on the one hand and more pragmatic on the other than his own conduct? He opposed war so long as it remained an idea or a prospect (war in general) but when the war was actual, he embraced it!

*   *   *

Dewey's attitude toward revolution was no less short-sighted than his approach to the problem of war. He wrote more about war than about revolution—and, in drawing lessons about this phenomenon, he was more likely to refer to the French and Russian experiences than to our native revolutions. He did not dwell upon these past events because for him revolution was no longer a live option for Americans.

He would not admit that revolutions have any lawful or necessary place in the progress of class society, even though they have erupted wherever and whenever long-standing social antagonisms have reached the breaking point—including two times in America's history.

Dewey anthologized Jefferson and admired Lincoln, and he claimed to be carrying forward their democratic ideals. But a decisive difference separated him from them. Jefferson and Lincoln staunchly upheld the right of revolution and headed the great revolutions of their time. Dewey, on the other hand, argued that revolution in the United States was antiquated, wrong, and harmful.

He preserved the democratic values of his mentors but discarded their revolutionism. Whereas they represented a *revolutionary* democracy, he was the philosopher of a liberalism that in principle rejected revolution in favor of gradual reform.

The struggles led by Jefferson and Lincoln had cleared away major obstacles to the expansion of American capitalism by violent means. The Progressives had to contend with a powerfully entrenched capitalist rulership. They tried to improve the conditions of the masses and defend their liberties without threatening or invading the property rights of the profiteers. Their efforts failed because the means they used and the forces they relied on were inadequate.

Dewey rejected historical determinism in the name of empiricism. He did not see that the determinism underlying the development of revolutions works itself out in a highly empirical way. So it was with the two previous American upheavals. The mass of their participants did not become revolutionized through long-range calculation or by conscious plan; they arrived at civil strife after trial and error. Having tried again and again to settle the fundamental issues at stake by half-measures and compromise, they were ultimately driven to the fateful choice of either submitting supinely to rampant tyranny or fighting to the death.

Liberal thinking ignores the fact that in the unfolding of irrepressible class conflicts revolution does not erupt without sufficient reason; it is made necessary by the provocations of reaction. Armed resistance was precipitated in both the War of Independence and the Civil War by the initiatives of the adversary (the British blockade of Boston, the firing on Fort Sumter).

Dogmatic aversion to revolutionary action contravenes the instrumentalist maxim that no means of achieving a purpose is to be ruled out in advance of the consummation of the process, the successful reconstruction of the troubled situation. Revolution is justified even on pragmatic grounds if and when the people have no other or better way available to remedy their social ills and solve the problems of their national development.

The liberals did not regard revolution as an inescapable climactic stage in the intensification of class conflicts within a nation but as an aberration that could be averted by reasonable leaders on both sides. It was out of place in an enlightened democracy like the United States.

Dewey and his disciples discounted the possibility that the defense and deepening of democracy itself could necessitate taking the road of revolution once again. While he gratefully accepted the democratic freedoms won through earlier revolutionary struggles and worked to preserve and extend them, he could not conceive that a third revolution, this time of a socialist character, might be rendered imperative by the assaults of capitalist reaction upon the rights and gains of the American people. Nor could he envision that the monopolists and militarists might one day try to emulate the British lords and Southern slaveholders and have to be combatted as sternly.

Unlike the liberals, the Marxists put no trust in the fidelity of the capitalist rulers to democratic institutions. Their perspective goes beyond the safeguarding of acquired liberties to the establishment of a thoroughgoing socialist democracy. (For a more extensive treatment of these questions, see my book *Democracy and Revolution,* chapter 10, "Two Traditions of American Democracy.")

*   *   *

Contrary to Dewey's belief, his mode of thought in sociology, history, and politics was less scientific than the method and conclusions of the historical materialists. Compared with them, he was like an experimenter who clung to the ideas of the alchemists after Boyle. Lavoisier, and Dalton had given chemistry a solid theoretical foundation. His theory of society as a heap of groups, organized by social contract, headed by an impartial state, guided by a value-free intelligence rid of all class characteristics—is the sociological equivalent of operating in chemistry with Aristotle's four elements (air, fire, water, earth) after the modern atomic theory of the elements had been devised.

Yet it must be recognized that Dewey's sociological theories and political positions had broad popular appeal. His way of interpreting history and approaching social problems accorded with the outlook, the hopes, the illusions and disillusions of progressive middle class Americans—and a large section of the workers, too—during his lifetime. These segments of the people were neither reactionary nor revolutionary in temper; they were liberalistic, not socialistic. They were eager for steady improvements in their conditions within the framework of an ascending capitalist society. They expected to gain their demands bit by bit, step by step. Dewey gave a general theoretical expression and a philosophical foundation to these prevailing sentiments, defended them from the assaults of the right as well as the arguments of the left, and applied them in fields ranging from education and the law to political activity.

The real class role of these views will emerge more clearly and sharply in a review of the way pragmatism actually functioned in the field of education and in the major political, economic, and social crises of American capitalism during Dewey's lifetime.

11

Progressive Education

Dewey's most valuable and enduring contribution to American culture came from the ideas he fathered in education. He won a greater international following for his reforms in this field than for his instrumentalist philosophy. In previously backward countries that were obliged to catch up quickly and use the most modern methods, as in Turkey, Japan, China, the Soviet Union, and Mexico—all of which he visited in the 1920s—the reshapers of the educational system turned to Dewey for guidance.

Most broadly considered, Dewey's work consummated the trends initiated by the pioneers in primary and secondary education, who were animated by the impulses of the democratic revolution. This was especially clear in his views on child education, which built on ideas first brought forward by Rousseau, Pestalozzi, and Froebel in Western Europe and by kindred reformers in the United States.

In its course of development on a world scale the democratic movement forced consideration of the needs and claims of one section of the oppressed after another. Out of the general cause of "the rights of the people" there sprouted specific demands voicing the grievances of peasants, wage workers, the religiously persecuted, slaves, women, paupers, the aged, the disabled, prisoners, the insane, the racially oppressed. Children, one of the weakest, most dependent, most defenseless sections of the population, were included among them.

Every mass struggle against antiquated social and political conditions since the French revolution has evoked demands for the reconstruction of the educational system. The kindergarten and child-play movement, now incorporated in the public schools, was part and parcel of the ferment created by the French upheaval. Thomas Jefferson first called for national free public schools to defend and extend the newly won American democracy. The utopian socialists, in accord with their understanding that people were molded by their social environment, gave much thought to the upbringing of children and introduced many now accepted educational innovations.

The communist colony in New Harmony, Indiana, founded by Robert Owen in 1826, pioneered a pattern in free, equal, comprehensive, and secular education that had yet to be realized throughout this country over a century later. From the age of two the children were cared for and instructed by the community. The youngest spent the day in play school until they progressed to higher classes. The Greek and Latin classics were discarded; practice in various crafts constituted an essential part of the program. The teachers aimed to impart what the children could most readily understand, making use of concrete objects and avoiding premature abstractions. They banished fear and all artificial rewards and punishments, appealing instead to the spontaneous interests and inclinations of the children as incentives for learning. Girls were on an equal footing with boys.

The educational reformers of the eighteenth and nineteenth centuries dealt with two distinct aspects of children's problems. One concerned the claims of childhood as a specific and independent stage in human growth. This perennial problem arises from the efforts of adults to subject growing children to ends foreign to their own needs and to press them into molds shaped not by the requirements of the maturing personality, but by the external interests of the ruling order. Rousseau had protested against this when he wrote: "Nature wants children to be children before they are men. . . . Childhood has ways of seeing, thinking, and feeling, peculiar to itself, nothing can be more foolish than to substitute our ways for them."

The other aspect involved efforts to reshape the obsolete system of schooling to make it fit the changes that had taken place ir social life. These two problems were closely connected. The play school, for example, was devised not only to care for the specific needs of very young children but also to meet new needs which had grown out of the transformation in the family caused by industrial and urban conditions. The home was no longer a unit of production as in feudal and colonial times but had become more and more simply a center of consumption.

Dewey's theories focused attention on the child as an individual with rights and claims of his or her own. They combined this with a recognition of the clash between the outdated and class-distorted educational setup inherited from the past and the urgent requirements of the new era.

The educational system had to be thoroughly overhauled, he said, because of the deep-going changes in American civilization. In the colonial days of agrarian, small-town life, the child took part in household, community, and productive activities which spontaneously fostered capacities for self-direction, discipline, leadership, and independent judgment. Such worthwhile qualities were discouraged and stunted by the new industrialized, urbanized, atomized conditions which had disintegrated the family and weakened the influence of religion.

In the city the training of children became distorted because intellectual activities were dissociated from practical everyday occupations, Dewey wrote.

> While the child of bygone days was getting an intellectual discipline whose significance he appreciated in the school, in his home life he was securing acquaintance in a direct fashion with the chief lines of social and industrial activity. Life was in the main rural. The child came into contact with the scenes of nature, and was familiarized with the care of domestic animals, the cultivation of the soil, and the raising of crops. The factory system being undeveloped, the house was the center of industry. Spinning, weaving, the making of clothes, etc., were all carried on there. As there was little accumulation of wealth, the child had to take part in these, as well as to participate in the usual round of household occupations. Only those who have passed through such training [as Dewey himself did in Vermont], and, later on, have seen children raised in city environments, can adequately realize the amount of training, mental and moral, involved in this extra-school life. . . . It was not only an adequate substitute for what we now term manual training, in the development of hand and eye, in the acquisition of skill and deftness; but it was initiation into self-reliance, independence

of judgment and action, and was the best stimulus to habits of regular and continuous work.

In the urban and suburban life of the child of today this is simply memory. The invention of machinery, the institution of the factory system, the division of labor, have changed the home from a workshop into a simple dwelling place. The crowding into cities and the increase of servants [!] have deprived the child of an opportunity to take part in those occupations which still remain. Just at the time when a child is subjected to a great increase in stimulus and pressure from his environment, he loses the practical and motor training necessary to balance his intellectual development. Facility in acquiring information is gained; the power of using it is lost. While need of the more formal intellectual training in the school has decreased, there arises an urgent demand for the introduction of methods of manual and industrial discipline which shall give the child what he formerly obtained in his home and social life.

The old schooling had to be renovated for still another reason. The curriculum and mode of education of colonial education had been largely shaped by medieval concepts and aims. The schools were controlled by the clergy and access to them was restricted to the favored few among the wealthy and well-born. The teacher tyrannized the classroom, imposing a schematic routine upon a passive, obedient, well-drilled student body.

In *The School and Society* (1899) Dewey pointed out how haphazardly the existing school organization had grown up. It was composed of oddly assorted and poorly fitting parts, fashioned in different centuries and designed to serve different needs and even conflicting social interests.

The crown of the system, the university, had come down from medieval times and was originally intended to train an elite for such professions as law, theology, and medicine. The high school dated from the nineteenth century when it was instituted to care for the demands from commerce and industry for better-trained personnel. The grammar school was inherited from the eighteenth century when it was felt that boys ought to have the minimum ability to read, write, and calculate before being turned out to shift for themselves. The kindergarten was a later addition arising from the breakup of the family and the home by the industrial revolution.

A variety of specialized institutions had sprung up alongside this hierarchy of education. The normal or teacher training school produced the instructors demanded by the expansion of public education in the nineteenth century. Trade and technical schools turned out the skilled craftsmen needed for industry and construction.

Thus the various parts of the educational system ranged from institutions of feudal formation like the university to such offshoots of industrial capitalism as the trade school. No single principle or purpose unified the whole.

Dewey sought to supply that unifying pattern by consistently applying the principles of democracy, as he interpreted them, throughout the educational system. First, the schools would be freely available to all from kindergarten to college. Second, the children would themselves carry on the educational process, aided and guided by the teacher. Third, they would be trained to behave cooperatively, sharing with and caring for one another. Then these creative, well-adjusted equalitarians would make over American society in their own image.

In this way the opposition between the old education and the new conditions of life and work would be overcome. The progressive influences radiating from the schools would stimulate and fortify the building of a democratic order of free and equal citizens.

The new school system envisioned by Dewey was to take over the functions of the crumbling institutions clustered around the farm community: the family, the church, and the small town. "The school," he wrote, "must be made into a social center capable of participating in the daily life of the community . . . and make up in part to the child for the decay of dogmatic and fixed methods of social discipline and for the loss of reverence and the influence of authority." Children were to get from the public school whatever was missing in their lives elsewhere that was essential for their balanced development as members of a democratic country.

Dewey therefore urged that manual training, science, nature study, art, and similar subjects be given precedence over reading, writing, and arithmetic in the primary curriculum. The problems raised by the exercise of the child's motor powers in constructive work would lead naturally, he said, into learning the more abstract, intellectual branches of knowledge.

Although Dewey asserted that activities involving the energetic side of the child's nature should take first place in primary education, he objected to early specialized training or premature technical segregation in the public schools, which was dictated not by the individual needs or personal preferences of the growing youth, but by external interests.

The question of how soon vocational training should begin had been under debate in educational circles since the days of Benjamin Franklin. The immigrants, the workers, and the middle classes regarded education not as an adornment or a passport to aristocratic culture, but as indispensable equipment to earn a better living and rise in the social scale. They especially valued those subjects that were conducive to success in business. During the nineteenth century private business colleges were set up in the cities to teach the mathematics, bookkeeping, stenography, and knowledge of English required for business offices. Mechanics' institutes were established to provide skilled labor for industry.

These demands of capitalist enterprise invaded the school system and posed the question of how soon children were to be segregated to become suitable recruits for industry. One of the early nineteenth-century promoters of free public education, Horace Mann, appealed to both the self-interest of the people and the cupidity of the industrialists for support of his cause, on the ground that elementary education alone could properly prepare youth for work in the field, shop, or office and would increase the value of labor. Mann said that "education has a market value; that it is so far an article of merchandise, that it can be turned to pecuniary account; it may be minted, and will yield a larger amount of statuable coin than common bullion."

Dewey, following his fellow educator Francis Parker, rejected so commercial-minded an approach to elementary education. They both opposed slotting children prematurely into the grooves of capitalism. The business of education is more than education for the sake of business, they declared. They saw in too-early specialization the menace of uniformity and the source of a new division into a master and a subject class. Education should give every child the chance to grow up spontaneously, harmoniously, and all-sidedly.

Each stage of child development, as Gesell's experiments and conclusions have proved, has its own dominant needs, problems, modes of behavior and level of reasoning. These special traits required their own methods of teaching and learning which had to provide the basis for the educational curriculum.

The kindergarten was the first to consciously adopt methods of instruction adapted to a particular age group. Dewey extended this approach from preschool age to the primary and secondary levels. Each grade ought to be child-centered, not externally oriented, he taught. "The actual interests of the child must be discovered if the significance and worth of his life is to be taken into account and full development achieved. Each subject must fulfill present needs of growing children. . . . The business of education is not, for the presumable usefulness of his future, to rob the child of the intrinsic joy of childhood involved in living each single day."

Children must not be treated as miniature adults or merely as means for achieving adult aims. They had their own rights. Childhood was as much a period of consummation and enjoyment of life on its own terms as it was a prelude to later life.

Socially desirable qualities could not be brought forth in the child by pouring a ready-made curriculum into a passive vessel. They could be most easily and fully developed by guiding the normal motor activities, irrepressible inquisitiveness, and outgoing energies of the child along the lines of their greatest interest. Inner urge, not outside pressure, mobilizes the maximum effort in acquiring knowledge as well as in performing work. The authoritarian teacher, the cut-and-dried curriculum, the uniform procession from one grade to the next, and the traditional fixed seats and desks laid out in rows within an isolated and self-contained classroom were all impediments to enlightened education. Whenever the occasion warranted, the children should be permitted to go outdoors and enter the everyday life of their community instead of being shut up in a classroom "where each pupil sits at a screwed down desk and studies the same part of the same lesson from the same textbook at the same time." The child could freely realize his or her capacities only in an unobstructed environment.

The child learns best through direct personal experience. In the primary stage of education these experiences should revolve around games and occupations analogous to the activities through which adults satisfy the basic material needs for food, clothing, shelter, and protection. The city child is far removed from nature and the processes of production: food comes from the store in cans and packages, clothing is made in distant factories, water comes from the faucet.

The school has to give children not only an insight into the social importance of such activities, but above all the opportunities to practice them in play form. This leads naturally into the "problem" or "project method" which has come to be identified with the essence of the progressive educational procedure.

When children are exposed to things that arouse their interest, they will soak up knowledge and retain it for later use. They progress fastest in learning not through being mechanically drilled in prefabricated material, but by doing work, experimenting with things, changing them in purposive ways.

Occasionally children need to be alone and on their own. But in the main they will learn more by doing things together. By choosing what their group would like to do, planning their work, helping one another do it, trying out various ways of performing the tasks involved and discovering what will advance the project, comparing and appraising the results, the youngsters would best develop their latent powers, their skill, understanding, self-reliance, and cooperative habits.

The questions and answers arising from such joint enterprises would expand the child's horizon by linking his or her immediate activities with the larger life of the community. Small children of six or seven who take up weaving, for example, can be stimulated to inquire into the cultivation of cotton, its processes of manufacture, the history of spinning devices. Such lines of inquiry emerging from their own interests and occupations would open windows upon the past, introduce them naturally to history, geography, science and invention, and establish vivid connections between what they are doing in school and the basic activities of human existence.

Participation in meaningful projects, learning by doing, encountering problems and solving them, not only facilitate the acquisition and retention of knowledge but foster the right character traits: unselfishness, helpfulness, critical intelligence, individual initiative. Learning is more than assimilating a fixed stock of information, Dewey kept repeating; it is the development of habits which enable the growing person to deal effectively and most intelligently with his or her environment. And where that environment is in rapid flux, as in modern society, the elasticity that promotes readjustment to what is new is the most necessary of habits.

Dewey aimed to integrate the school with society, and the processes of learning with the actual problems of life, by a thoroughgoing application of the principles and practices of democracy. The school system would be open to all on a completely free and equal basis without any restrictions or segregation on account of color, race, creed, national origin, sex, or social status. Self-governing group activity would make the classroom a miniature republic where equality and consideration for all would prevail.

This type of education would have the most beneficial social consequences. It would tend to erase unjust distinctions and prejudices. It would equip children with the qualities and capacities required to cope with the problems of a fast-changing world. It would produce alert, balanced, critical-minded individuals who would continue to grow in intellectual and moral stature after graduation.

The transformed schools would remake American society in two ways. First, by bringing forth the most desirable attitudes in the student body, experimental education would create new generations of inquiring, equalitarian-minded, scientifically-oriented individuals. These in turn would intervene in the solution of social, economic, and political problems and remodel our culture after the pattern of their school experiences.

Progressive teachers would thereby become leaders of social advancement. By their guidance of the youth and their partnership with the parents in Parent-Teacher Associations, they would convert the school into a central powerhouse of democratic doctrine which would enlighten and energize the community and eventually the nation.

The Progressive Education Association, inspired by Dewey's ideas, later codified his doctrines as follows: (1.) The conduct of the pupils shall be governed by themselves, according to the social needs of their community. (2.) Interest shall be the motive for all work. (3.) Teachers will inspire a desire for knowledge, and will serve as guides in the investigations undertaken rather than as task-masters. (4.) Scientific study of each pupil's development, physical, mental, social, and spiritual, is absolutely essential to the intelligent direction of his or her development. (5.) Greater attention should be paid to the child's physical needs, with greater use of the outdoors. (6.) Cooperation between school and home will fill all needs of the child's development, such as music, dancing, play, and other extracurricular activities. (7.) All progressive schools will look upon their work as of the laboratory type, freely giving to the sum of educational knowledge the results of their experiments in child culture.

These rules for education sum up the theoretical conclusions of the reform movement begun by Colonel Francis Parker and carried forward by Dewey at the laboratory school he set up in 1896 with his first wife in connection with the University of Chicago. There, with his instrumentalist theory of knowledge as a guide, Dewey tried out and confirmed his new educational procedures with children between the ages of four and fourteen.

This work was subsequently popularized by the leading faculty members of Teachers College at Columbia after Dewey transferred there from Chicago. From this fountainhead Dewey's ideas filtered throughout most of the teacher training schools and all the grades of public instruction below the university level. His disciples organized a John Dewey Society and the Progressive Education Association and have published numerous books and periodicals to propagate and defend his theories.

*   *   *

Dewey's progressive ideas in education have had a parodoxical career. Despite attacks from the right and criticism from the left (and to some extent within progressive educational circles), they have had no serious rival. In whatever diluted or distorted form, they are the entrenched creed in education from Maine to California.

Yet this supremacy in the domain of educational theory has not been matched by an equivalent reconstruction of the educational system. His ideas inspired many modifications in the traditional curriculum, in the techniques of instruction, in the pattern of school construction. But they have not changed the basis or the essential characteristics of the school system, and certainly not the class and racial stratification of American society.

Such restricted results are not a very good testimonial for the principal product of a philosophy which demands that the merits of a theory be tested and judged by its ability to transform a defective situation.

How is this ineffectiveness in practice to be explained? If Dewey's procedures, ideas, and aims are so admirable—and they are—why after seventy-five years haven't they succeeded in accomplishing more in the spheres of educational and social reform? Why have they fallen so far short of expectations?

Dewey went wrong not in what he proposed for the school itself, but in his lack of understanding of the forces at work in American society and of the real relations between the educational and economic systems under capitalist rule.

For Dewey, education was to be the main means for correcting economic evils and attaining progressive political ends. The school system was to serve as the major institution for carrying the democratic processes initiated by the founding fathers to their logical conclusion. He fervently believed in Emerson's prophecy: "Efficient universal education . . . is the mother of national prosperity. . . . We shall one day learn to supersede politics by education."

"Education," Dewey declared in "My Pedagogic Creed" (1897) "is the fundamental method of social progress and reform." This key proposition, however modified, exposes the fundamental flaw in his position. He assumed that either his aims of democratic education could be fitted into the priorities of the capitalist regime, or, where these came into conflict, the democratized schools, with their supporters and graduates, would prevail against the forces of reaction. He staked the whole fate of progressive education and the future of American life on the latter assumption.

In reality, the kind of education he urged went counter to the demands of monopoly capitalism. The ruling class does not want a populace made up of outspoken, critical-minded, inquisitive individuals. It has to keep its labor market stocked with people trained not only to operate its factories and offices, but to be voting sheep for its parties as well.

The modes of life and learning inside the schools were at variance with the realities of the business civilization outside. Dewey was aware that the school provides only a fraction of the social influences at work upon the child's development, and usually not the most decisive ones. The emotional responses, behavior, and standards of children are shaped far more by circumstances in the home and family, the neighborhood, and the streets, by the social level they occupy, and by the media of commercialized mass culture than by the classrooms. James T. Farrell's *Studs Lonigan* and Richard Wright's *Black Boy* present two extreme cases of this predominance of the external environment over the school.

The spotlight has been thrown on the "blackboard jungles." But children made miserable, resentful, and rebellious by poverty, malnutrition, discrimination, broken homes, and lack of recreational facilities are only the most obvious victims of the capitalist environment. The sharp contrasts between the intellectual habits, moral values, and code of conduct instilled in the schools and what they experience around them generate deep uncertainty, confusion, and frustration among young people in all walks of American life.

Even if children are treated as equals at school, they encounter many gradations of poverty and wealth outside. If students are taught to be mutually helpful, considerate, and cooperative, the first commandment of the acquisitive and competitive world around them is "look out for number one." Teachers prate about decency and kindness while TV, movies, and comic books glorify crime, brutality, and violence. Honesty may be the best policy—but what about the bribed politicians and their corporate corrupters? How can education proceed with serenity and security when fears of war and H-bomb annihilation are ever-present? The more enjoyable learning is made in progressive schools, the more intolerable is the monotony and drudgery of factory and office occupations afterwards.

The liberal thinkers of the Progressive school found themselves in a dilemma whenever they bumped up against these realities of capitalist life. They opposed any indoctrination in the schools. As advocates of "the open mind," they said that children should not have any preconceptions imposed upon them by their elders but should be encouraged to inquire freely and arrive at their own conclusions.

How were neutral and impartial teachers in neutral and impartial schools to produce progressive-minded students? After all, the "free intelligence" they hoped to cultivate did not operate in a void or in a society where everyone shared what Dewey called "a common knowledge, a common worth or a common destiny." Progressive education had to make its way within a society torn by antagonistic class interests. The disciples of Dewey could not in fact adhere to their angelic impartiality if they wished to further the cause of progressive education itself. The progressive educationists were in a small minority pitted against a majority of teachers with orthodox views not only on education but on most other matters. If they were not to be rendered impotent by conservatism, the Deweyites were forced to cast aside their assumed neutrality on disputed issues and lead their students along the path of liberalism.

Even their efforts to obtain reforms restricted within the confines of capitalism stirred up fierce resistance from the business interests, who insisted that the schools serve aims geared into the operations of capitalist enterprise. They could no more tolerate free discussion and unhindered consideration of social and political questions in the classrooms than in the country at large. Teachers with unorthodox views were liable to infect the younger generation.

In the 1920s Upton Sinclair wrote *The Goslings* and *The Goose-Step,* which documented how subservience to big business was bred and enforced in the schools. In the early 1930s the more respectable Commission on Social Studies in the Schools subsidized a study of freedom of teaching since the First World War by the prominent American historian Howard K. Beale. Here are some of his findings: School administrators were usually unsympathetic to the inquiry. They "are not interested in freedom." Many teachers "care nothing about freedom or a study of freedom and want only to draw their salaries with as little effort as possible. . . . The multiplicity of examples of fears of teachers about supplying facts is in itself eloquent testimony of the lack of freedom in the schools."

In conclusion, Beale exclaimed: "Can teachers who are cringing, obedient, 'hired men,' cowards, and hypocrites create citizens of courage and integrity? As the author completes this study, he is appalled by the extent to which American teachers are dominated by cowardice and hypocrisy. There are admirable exceptions. Yet almost universally teachers teach not what they would like, but only so much of it as they dare " (*Are American Teachers Free?* p. 775).

This was said at the height of the New Deal, when teachers had some latitude in expressing unorthodox opinions. The area of freedom became appallingly contracted under McCarthyism when public school and college teachers were bedeviled by conformism, loyalty tests, and witch-hunts. The processes of radicalization and unionization of the sixties and early seventies have only begun to mitigate the timidity of this section of white collar public employees.

The situation of social studies teachers in the secondary schools had grown so untenably oppressive that in 1954 the noted sociologist David Riesman proposed "that social studies be abandoned in the public schools, since they could not, without more protection for the teachers, be taught with any candor or vigor . . . *(Constraint and Variety in American Education,* pp. 127-28). The remnants of his own liberal conscience prompted Professor Riesman to remark that "John Dewey, with his orientation towards problem-solving as the principal basis of thought, and towards the school as a factor in the life of the community, would probably have regarded my view as an unwarranted concession to reaction." So it was. But the fact that the suggestion was put forward in earnest indicates how much the capitalist steamroller had succeeded in flattening out the spirit of inquiry and the will to struggle of the progressive educationists.

The "cowardice and hypocrisy" which so disturbed Professor Beale was imposed upon the teachers from above. State and city administration once meant liberating education from religious control; it now means subordinating education to the upper classes who dominate the government, determine the school budget, and police its personnel. As early as 1922 the *Brooklyn Eagle* asked: "Why should public money be employed to produce teachers disposed to break the established order rather than sustain it?" The representatives of the money masters take care to insure that the hand that writes the teachers' paychecks is the hand that rules the schools.

"Perhaps the most dangerous, because the most general and most subtle, control over teachers is that exercised by business," reported Beale. "Businessmen . . . dominate most boards of school trustees whether private or public. . . . Business's chief interest in the schools is the indoctrination of pupils and teachers with concepts that will silence criticism of business and its methods and insure large profits for the future. Reforms, which might limit its profits, must never be discussed in the schools. . . . Men are so used to confusing their own desires with fine principles that most men seeking to control the schools in order to protect their business probably have really convinced themselves that this is an act of pure public service," he ironically comments (ibid., pp. 545-47).

Business, big or little, directly or indirectly, has the economic, political, and propaganda power to exercise a veto over the whole realm of American education. For Dewey the schools came first. But good education for the masses has no such priority for the plutocracy. During the depression of the 1930s businessmen slashed educational appropriations and crippled the schools to save their own pocketbooks. During the big boom of the fifties and sixties Congress passed a forty billion dollar program for building highways because the Defense Department and the steel, cement, auto, and oil corporations were behind it—and then voted down sizeable monies for school construction. Federal appropriations for education hold a low place in a budget of which two-thirds goes for military purposes. Evidently missiles with atomic warheads are more important for capitalist survival than students with critical minds.

Dewey looked to the educational system to lift American culture, like a giant crane, to ever greater heights and lead the American people to a wider democracy, step by step, generation by generation. But the level of education cannot be higher than the surrounding social structure permits. Dewey loaded onto the institution of education more than it could be expected to bear. The forward movement imparted by his ideas proved considerably weaker than the backward pressures of the monopolist regime, which kept dragging education down to its own level.

So it was that the progressive crusade registered such disappointing results over the past half century. Today the exhilarating experimental élan of the early years has evaporated. About as much of the progressive proposals as can be accommodated to the status quo has been incorporated into current public school practice. But the movement itself appears afflicted with hardening of the arteries, like the rest of contemporary liberalism. Enlightened educators are asking in bewilderment: Where do we go from here?

The evolution of the strictly experimental schools has been exceedingly ironic. These laboratory schools were to serve as pilot plants where new methods were to evolve and be tested, and where the ideals of progressivism would flourish. Instead they have become private precincts of a narrowing cult, almost exclusively patronized by the offspring of well-to-do parents dissatisfied with the public schools. They have not come closer to the community and the workaday world, as Dewey projected, but have grown more isolated and turned back upon themselves.

Professor Harold Rugg of New York University, himself a leading light among the progressive educationists, detected this retrograde trend and described it in *Foundations For American Education* (pp. 19-21):

From 1942 to 1945 I spent forty-odd days in a score of older progressive schools, choosing principally those that had had the advantage of many years of uninterrupted experiment under fairly continuous administration. I saw some good teachers in action—occasionally true artist-teachers—who respected their young people as Persons and carried on their groups as societies of equals. I saw them reflecting the American psychology of freedom and action—the young people free to move about and talk, and each one expected to speak of what he sees in his own unique way. . . . Their climate of opinion was marked by a spirit of inquiry rather than of dogmatism; teachers sent young people to sources and put responsibility on them for organizing material and for facing issues. Thus the old dissectional atomism of the mechanical school had largely disappeared and young people were being offered a program in which total jobs, total enterprises, could be confronted and to which each could bring as much of himself as possible. In psychological terms this was no mean achievement. . . .

But . . . something seemed to be missing in these schools. . . . A strange aloofness from society seemed to mark them. . . . They seemed afraid of forthright realistic dealings with the actual conditions of their local communities; certainly they dodged most of the major controversial issues of the day. . . . After fifty years of creative study and innovation our people had found no effective way to incorporate youth into the actual design and operation of society; they are still regarded as onlookers, as observers—and unofficial at that. This revealed itself clearly in the inability of the schools— except in two of those I have seen, where an excellent program is under way—to engage the young people in socially useful work which is significant in their personal lives.

The oases of progressive experimentation remain encircled by a system that fails to fulfill elementary educational tasks. Very few parents expect schools to end poverty and transform society; they simply want their children to be taught to read. Yet the U.S. Office of Education estimated that 40 to 50 percent of the pupils in American cities have serious reading problems; 25 percent of all high school students drop out before graduation. The dropout rate for Blacks and Puerto Ricans is twice that of whites.

Dewey's fears that premature slotting would intensify social stratification have been borne out. The tracking system that goes into effective operation at early grades sorts out and channels the student body into the grooves imposed by their social status and prospective roles in the capitalist setup. An upper layer is directed toward the professions; the bulk is prepared for the general labor market; dropouts, mostly Black, Chicano, or Puerto Rican, end up on the scrapheap. Even though many more high school graduates now go on to college, the distinctions between rich and poor, middle class and working class, Black and white widen from one level to the next.

*   *   *

At the bottom of Dewey's naive and almost magical belief in the omnipotence of education in relation to the rest of social life was the implicit assumption that progressive education could find everything necessary to realize its aims within the existing social system. He shared this outlook with the entire Populist-Progressive mass movement, which tried in vain to smash the stranglehold of the monopolies upon American life—on the assumption that it could manage capitalism more fairly than the capitalists.

Dewey's exaltation of education as the prime solver of social problems was a direct translation into general theory of the aspirations of the rising middle classes, who looked to the education of the younger generation as the justification of their own struggles and sacrifices and as the guarantor of progress. The immigrants envisaged their sons becoming lawyers, doctors, dentists, professors, or successful businessmen—and their daughters marrying such prizes—as the way to achieve higher social status along with financial security. Native-born workers likewise cherished the hope that education would enable their children to raise themselves out of the working class.

The specific demand for the innovations of progressive education came, however, mostly from middle-class intellectual circles who were not very radical in their political outlook but were keenly cognizant of the deficiencies of traditional schooling. "These [progressive] schools were 'protest' schools, expressions of the parents' rebellion against the regimentation of childhood," writes Rugg. "They were formed in the years of the nation-wide shift from the conventional practices and allegiances of the nineteenth century to the new ones of the twentieth. The parents were themselves caught in a period of rebellion against the old ways of living and of hectic attempts to improvise new ones. It was natural that this same spirit of revolt and improvisation should mark the work of these schools in these first years. It was in the spirit of 'Try anything once and see if it works.' I recall dozens of times when that phrase was bandied about in the early days of the Lincoln School. It was educational innovation—not thought-out, designed experiment."

*   *   *

Disappointment with the fruits of progressive experimentation is one factor in the widely discussed "crisis of American education." Conservative spokesmen exploit its shortcomings to discredit the entire venture of progressivism. Their attacks were especially intense during the cold war period.

They have made Deweyism the scapegoat for the failures of the educational system. Johnny, they cry, isn't taught to read, spell, or figure. The schools are too full of "frills and fads." Deweyism is almost un-American and the abettor of "creeping socialism."

It may be true that here and there overindulgent teachers have placed too little emphasis upon the acquisition of the elementary tools of learning and that this unbalance in the curriculum needs correction. Dewey himself never slighted the importance of the formal elements in instruction but simply insisted that they be fitted into a rounded educational development.

The right-wing critics, however, want to do more than correct one-sidedness. They aim to wipe out the "newfangled notions" and go back to the old-fashioned ways. They urge a revival of the classical curriculum through study of "the great books," the institution of more discipline and uniformity, the reinstatement of the three Rs as the core of primary instruction, the inculcation of religion and moral lessons, even restoration of corporal punishment. Their prescriptions would not only sweep away whatever advances have been made under progressive tutelage. They would shift the responsibility for the defaults of American education from the capitalist culprits to the liberal educators who did their best to improve the schools.

American education cannot go back where it came from, either to the obsolete traditional methods or to the utopian premises of the original progressives. It has to move to higher ground, taking off from the ideas and achievements of Dewey's school.

"To educate on the basis of past surroundings is like adapting an organism to an environment which no longer exists. The individual is stultified, if not disintegrated; and the course of progress is blocked," Dewey once wrote. Those in quest of a fresh approach to the problems of American education should heed these words.

The conditions which confront the present generation are vastly different from those at the beginning of the century when Dewey first put forward his ideas. The changeover from colonial and rural to urban and industrial life which so preoccupied him has not only been completed; the countryside itself has become modernized and mechanized. The mighty influences of corporate wealth, the rise of organized labor, the upsurge of the oppressed nationalities dominate our national life. The world arena is the stage for a prolonged struggle for supremacy between a capitalism in retreat and the advancing forces of socialism, with the middle classes caught in between.

The old social fabric is rotting and a new one is being woven before our eyes. Any theory of education which refused to take these fundamental developments of our era as its starting point would be divorced at its roots from social reality. Dewey maintained that education must be socially and practically useful—and what is more useful than a correct understanding of the class forces operating around us and their effects upon the educational process?

Dewey himself learned from the setbacks of the Progressive r_ovement and drew certain conclusions from them. In the thirties he came to recognize that the schools in and of themselves could not be the prime instrument of social change. "It is unrealistic, in my opinion," he wrote in 1937, "to suppose that the schools can be a *main* agency in producing the intellectual and moral changes, the changes in attitudes and disposition of thought and purpose which are necessary for the creation of a new social order. Any such view ignores the constant operation of powerful forces outside the school which shape mind and character. It ignores the fact that school education is but one educational agency out of many, and at the best is in some respects a minor educational force" ("Education and Social Change," *Social Frontier,* vol. 3, p. 239).

He advocated that progressive education associate itself more closely with the labor movement. He had earlier taken the initiative in organizing teachers into unions and was one of the founders of the American Federation of Teachers. He called upon teachers to "ally themselves with their friends against their common foe, the privileged class, and in the alliance develop the character, skill and intelligence that are necessary to make a democratic social order a fact."

Under the impact of the Great Depression he took the further step of proclaiming his belief in a tame socialism of the Norman Thomas type: a vague ideal of justice, equality, and democracy which would ensure the material welfare of everyone in the community and the spiritual self-realization of the individual. His creed hovered on the borderline between liberalism and socialism.

He rejected scientific socialism, which taught that the independent struggle of the working class for power was the only way to abolish capitalism and achieve genuine democracy. This cut straight across his own supraclass outlook. Neither in his politics nor in his educational theory would Dewey admit that the differences between capital and labor might be irreconcilable. He tried to prevail upon both to subordinate any specific class aims to some more comprehensive national interests, hoping that intelligent, forward-looking members of all social strata would unite in a common endeavor to democratize America.

Some of his left-wing followers abandoned the original injunction of the progressive educators that the teacher and the school should abstain from taking sides on controversial issues; they openly proclaimed the need for active alignment with the forces working for a new social order. Among these was Professor George S. Counts of Columbia Teachers College, who wrote a book in 1932 with the challenging title, *Dare the School Build a New Social Order?*

This reorientation, though later abandoned, was in line with what Horace Greeley, the radical editor of the *New York Tribune* before the Civil War, wrote in his *Hints Toward Reforms:* "Before Education can become what it should be and must be, we must reform the Social Life whence it proceeds, whither it tends." Dewey and his fellow progressives tackled the problem from the other end. They tried to reform the education system before and without effecting a thoroughgoing reorganization of the social system. Consequently their experimentation did not yield the desired results.

*   *

Does Dewey's vision of democratically functioning schools in a free and equal society have to be given up, as reactionaries demand and despairing liberals fear? The guiding principles of his educational proposals remain the most viable cultural creations of the defunct Progressive movement. But experience has shown that their admirable objectives cannot be achieved within the framework of an increasingly monopolistic and militaristic capitalism.

In his *Impressions of Soviet Russia* (1928), Dewey tells about the pilgrim's progress of a Russian educator he met who passed over from pedagogic reform to communism after his attempts to implant progressive educational practices were foiled by the prerevolutionary regime:

> There are, as he puts it, two educations, the greater and the smaller. The lesser is given by the school; the larger, and the one finally influential, is given by the actual conditions of life, especially by those of the family and neighborhood. And, according to his own story, this educator found that the work he was trying to do in the school, even under the relatively favorable conditions of his experimental school, was undone by the educative—or miseducative—formation of disposition and mental habit proceeding from the environment. Hence he became convinced that the social medium and the progressive school must work together, must operate in harmony, reinforcing each other, if the aim of the progressive school was not to be constantly undermined and dissipated; with the growth of this conviction he became insensibly a communist. He became convinced that the central force in undoing the work of socialized reform he was trying to achieve by means of school agencies was precisely the egoistic and private ideals and methods inculcated by the institution of private property, profit and acquisitive possession. [pp. 69–71]

The benefits of Dewey's work have likewise been frustrated and dissipated by the predominant trends of the capitalist environment. The crisis of American education has grown more acute since his death. The root cause was indicated by the instructive experience of his Soviet counterpart decades ago. This is the impossibility of harmonizing the most progressive educational ideas with the institutions of private property, which subordinate the needs of the pupils to the dictates of the profiteers.

Dewey himself was almost convinced of this incompatibility in 1928. In this same book he went on to say: "The Russian educational situation is enough to convert one to the idea that only in a society based upon the cooperative principle can the ideals of educational reformers be adequately carried into operation" (p. 86).

Indeed, the socialist alternative would treat the youth of the country as the most precious of social assets. Its regime would give the highest priority in its planning and allotment of resources to fostering the best character formation and creative potential of the oncoming generation from infancy to maturity, and thereby realize the promise of a genuinely progressive educational system.

12

Dewey's Views
on Ethics

Ethics is the branch of philosophy concerned with the good and bad, the virtuous and vicious, the right and wrong, the just and unjust; it examines the grounds for making moral judgments one way or the other. The Sophists and Socrates were the first to formulate a rational moral theory in place of religious commandments and fixed custom as a guide to social conduct. Dewey sought to do for his time what these Greek thinkers had done for theirs.

He was highly critical of the existing state of moral theory. Toward the close of his long life he wrote in an introduction to *Reconstruction in Philosophy* that morality, in both senses of the word ("as a practical socio-cultural *fact* in respect to matters of right and wrong, good and evil, and for theories about the ends, standards, principles according to which the actual state of affairs is to be surveyed and judged") is "pre-scientific when formed in an age preceding the rise of science as now understood and practiced" (pp. 19-20). Dewey regarded the preparation of a new moral order which would cap the scientific, industrial, and political changes of modern times as one of the principal tasks of his instrumentalism.

Certain contemporary philosophies, such as positivism, intuitionism, and existentialism, sever knowledge of matters of fact from judgments of value and invoke different ways of handling these dimensions of experience. The one is amenable to scientific treatment; the other only to arbitrary subjective criteria. Thus the neopositivist A.J. Ayer maintains that ethical statements do not describe anything and are therefore not really statements at all. This is why some people regard a thing as true and good while others regard the same thing as false and evil. (See his *Philosophical Essays,* pp. 231, 247.)

Dewey insisted, against this dualism, that scientific and moral conclusions could be arrived at by the same method and, as related aspects of intelligent action, were both subject to the same tests of validity. "Because I hold that experimental method as union of theory and practice, of ideas and operations directed by them, has supremacy over an antecedent situation, I also hold that one and the same method is to be used in determination of physical judgment and the value-judgments of morals." Like the eighteenth-century French materialists, he even went so far as to project that the directive standards of the new morality would come "largely from the findings of the natural ;iences" (*Philosophy of John Dewey,* pp. 328, 583). This "nati ·alistic" approach was off the mark, since morality, which deals with the relationships of people, is exclusively social and cannot be based on natural law, contrary to Hobbes and Spencer.

Together with James H. Tufts, his colleague at the University of Chicago, he wrote a popular textbook on *Ethics* (1908) that was designed to give a reasoned foundation to the views and values of a liberal democratic morality adjusted to the progressive capitalism that existed before the First World War. Despite the vast changes following that catastrophic event, they set forth essentially the same positions in the second revised edition published in 1932.

The two men took a historical, secular, rational, and relativist approach to moral questions. Morality was a product of social development and had changed its content as humanity progressed. They rejected invariable norms of conduct and absolute standards of moral evaluation, sanctified by religion or legal decree. All such bases for morality belong to the prescientific past. No one is obligated to conform to any axiomatic precepts or categorical imperatives of the Kantian type. Every moral judgment is a practical one and must take into account the concrete circumstances of the situation and the ends its participants aim at.

Real moral beliefs are expressed in action, according to Dewey. An act is good not because of any general principle it exemplifies, but by virtue of its specific consequences. Indeed, a conscientious person will not only measure his or her conduct in accord with a given standard but, if conditions warrant, should be ready to revise the standard and replace it with a better, more applicable one.

Moral problems, along with the urge to find the means to resolve them, arise from situations of conflict where alternatives present themselves and choices must be made. In private life an individual can be torn by warring impulses and desires or between incompatible aims. In social and political affairs conflicting values can be esteemed and enforced by different countries, parties, classes, movements, and groups. The role of responsibility comes forward when people are impelled to choose one objective over another, take one course of action rather than another, and align themselves with one side or the other.

By what moral standards are their decisions to be considered right or wrong? According to Dewey, the moral quality of conduct in general, or of any particular act, is not certified by benevolent motives or any inner intuition of what is right or just. He expressly disclaims "subjectivistic" views that identify meaning well with moral good. The axis of morality revolves around the improvement of institutions rather than the self-regeneration of the individual.

The worthiness of choices made or courses taken is tested and ascertained by their success in removing the original trouble, to the benefit of the individual and community. They are morally justified if they actually lead to greater equity, progress, harmony, and order.

The laudable consequences of successful action (which are likewise the ends-in-view sought by the intelligent person) comprise a catalog of the liberal virtues and democratic ideals. Actions that tend to increase wealth and equalize its distribution, extend freedoms, institute and ensure peaceful relations, open more opportunities for more people, enhance their sensitivities, add to their understanding and control over their lives, are good. Conduct that has the contrary consequences must be censured. This adds up to the common-sense moral outlook of the ordinary law-abiding citizen living under stable and tranquil conditions in bourgeois society.

Dewey and Tufts were well aware of the relativism of ethical conceptions and the contradictory character of moral judgments. In an autobiographical statement of his credo Tufts wrote: "Justice, I found, meant different things to different persons and different groups" (*Contemporary American Philosophy,* p. 340).

They also knew that "moral ideas are shaped under the influence of economic, social and religious forces." What is right for the worker is often wrong for the employer. Tufts cites the example of the mine owner who makes his workers sign contracts not to join any union. The mine unions oppose such "yellow-dog" agreements imposed by economic compulsion because they deprive the workers of the right to improve their conditions. "The right of property and the right to combine are here in flat contradiction." Even the courts that decide who is right and who is wrong in this collision of opposing rights are themselves under the influence of social forces and render their verdicts, not by appeal to abstract justice, but under the coercion of class pressures, says Tufts.

Tufts also understood that ethics cannot be divorced from politics and economics. The great ethical question of the day, he wrote, "is the question of the ethical principles which are now on trial in our social-economic political system." Capitalism in the United States and communism in the Soviet Union are each conducting a gigantic experiment to see which can provide the best way of life for its people. Tufts expressed the hope that "the equality of opportunity afforded by education could offset the inequality of property and income under American capitalism" (ibid.). Writing in 1930, the pragmatic philosopher suspended his judgment on the outcome of the competition between the two systems. He would hardly have been permitted such neutrality twenty-five years later when McCarthyism was rampant. And educational opportunities have not appreciably narrowed the gap between rich and poor after half a century.

While Dewey rejected theological, idealistic, intuitive, emotive, subjectivist, and absolutist ethical theories, he polemicized with increasing vigor against the premises and practices of historical materialism, which challenged his positions from the left. The extremes of reaction and revolution were equally repugnant to his reformism.

Dewey's junking of immutable principles, and his conception of morality as bound up with effective social action, are agreeable to Marxism. A moral code largely preoccupied with private virtues and vices in a clerical manner is not only petty but evades the major moral issues facing the mass of humanity, such as war, poverty, oppression, inequality. Sexual peccadilloes which horrify the religious and respectable are trivial compared with the momentous question of conscience presented by the danger of nuclear extermination and how to prevent it.

Nevertheless the main thrust of Dewey's ethical outlook clashed with Marxist teachings at vital points. They fundamentally disagreed on the relation of moral conflict to class conflict. Dewey advocated a classless morality to be shared by all and impartially applied as a poultice in ameliorating or resolving conflicts. He denied that moral criteria necessarily had a class nature in capitalist society or that moral values and judgments upheld by antagonistic class forces could acquire an irreconcilable edge.

He recognized that morality has subserved special interests and ends in the past. But he hoped that the advancement of science and the diffusion of the method of experimental inquiry through a proper educational system under American democracy could enable an enlightened, socially responsible citizenry to set aside selfish class considerations and act for the good of the whole. He offered his ethics as an intellectual tool for converting class strife into social harmony, the most desirable of goals.

Dewey meant well. But as he himself averred, what counts in morality is not benevolent intentions but practical efficacy. The prime premise of his ethics unrealistically disregarded the fundamental facts about the nature of capitalist life. For two millennia Christians have preached the desirability of brotherly love under material circumstances that militated against it. Dewey's prescriptions for morality did not shake off this defect. The fiction of a classless morality accompanied the illusory vision of a homogeneous capitalism in which the deepest differences could be indefinitely tolerated and ultimately overcome. This fit the mythology of bourgeois-democratic ideology.

The common morality Dewey recommended is not followed in everyday affairs. It would inevitably be wrecked by the insuperable contradictions built into capitalist society. He denied that the relations between the ruling rich and the working masses were at bottom as antagonistic as those between lords and serfs under feudalism. In Tufts's example, the contest of opposing rights between mine owners and miners over unionization, the opinions of the two sides on what was right and wrong flowed from their respective class positions. In most cases up to now this sort of difference has been settled by arbitration—but only after fierce battles have established the relationship of forces.

In such situations Dewey's compromise procedure can be

applied—though it favors the more powerful side, which is usually the property owners backed by their government. The gulf between liberal and Marxist moralities is most evident in extreme situations of social crisis when the safety valves of compromise no longer function smoothly and the class struggle acquires its sharpest, most violent, most decisive forms.

Suppose the miners should one day decide upon more drastic moves and set out with their fellow workers to expropriate their employers' holdings and operate them under their own democratic control. Would there then be a sufficient basis to implement the art of conciliation between the classes contending for power and supremacy? The Civil War, which was the central testing ground for moral decision and political alignment in the nineteenth century, showed how mutually shared moral norms are shattered under the hammer blows of social conflict.

The disparity in the ethical outlooks of liberals and Marxists also stemmed from their different perspectives for the evolution of American society. Dewey looked forward to the softening of antagonisms between its class components and precluded the possibility of upheavals from the right or the left, even though the twentieth century has witnessed revolutions and counterrevolutions elsewhere. He tacitly presupposed the continuance of the status quo—with some amendments.

So long as the demands for change are kept within the limits of reform affordable by the rulers, and all opponents accept the legitimacy of the established order, the precepts of liberal morality can be more or less operative. But when high-voltage tensions take over, common moral values are displaced by conflicting ones. In 1861, fidelity to the Union was superseded by loyalty to the Confederacy among white Southerners—and fratricide became the highest virtue.

Since morality is indispensable to the maintenance of social life, certain moral injunctions are found in most communities. Often, however, these elementary stipulations are so general and vague that they are easily ignored in practice. One of these universal rules is the prohibition against killing. This mandate is waived in cases of self-defense and excused in cases of insanity. What is criminal during peace is the greatest glory in wartime.

Liberal moralists can justify such violations of the rule on the ground of exceptional circumstances. They run into more difficulty when they have to explain those internally contradictory cases where the same action calls forth contrary moral judgments that cannot be reconciled. Violence, it is agreed, is generally to be condemned. But when strikers clash with scabs, Blacks with racists, or workers with fascist gangs, what justifies the resort to force by one and not the other? Both sides will offer different sets of justifications. By what criteria are these to be judged?

Emotional sympathies or antipathies will not settle the matter. The causes underlying moral disagreements are traceable to the concrete relations of the contending classes and social strata. Just as differences in color correspond to different wavelengths of radiation, so differences in evaluations, and in the moral codes themselves, flow from objective social and economic differences.

For Marxism the socioeconomic position and historical function of a given class and its individual members are decisive in laying out its path of conduct, shaping its moral criteria, and arriving at its judgments of value. A higher morality, or a better moral act, is distinguished from a baser one by the service it renders to the satisfaction of human needs and to the necessities of social progress. Its rational goals are the acquisition of greater command over nature and increased capacities of producing wealth in order to reduce and eliminate the perennial causes of oppression by a ruling minority over the bulk of humanity.

The main agency delegated by its position in the economy to promote these paramount progressive tasks in this epoch is the working class. This historical responsibility invests its defensive and offensive actions and organizations with their ethical authority and moral worth. Conversely, since the capitalists and colonialists are the principal upholders and beneficiaries of reaction, their rulership is immoral as well as parasitic.

Dewey denies this objective basis for moral appraisal, which proceeds from the laws of social development and is anchored in the contradictory motive forces of contemporary life. He could not see that the ethics of a subjugated people or an exploited class struggling for its emancipation are *ipso facto* superior to those of a dominant class bent on preserving its privileges by any means necessary. This standard is warranted because the conditions required to liberate the oppressed from the exploitation of labor lead to the widest human good, coincide with the necessities of progress, and help lift humanity to a higher level of wellbeing.

These propositions of Marxism, Dewey contends, are unintelligent, dogmatic, nonexperimental—in a word, unscientific. Here is the gist of his argumentation: "The method of intelligent experimental action is criticized on the ground that class interests are too strong to permit its use, so that the only alternative is the method of class war with victory to the strongest. . . . The alternative is not an extreme pacifism which makes a fetish of passivity. The basic difference is that one theory, that of inevitable class conflict and inevitable victory for one class, takes situations in a mechanical and wholesale manner, whereas the method of intelligent action insists upon analysis *at each step* of the concrete situation then and there existing, basing its hypothesis as to what should be done upon the results of that analysis, and testing moreover the adequacy of the hypothesis at every step by the consequences that result from acting upon it. The question is one of choice—choice between a procedure which is rigid because based on fixed dogma, and one which is flexible because based upon examination of problems actually experienced and because proposing policies as hypotheses to be experimentally tested and modified" (*Philosophy of John Dewey,* pp. 592-93).

This procedure has a reasonable ring and could be followed on many occasions. But it has certain shortcomings. The method is purely empirical and does not rise to the higher levels of scientific insight which are based on a knowledge of the laws of the phenomenon in question. Science does not consist solely of experiments to enlarge the boundaries of knowledge or check on acquired results. It proceeds from an ample and growing stock of verified information, tested generalizations, and validated truths which disclose the nature of reality.

Not the least of these truths is that the class struggle is the central law of capitalist development. In Dewey's eyes this is not a part of scientific sociology but a dogma or fetish. In reality, the generalization is derived from the historical experience of all civilized social formations and an analysis of the structure and operations of the capitalist system. Like any other law, it can be used to predict further developments and direct analysis and action within its field of application.

Dewey refused to believe that class conflict arises from deep-seated, compelling, and ineradicable causes in the capitalist system. It was an occasional and subordinate phenomenon that could be overcome by joint effort, good will, mutual give and take. He therefore looked to different agencies and means than the Marxists for achieving the desirable goals of a better life. He wrote: "That work can be done only by the resolute, patient, cooperative activities of men and women of good will, drawn from every useful calling, over an indefinitely long period" (*Reconstruction in Philosophy*, p. 25). In other words, class collaboration is the preferable means of social reformation, political action, and moral improvement. Class struggle goes in the wrong direction and gives disastrous results.

That was not the case in the 1930s when the industrial workers fought the monopolists and battered down the open shop in unionization battles verging on civil war. The powerful labor organizations of today are the product of that class struggle.

Plenty of experiments have been conducted in the laboratory of contemporary politics over the past two decades with the contrasting methods of class struggle and class conciliation. In Latin America alone, Cuba testifies to the efficacy and benefits of class struggle carried through to socialist revolution. The bloody catastrophe suffered by the workers in Chile demonstrated, to the contrary, the maleficent consequences of relying on the "method of intelligent action" based on gradual reform urged by Dewey and practiced under Allende.

Dewey's theory of ethics suffers from the same faults as his theory of knowledge. Just as ideas have no validity before all the returns are in but must be tested afresh in each instance, so moral judgments have no verifiable value or weight in advance of their results in action. Instrumentalist morality goes from case to case and from one step to the next without reaching any general standards of right or wrong and what makes them so. The most it can offer is a reasonable assumption or hopeful expectation that this way may be better than that, without examining the requisite objective grounds for the hypothetical belief.

Moral abstractions, as Dewey acknowledged, take on flesh and blood in concrete cases. The Vietnam war posed the greatest moral issue to the American people in the 1960s. Should U.S. intervention be supported or opposed, approved or condemned? This dilemma also put the moralities and methods of liberalism and Marxism to the test.

At the outset the heterogeneous liberal community held views ranging from doubt to whole-hearted support for Washington. Whatever hypothesis they started with, most agreed with the instrumentalist axiom that the political and moral nature of the conflict was not determined by objective factors and could not be defined in advance of the results. It was the better part of wisdom to reserve final judgment on whether it was good or bad, check at each step along the way, and then see how the affair would turn out.

The Marxists took no such conditional attitude. On the basis of their socialist principles, they categorically stated that U.S. intervention was unwarranted and unjust and had to be unequivocally opposed. It was wrong to endorse imperialist aggression against a small nation striving for self-determination and social liberation—or even to abstain from siding with the victim, just as it would have been wrong to remain neutral or back Great Britain against the colonial rebels in the War of Independence. Marxists did not have to wait for the casualties, costs, and horrors to mount up before arriving at this definitive judgment.

To be sure, millions of Americans came to this same conclusion as the war dragged on, though for different reasons; their moral indignation was aroused by the accumulated evidence of the war's criminality. The point is that the farsighted position of the Marxists was not only morally and politically but *methodologically* superior to the hindsight of the liberals, who pride themselves on their allegiance to science and freedom from dogmatism.

The difference between the two showed up in the results, enabling the radicals to take the lead in organizing the mass antiwar movement. The pragmatic-empirical approach that waited for the facts to be accomplished before moving into opposition was less scientific and effective as a guide to political conduct and moral evaluation than the Marxist method of analysis which looked to the causal forces at work and predicted the consequences.

*   *   *

Dewey's specifications for an appropriate morality for the new age were out of synchronization with the main trends of the time. The twentieth century is not only an era of science, technology, and large-scale industry but of wars, revolutions, and colonial uprisings. The democracy that was the offspring of a progressive capitalism is being eroded under the domination of a predatory monopoly capitalism that has scant respect for the rights of the American people and even less for the liberties of other nations.

The supreme moral task confronting the American people is the struggle against the misrule of the monopolists and militarists, leading to the overthrow of class society. The highest moral ideal is the making of that emancipatory revolution and ensuring its success. These ends, and the means required to achieve them, were declared out of bounds by Dewey. His moral code and method are destined to frustration because they fail to provide adequate answers to the most crucial questions: What is to be done, how is it to be done, and who will be able to do it?

13

Instrumentalism
Put to the Test

The pragmatists denounced traditional idealism, among other reasons, for its refusal to acknowledge that ideas are to be judged by their results in practice. According to its pioneers, pragmatism had the singular merit of overcoming the defects of previous philosophies by doing justice to "the truth of things in their living fullness" and satisfying the demands upon theory put by practical life. They insisted that ideas must prove their worth and power through controlled experiment under real conditions. The only reliable indicator of the truth of general conceptions was to be found in their actual consequences in social experience.

The snobbish and theological-minded guardians of American idealism retorted by ridiculing the insistence of the pragmatists that theories prove their "cash value" by competing with rival ideas in the marketplace. This was unworthy, they thought, of the holy office of philosophy. They spread the inane notion that philosophy and logic had no essential connection with social struggles and political issues.

The pragmatic school had no sympathy with this sterile viewpoint. It insisted upon the unity of philosophy with social and political action, maintaining that the principal purpose and final justification of philosophy lay in its social utility. "Philosophy," said Dewey, ". . . can make it easier for mankind to take the right steps in action by making it clear that a sympathetic and integral intelligence brought to bear upon the observation and understanding of concrete social events and forces, can form ideals, that is aims, which shall not be either illusions or mere emotional compensations" (*Reconstruction in Philosophy,* p. 112).

The supreme criterion of the merit of ideas was, for Dewey, their proven capacity to reconstruct the reality around us to effect our aims. "*If* ideas, meanings, conceptions, notions, theories, systems are instrumental to an active reorganization of the given environment, to a removal of some specific trouble and perplexity, then the test of their validity and value lies in accomplishing this work. If they succeed in their office, they are reliable, sound, valid, good, true. If they fail to clear up confusion, to eliminate defects, if they increase confusion, uncertainty and evil when they are acted upon, then they are false. Confirmation, corroboration, verification lie in works, consequences. Handsome is that handsome does. By their fruits shall ye *know* them. That which guides us truly is true—demonstrated capacity for such guidance is precisely what is meant by truth" (ibid., p. 128).

The pragmatic school performed a service to American thought by bringing forward the indissoluble connection between ideas and action and stressing the primacy of practice in determining the worth of theories. The pragmatists were right as against those idealists who feared to bring their ideas down to earth and show what they really meant and could do in social practice, preferring to store up unused credits in a heaven accessible only to an initiated elite. Ideas do not fall from the skies or remain suspended in midair. They grow up out of the soil of society—and must submit to its judgment. Ideas that misdirect action do so by falsifying the real state of affairs. They have to be discarded or corrected if they cannot vindicate their truth in practice. Marxism can align itself with instrumentalism against philosophies which scorn to send their ideas into the centers of everyday life.

Dewey recommended instrumentalism both as a valid interpretation of reality and as the most accurate and efficient guide to action. Taking him at his word, let us see how his ideas worked out in practice during the first half of this century. What capacities for guidance did the pragmatists demonstrate? How did they deal with the life-and-death problems of their time? How far did these liberals succeed in "reorganizing the given environment" in line with their program, aims, and ideals? What have their intelligent experiments in social action actually come to?

Since pragmatism took to the field, American capitalism has passed through several major crises; including two world wars and a Great Depression. Any philosophy which had not lost contact with the realities of social life should have been able to foresee, at least in broad outline, the growth and outbreak of these upheavals; to have interpreted their meaning; to have prepared and equipped people to cope with them; and thereby to have helped influence the course of events in a progressive direction. Certainly a philosophy like instrumentalism, which claims to be so realistic and practical, should have done no less.

However, the record shows that at every critical turn of American history in the twentieth century, Deweyism has been caught off guard and overwhelmed by the sweep of events. Instead of playing a directing role, its adherents have been towed along in the wake of the more aggressive and dominant forces of plutocratic reaction. Their perplexity and powerlessness was first exhibited in the First World War; it has been duplicated in every serious crisis convulsing the United States since that time.

Dewey and Bourne

In the tributes to John Dewey on his ninetieth birthday in 1949, no mention was made of the searing public rupture between him and his disciple Randolph Bourne during the First World War. This silence was not due to a polite desire to refrain from unpleasant memories on a festive occasion. It indicated how the anti-war and anti-imperialist sentiments which blazed among the liberal intellectuals in the first decades of the century had died down three decades later. It did not strike the celebrators, who had mobilized behind the Second World War and ideologically enlisted in the cold war, that anything was wrong with Dewey's support of World War I.

Yet Dewey's betrayal of his liberal traditions to the imperialist war-makers of Wilson's generation, which impelled Bourne to break with him and with pragmatism, was one of the most revealing episodes in his intellectual and political biography. It marked a turning point in the development, or rather the degradation, of twentieth-century liberalism.

Randolph Bourne was one of the most penetrating and incorruptible critics of American life during the First World War period. He was an ardent spokesman for the most sensitive, dissatisfied intellectuals of the younger generation who were in revolt against plutocratic rule and groping toward a better America. He aimed to become the herald and creator of a liberalized culture freed from conformity to the monied powers.

Bourne fixed his hopes for a regenerated America upon education. Dewey's experiments and proposed reforms in this field seemed to be the sovereign remedy for social evils. Dewey's philosophy, he wrote, was regarded "almost as our American religion." He and his associates in the lively Progressive circles, bent upon renovating American literature, culture, and politics, looked upon Dewey as the incarnation of enlightenment and the incorruptible guardian of democracy; his ideas and methods were the sole alternative to conservatism. Their trust in his pragmatic philosophy and Progressive program was boundless.

With the advent of the First World War, followed by the Russian revolution, Deweyism and the Progressive movement were put to a supreme test. These two interlinked events shook Bourne's faith in pragmatism and transformed him into a militant socialist.

When war engulfed Europe in 1914 and threatened to draw the United States into it, liberal intellectuals and pacifist-minded youth looked to Dewey for leadership. Instead of resisting the war hysteria, however, Dewey began as early as 1916 to adjust himself to its approach.

A training camp to convert businessmen into army brass was set up at Plattsburgh, New York. Dewey hailed such volunteer officers' camps as a beneficial form of contemporary education!

This theoretical justification for capitalist military training, in preparation for conscripting the youth, shocked and disgusted the consistent socialists and pacifists, Randolph Bourne among them. Then came the intervention of the United States in the war. This confronted the Progressives with a major decision. In the ensuing struggle the ranks of the pragmatists split. The majority of Dewey's followers, having learned the virtues of middle-class instrumentalism, speedily converted themselves into instruments of the war-makers—with Dewey himself at their head.

Bourne refused to go along. In a famous philippic on "War and the Intellectuals," published in June 1917, he flayed the "war-liberals" for this betrayal of their own ideals and of his generation. "The war sentiment," he wrote, "begun so gradually but so perseveringly by the preparedness advocates who came from the ranks of big business, caught hold of one after another of the intellectual groups. . . . the intellectuals, in other words, have identified themselves with the least democratic forces in American life. They have assumed the leadership for war of those very classes whom the American democracy has been immemorially fighting. Only in a world where irony was dead could an intellectual class enter war at the head of such illiberal cohorts in the avowed cause of world liberalism and world democracy."

The pro-war liberals, along with the ex-socialists, argued that a democratic world and a lasting peace would come out of American participation in the war, provided the intellectuals did not stay on the sidelines but flung their full forces into the dogfight. Bourne asked Dewey this pertinent question: "If the war was too strong for you to prevent, how is it going to be weak enough for you to control and mould to your liberal purposes?" Indeed, the war and its immediate aftermath abruptly ended the liberal movements in economics and politics which had flowered before the war.

Bourne foresaw and feared this outcome. He also saw that Dewey's surrender to these "illiberal cohorts," his abandonment under stress of the struggle for peace and democracy, was not a mere personal dereliction or accidental deviation. It was a political conclusion implicit in the theoretical premises and social outlook of pragmatic philosophy.

Pragmatism, Bourne pointed out, assumed that all people of good will, regardless of their class interests, could work together for the common welfare. But he saw that in the showdown, the predatory aims of the capitalists overrode the needs and desires of the American people. Profit-making—and war-making to defend the institutions of profit-making—took precedence over the recommendations of the liberals and shoved them aside. "What concerns us here is the relative ease with which the pragmatic intellectuals, with Professor Dewey at the head, have moved out their philosophy, bag and baggage, from education to war," Bourne exclaimed.

Challenging Dewey and the other prophets of instrumentalism, Bourne demanded that they be precise in their definition of "democracy." "Is it the political democracy of a plutocratic America that we are fighting for, or is it the social democracy of the new Russia? Which do our rulers fear more, the menace of imperial Germany, or the liberating influence of a socialist Russia? In the application of their philosophy and politics, our pragmatists are sliding over the crucial question of ends."

The prostration of Deweyism before the plutocracy exposed to full view the hitherto concealed weaknesses in the instrumentalist method and views. "What I came to," Bourne wrote in

"Twilight of Idols," "is a sense of suddenly finding a philosophy upon which I had relied to carry us through no longer works." Pragmatism, like do-goodism, "cooled off rapidly before it reached the boiling point" in the struggle against capitalist reaction.

Bourne correctly reasoned that there could not be a more definitive condemnation of pragmatism. This philosophy had won so many adherents on the ground that it worked—and worked better than any other mode of thought available to intelligent Americans. Yet in the life-and-death questions of imperialist war and social revolution, pragmatism proved itself to be bankrupt. Bourne concluded it had to be repudiated because it failed to pass its own supreme test of application in practice.

Why did Deweyism turn out to be so worthless a pilot in stormy weather—when reliable pilots were most urgently needed? The answer is that pragmatism slides over the surface of things, ignoring their profound inner contradictions. It is a philosophy that lives from day to day and from hand to mouth. It prospers so long as social conditions change little, or only little by little; so long as class relations are in a temporary equilibrium; so long as the political skies are clear and shining.

But when underlying class antagonisms erupt and upset the balance of social forces, then pragmatism, which bases itself upon social calm and class cooperation, becomes weak and helpless. In the decisive question of war its proponents are compelled to choose between contending and irreconcilable class interests. When the chips are down, the organic conservatism of many middle-class elements displaces their fair-weather liberal mask and draws them into reconciliation with other defenders of the status quo.

Thus, in the hour of supreme danger, instrumentalism disclosed its real class character as a liberal extension of bourgeois ideology, just as progressivism turned out to be but a left shadow of capitalist politics. Step by step, the bulk of the pragmatists became dupes and defenders of the lies and pretensions of the most reactionary forces in American life.

That was the lesson Randolph Bourne learned the hard way. Once having learned it, he felt the need for a more profound and correct philosophical doctrine and for a more realistic program that would take into account the real relations of social forces and their movement in modern life. He looked from the imperialist United States to revolutionary Russia, from liberalism to socialism, from Dewey to Marx and Lenin. Against Dewey's call for continued confidence in the democratic aims of America's plutocracy, he counterposed the accomplishments of the young Russian revolution:

"Young pacifists do not see that democratic peace can come out of the war. They are skeptical of the war professedly for political democracy, because at home they have seen so little democracy where industrial slaves are rampant. They see the inspiring struggle in the international class struggle, not in the struggles of imperialist nations. To Russia, the socialist state, not to America, who has taken a place on the old ground—do they look for realization of their ideal."

Bourne's life was cut short in 1918 at the age of thirty-two. This brilliant young social critic was unable to pursue his new path. But his decision was important. He turned in the right direction at the right time. Both his negative conclusion—that Dewey's instrumentalism with its reliance upon class collaboration as the method of social progress had proved its bankruptcy in practice— and his positive proposal—that the philosophy of socialism and the program of international class struggle should replace it— deserve to be recalled and engraved upon the minds of the present generation.

Between the Two World Wars

Once U. S. capitalism returned to "normalcy" after the Palmer witch-hunt and "the deportations delirium" at the close of Wilson's administration, the instrumentalists likewise recovered their intellectual equilibrium and even their self-confidence. They adjusted themselves comfortably to the prosperity and social calm of the 1920s by coming forward as the champions of liberalism against the encircling political reaction personified by Harding, Coolidge, and Hoover. In *The Nation, The New Republic, Survey,* and similar journals they pushed for reforms at home and appeared as sympathizers of the "Soviet experiment" abroad. In 1928 Dewey went to the Soviet Republic and brought back friendly and hopeful reports of progress there.

But despite criticisms and proposals for improvement, these left liberals maintained full faith in the fundamental stability of the capitalist system. They had no premonition of the collapse of 1929 and did not prepare themselves or their disciples for its advent and consequences. As a result, the economic crisis promptly produced a crisis in the ranks of the pragmatic liberals; capitalism's loss of credit was reflected once more in a sharp drop in the prestige of pragmatism.

Rationalists assume that philosophies are refuted primarily by intellectual argument and that one philosophy can replace another merely by virtue of its superior appeal to critical reason. If this were so, mankind would have shown more steady progress in thought about the world since the days of the ancient Greeks. Actually, philosophies are refuted far more by the criticism of events than by the persuasiveness of ideas as such. Or rather, new developments lend fresh force to previously disregarded positions. One philosophy displaces another because new trends disclose to the more perceptive minds that the old ideas no longer fit. In the most universal realm of thought, as elsewhere, social need has the last word and practice is the supreme judge. Galileo, for example, did not bother to refute Thomas Aquinas's views on motion; he simply swept them aside as irrelevant to his work in mechanics.

Much the same happened with Dewey's instrumentalism following the 1929 crash. After having held the field during the preceding decade of economic advance and class peace, instrumentalism all of a sudden appeared outmoded because its ideas were so far out of touch with the changed situation. It was not so much refuted as jettisoned by the radicalized intellectuals. They felt that pragmatic liberalism had left them in the lurch, not by direct desertion as in 1917, but rather in a negative way. It was as though formerly solid ground under their feet in the fields of philosophy and politics had turned into a bog. The representative thinkers of the liberal school began to go unheeded and were themselves in need of rescue. The advanced intellectuals looked elsewhere for guidance, especially to the left.

Instrumentalism, however, is extremely agile; it can shift its positions and switch fronts quickly. Knocked off its old perch by the onset of the crisis, pragmatism soon began to adapt itself to the changed circumstances. The command of the hour was: "To the left, march!" For the next few years, Dewey, along with his entire movement, became radicalized in his social thinking and political positions. Dewey, who had voted for the Democrat Al Smith in 1928, moved over to support the Socialist Norman Thomas by 1932. As chairman of the League for Independent Political Action and president of the People's Lobby, he worked toward the formation of a Farmer-Labor Party.

Inspired by the example of the first five-year plan in the USSR, the liberals talked of regenerating American capitalism through national planning. They wanted to enjoy the fruits of social revolution without the back-breaking work of turning over the soil.

Dewey's *Liberalism and Social Action*, published in 1935, showed how far the radical atmosphere of that time affected pragmatic thought. After World War I pacifism, especially in respect to internal class conflicts, had been a prime article of faith in the liberal creed. But under the impact of the collapse of capitalism and the spread of fascism, Dewey somewhat altered the old attitude of "resist not evil with violence." In that book he modified his former blanket rejection of the use of force by saying that under certain conditions it would be necessary and proper for the progressive forces and the working class to resist the onslaughts of fascist reaction by any means at their disposal.

This was the extreme limit of radicalism reached by the social thought of the pragmatists. Indeed, it was not possible to go much beyond that point without passing into the orbit of Marxism. A section of ex-pragmatists did take this road. But the main body did not follow through; after taking a step forward under the blows of the economic crash, they slipped two steps backward when it eased off.

Having turned away from capitalism in its collapse, in its revival they returned to it by way of the New Deal. In their eyes the "Roosevelt revolution" was to achieve what the Russian revolution had done—in a cheaper and easier form. Did not the warriors of the New Deal promise to "throw the money-changers out of the temple," introduce national planning, oust the monopolists, bring progress, peace, and prosperity, and usher in "the Century of the Common Man"?

Roosevelt's reforms were more successful in quieting the pragmatists than in eliminating unemployment or dislodging the monopolists from power. Before the decade was over, his New Deal was succeeded by the War Deal. In the face of the oncoming threat of war, the liberals were confused and divided. One section, led by such people as Lewis Mumford, joined the battle chorus of the "interventionists"; another, headed by the historian Charles Beard, supported the "isolationists." Dewey wavered for a time between these two tendencies. But once the United States entered the war, he and his followers again backed the imperialists en masse. It was easier for them to do that the second time. Their consciences were clear because now they were fighting to destroy fascism, even though under the leadership of big business.

In 1944 Dewey voted for Roosevelt as the man most likely to "lead us forward." He was even able to point out how his own methods of progressive education had contributed to the war effort. "The conduct of the boys on the battlefields," he said, "shows what a democratic discipline and development from within is capable of accomplishing."

The Real Results

When we review the results of the work of the pragmatic liberals in the three decisive fields of politics, economics, and education from 1900 to 1950, what do we find?

Politics provides the main arena for conscious collective action by any movement dedicated to social change. According to their own standards, the Deweyites should have functioned as the most farsighted, progressive, and powerful of leaders. Actually, they were shortsighted and helpless in dealing with the major developments in American life over the last half century.

Instead of foreseeing wars and crises, the pragmatic liberals were taken by surprise and tumbled over by them. Instead of standing at the forefront of the political procession, they lagged in the rear of events. Instead of playing an independent role in the class struggle, they found themselves at decisive moments either trailing the representatives of the plutocracy or seeking some connection with the working-class movement.

Dewey's personal record of political activity was typical of the entire Progressive movement. From Bryan to Roosevelt there was hardly a demagogue of capitalist reform he did not trust for a time. Con men have sucker lists made up of "marks" who can be swindled over and over again. The con men among the capitalist politicians have found that liberals are among the easiest marks; they fall for the same line of bogus promises time after time.

In 1896 Dewey supported Bryan; in 1912 Theodore Roosevelt's Bull Moose campaign; in 1916 Wilson; in 1924 La Follette; in 1928 Al Smith. Then in 1932 and 1936, when the middle classes were spinning to the left, he voted for the reformist socialist Norman Thomas. By 1944 he was back with the Democratic Party under Franklin Roosevelt. His last vote in a national election was cast for Truman, the banner-bearer of the cold war.

The principal aim of the Progressives was to dislodge the

plutocrats from Washington and place the power of determining national policy in the hands of "the people." Today the monopolists and militarists are more securely entrenched in the government apparatus than at any time in the century. The harmony of the Democratic and Republican parties on the main issues of foreign policy demonstrates that.

The liberals dedicated themselves to the defense and extension of democracy. Yet their own chosen candidates delivered the greatest blows to civil liberties during their administrations: Wilson, the advocate of the "New Freedom," presided over the Palmer Raids; Roosevelt, champion of the "New Deal," signed the Smith "Gag" Act; Truman, their "Fair Deal" friend, instituted the loyalty purge.

The liberals worked to preserve peace within the framework of the capitalist system. Wilson took the country into the First World War, Roosevelt went into the second, and Truman engaged in the Korean "police action."

In the economic domain the liberals opposed the growth of monopoly. Is it necessary to cite facts to prove the increased predominance of big business and high finance in the American economy? In 1957, five years after Dewey's death, former Assistant Secretary of State Berle described the uninterrupted growth of monopoly power in a pamphlet called *Economic Power and the Free Society*, published by the Fund for the Republic: "Today approximately 50 percent of American manufacturing is held by about 150 corporations. . . . 500 corporations control two-thirds of the non-farm economy. This is, I think, the highest concentration of economic power in recorded history. . . . It makes the medieval feudal system look like a Sunday School party."

And the trend has considerably accelerated since then. The column "TRB from Washington" in *The New Republic* of February 22, 1975, reported: "The top 500 corporations in America have increased their share of all US manufacturing and mining assets from 40 to 70 percent in 15 years and they are virtually all global. Interlocking directorates tie them with the top dozen or so banks. . . . These largest corporations are not merely richer than many countries; they often have their own foreign policies, like ITT in Chile, which helped overthrow left-wing Allende with the aid of the CIA. General Motors' yearly operating revenues exceed those of all but a dozen nation-states. . . ."

The most ironic results have occurred in the field of education, where Deweyism held out the brightest promise. Progressive education was intended for the many. In practice it has been largely restricted to the few, flourishing in private schools detached from the public system and patronized for the most part by the offspring of well-to-do families. The influence of progressive educational methods was going to promote democracy through the schools. Instead of the educational system democratizing society, the control exercised by conservative monied interests has throttled freedom of expression and experimentation in the school system itself to such an extent that in many places the disciples of Dewey are under a cloud.

The excellent aim of integrating theory with practice in the educational process, thus preparing the child for later life, has not been realized to any extent for the masses of students and is a mockery in the inner-city ghettos from coast to coast.

In "Humanism and Truth" William James beseeched the opponents of pragmatism "to give the theory plenty of rope and see if it hangs itself eventually." That is precisely what has happened. The balance sheet of its own achievements is the most annihilating refutation of the pretensions of the pragmatic liberals.

Why has instrumentalism proved useless in attaining its objectives? It did not fail because of lack of talent in its leaders or energy in its ranks, because of poverty of resources or lack of opportunities. It had these in abundance over the years.

Instrumentalism turned out to be untrustworthy in practice because it was not correct enough in theory. First of all, its theory of society was wrong. Dewey correctly remarked: "The first distinguishing characteristic of thinking . . . is facing the facts" (*Reconstruction in Philosophy,* p. 118). He and his followers did not face the fundamental fact about present-day society: that it is not a harmonious and homogeneous whole but is divided into antagonistic classes with divergent interests.

They classified the American population into prejudiced mossbacks and individuals of intelligence and goodwill; both were scattered through all the ranks of society. If the progressive elements were enlightened and mobilized, they would overcome the reactionaries. That was the starting point of their reasoning, the foundation of their illusions, and the ideological source of their fiascos in politics.

The instrumentalists failed in the second place because the

methods of action based on these unsound premises were misleading. They continued to view middle-class elements as the pacemakers of social betterment long after the working class had become the main force for progress. They sought to yoke the movement of the working class to a program restricted to the reform of capitalism. But the aims they set for themselves could not be attained that way. They required the independent organization and revolutionary struggle of the workers against all forms of monopolist domination. This, however, was the road of Marxism, which the pragmatic liberals did not care or dare to take.

While instrumentalism has ruled the roost in the domain of general ideas for most of the twentieth century, it has not succeeded in changing any of the decisive departments of American life according to its aims. What a paradoxical outcome for a philosophy which holds that the supreme test of the value and validity of theories lies in "an active reorganization of the given environment"! Something must be radically wrong with a philosophy that ends up in such contradiction with its own premises and objectives.

There is a well-known game called "truth or consequences." The contestant who cannot give the right answer to the questions posed must pay a penalty. The same punishment awaits the pragmatist who asserts that consequences are the gauge of truth. Since pragmatism has demonstrated its incapacity in social reconstruction and its ignorance of the most common realities of American life, it cannot escape the proper punishment. It must be set aside in favor of a philosophy which encompasses and expresses the essential truth about natural and social reality and is able to apply its ideas in action with more fruitful results.

The Durability of Pragmatism

It may well be asked: Why, if Deweyism has exhibited such weaknesses at times of social crisis, has it not been more completely discredited and discarded? The reason for its endurance must first of all be sought in the field of social relations. The positions and prospects of pragmatism are closely bound up with those of the capitalist regime, and with the attitude of the educated middle classes toward it. When capitalism is shaken and the middle classes become unsure of their future, pragmatism suffers accordingly. But the social forces behind it endure, even though the inadequacy of the ideas and methods of pragmatism may be exposed to discerning eyes.

These forces come to prop it up again at the next turn of events. The United States came out of two world wars as the strongest sector of a weakened world capitalism. American capitalism possesses immense reserves inherited from the national past and reinforced by its supremacy in the world's markets. It not only draws upon this enormous wealth for recuperation and resistance, but also upon all that belongs and clings to the past.

One of its ultimate reserves in the theoretical field is instrumentalism itself. In extremities this school of thought can be relied upon to rush to the rescue, as it did during two imperialist world wars, by finding high-sounding and opportunistic justifications for the policies and actions of the capitalist regime and restraining critical minds from passing over to Marxism.

The richness of U.S. capitalism, based upon its worldwide exploitation, gives it tremendous capacities for corruption. The ruling classes of many countries have become dependents of Washington. At home, many layers of the population—from the politicians, white and Black, to the labor bureaucracy—are tainted with this corruption.

Intellectuals, too, who pretend to a higher code of honor, are not disinclined to find reasons why they should have a seat at one end of the banquet table. For example, quite a few ex-Marxists have served as mouthpieces for big business on the staffs of the Luce publications. And where high salaries and academic preferment alone have not induced conformity, the intimidation of the heresy-hunt has added the final squeeze.

There are important factors on the other side which have helped prop up pragmatism. Among these have been the theoretical backwardness of the labor movement, the weakness of its socialist component, and most of all the adverse effects of Stalinism. Just as the rise of the Russian revolution pulled intellectuals like Randolph Bourne away from pragmatism and toward Marxism, so the degeneration of that revolution repelled many honest intellectuals from the Stalinist perversion of Marxism and left a void where instrumentalism could operate. For all its defaults and defects, Deweyism managed to pose as a progressive alternative against the background of Stalinist totalitarianism, deceit, and betrayal. Thus Dewey summarized his attitude on the conflict between capitalist counterrevolution and the proletarian revolution in the following formula: "To be asked to choose between Bolshevism and Fascism is to be asked to choose betwen the GPU and the Gestapo."

This became a popular excuse for the retreat of the radical intellectuals from revolutionary socialism during the late thirties and the forties, and their reconciliation throughout the cold war years with the imperialist democracy they had earlier abjured.

In defending bourgeois democracy Dewey remained true to himself, his creed, and his class to the end. There was nothing hypocritical or cowardly in his beliefs. He held them honestly and fought for them consistently. To fight for one's convictions openly, candidly, without care for personal inconveniences is rare. In this respect Dewey is entitled to honor; he fulfilled his obligations to his social group and never failed to speak what was on his mind, which so well coincided with their thinking. His inconsistencies and shortcomings were not due to any lack of moral courage or intellectual integrity but to the intrinsic limitations of his ideas. As a moral personality, Dewey stood above his philosophy. Many of his later followers, who became Marxists during the 1930s and then returned to the defense of bourgeois values, did not have his moral stature.

Pragmatism will survive and even thrive so long as American capitalism appears impregnable. But it does not have an indefinite lease on life. Every severe crisis of the capitalist order will generate as a reflex a parallel crisis in its liberal projection. This happened during the ferment surrounding the Vietnam war and continues as economic crisis and social disaffection grow deeper.

What is shown by the radicalization of younger minds is negatively corroborated by the moods of discouragement and disarray among the aging liberals of the older generation as they face the seventies. On the basis of his findings in more than a hundred intensive interviews with the leaders of American intellectual opinion, Charles Kadushin wrote in 1974: "They have been leaders and influentials in the development of ideas on domestic reforms and foreign affairs. But most count their work as a failure and seem to find no way at present of carrying out their goals, or even influencing others to join the battle. It would not be fair to say they are in despair, but optimism based on a step-by-step plan for achievement is simply not present" (*The American Intellectual Elite,* p. 291).

14

Deweyism
and Marxism

Pragmatism's Attitude to Marxism

Two different phases can be distinguished in the evolution of pragmatism's attitude to Marxism.

At the turn of the century, as the socialist movement began to spread in Europe and even stir America to some extent, Marxism attracted the attention of some alert American scholars and intellectuals. Its economic doctrines in particular were welcomed by the more radical members of the Chicago school as an auxiliary aid to their own work in economics, sociology, and social reform. They valued socialism for its criticism of the more blatant evils of capitalism, and they were well disposed toward Marxism's historical method for its emphasis that the social environment was decisive in forming social institutions and individual characteristics.

Veblen wrote in 1906 that "there is no system of economic theory more logical than that of Marx." Albion Small, founder of the first department of sociology in an American university, stated in the May 1912 *American Journal of Sociology,* which he edited: "Socialism has been the most wholesome ferment in modern society." And he concluded: "Marx will have a place in social science analogous with that of Galileo in physical science. . . ."

These Midwest scholars were much more interested in the light Marx's analysis could shed on economic and social problems than in his philosophical positions or dialectical logic. Marxism was not taken any more seriously in philosophy than its revolutionary conclusions were in politics. Just as the industrial workers did not then bulk large as an independent political and cultural force in relation to the middle classes, so the theory and program of their most advanced representatives could be easily disregarded as irrelevant to American life.

Dewey was simply indifferent, not antipathetic, to the doctrines of Marxism. After having rejected Hegel's logic of contradiction, he felt no obligation to come to terms with its materialist successor.

Such leading thinkers among the Progressives as Veblen, Beard, Small, and Dewey borrowed from Marxist sources whatever seemed useful for any particular purpose. But there was no consistency in their materialism. Although Dewey explained the special features of Aristotle's logic by reference to the role of the slave aristocracy in ancient Athens, he shrank from extending the same materialist method of analysis to the development of his own logical theory. As a rule, in order to make materialism fit into their scheme of things and their habits of thought, the Progressive thinkers had to round off its sharp edges and excise its revolutionary essence.

Despite their political disagreements, the earliest American Marxists had a reciprocal benevolence toward the pragmatists. There is no evidence of any clash on the philosophical plane in the writings of A.M. Simons, the pioneer socialist historian, or such popularizers of Marxian political economy as Louis Boudin. This period of friendly neutrality between pragmatism and Marxism coincided with the alignment of the Progressives and labor against the plutocracy—with liberalism in the lead. This amity persisted until the early thirties, when it began to give way to a mistrust that finally hardened into open hostility.

Two main factors were behind this change. One was the weakening of world capitalism and its ideological props. The other was the reemergence of genuine Marxism through the Bolshevik victory in the Russian revolution. As the working class came forward as the revolutionary power of first magnitude, its doctrines and methods were more and more sharply counterposed to all others and came under ever more vigorous attack.

Although it took a while, this development affected the relations between pragmatism and Marxism in this country too. From an ally against entrenched conservatism, Marxism turned into a menace to the most cherished ideas and basic positions of liberalism. Despite a few feeble and futile efforts at reconciliation and combination of the two tendencies, the leading pragmatists grew more antagonistic to the revolutionary implications of Marxism. At the same time, inspired by the revival of Marxism by the leaders of the Russian revolution, a few authentic American Marxists assisted in the work of demarcating the rival schools of philosophy.

This mutual repulsion was further hardened by the rise of Stalinism, the increasing intervention of imperialism into American intellectual life, and the bending of pragmatism under its pressures. The principal pragmatists took an unreserved stand as defenders of capitalist democracy, not only against the Stalinist counterfeit, but also against the genuine representatives of Marxism.

Until the thirties Dewey had felt no inclination to get well acquainted with Marx's ideas. The capitalist crisis and the spread of Marxism on its heels made this gap in his knowledge less tolerable. He utilized his work as chairman of the Commission of Inquiry into the Moscow Trials to make a study of Marxism and Bolshevism. His final verdict was that Marx's theory was incurably tainted with Hegelian idealism and led to the absolutism proper to theology. Bolshevism was the negation of all democracy and inexorably resulted in the totalitarian regime and crimes of Stalinism. Civilization and culture could be promoted only through renewed faith in the virtues of an instrumentalism devoted to the defense and extension of a democracy exalted above the class arena.

Marxism's Attitude Toward Pragmatism

Illusions about the merits of Deweyism and its compatibility with Marxism have been current among a certain section of radical intellectuals with academic affiliations. These fellow travelers of the socialist movement have created considerable confusion about their real relations.

The first attempts to mate Marxism and pragmatism were made before the First World War by ideologues of the Socialist Party's right wing. In *The Larger Aspect of Socialism* (1913) W. English Walling took many of his ideas on education, philosophy, and psychology from Dewey and tried to demonstrate that Marx and Engels were pragmatists before that school emerged on this side of the Atlantic.

Most prominent among the later conciliators have been several professors of philosophy who pride themselves on being "undogmatic" thinkers. This enables them to assert that pragmatism and Marxism are, if not identical, at least in harmony with each other on most fundamental questions of philosophy. There is a touching coincidence of opinion on this score between two pupils of Dewey. One is Corliss Lamont, the noted civil libertarian, who taught philosophy at Columbia and was for a while an uncritical collaborator of the Stalinists before breaking with them; the other is Sidney Hook, retired professor of philosophy at New York University who, after immersion in left-wing politics up to 1940, made a career as a social democratic apologist for the U.S. State Department and supported Nixon in 1972.

In a debate on this question in the February 25, 1947, *New Masses,* Lamont wrote: "It is incontestable in my opinion that the main import and intent of Dewey's massive philosophic system is thoroughly anti-idealistic and in agreement with the general world-view of dialectical materialism." In *Reason, Social Myths and Democracy,* published in 1940, Hook asserted: "The most outstanding figure in the world today in whom the best elements of Marx's thought are present is John Dewey. . . . They were independently developed by him and systematically elaborated beyond anything found in Marx."

Lewis Feuer backs up this judgment. "Classical American social science, in the persons of such men as Beard, Veblen, and Dewey, was not only influenced by Marx, but shared with Marx the same basic tenets. The faith of these Americans in the ordinary man, in the underlying population, was also the messianic socialist one; their faith in science as the method of liberation and their belief in the primacy of the economic factor in human history were as powerful as Marx's. Classical American social scientists were indeed historical materialists in the way they regarded their social world, and this was one reason why many of their students found an evolution toward systematic Marxism a natural development in the thirties" (introduction to *Basic Writings in Politics and Philosophy,* by Karl Marx and Friedrich Engels, pp. ix-x).

On the purely ideological plane such attempts to lump together the two philosophies represent either a relapse into the theoretical infancy of American socialism or an incapacity to grow out of it. But this identification fulfilled a more definite function in the cases of Lamont and Hook. In their political careers both avoided the responsibility of lasting commitment to any party or program on the left. They looked for ways of blunting the conflicts of interest between the capitalist rulers and the working masses or finding some common ground on which to reconcile them. Their theoretical starting point in this quest for compromise was to deny the fundamental difference between the respective world views of these classes. Lamont did this in the name of humanism; Hook in the name of a sterilized and servile "democratic socialism."

They maintained this mistaken position not only in violation of obvious facts but in defiance of the most authoritative voices of the rival philosophies. Dewey himself was aware that instrumentalism and Marxism were essentially opposed. Bertrand Russell reports that Dewey bracketed dialectical materialism with theology: "I heard him say once that, having emancipated himself with some difficulty from the traditional orthodox theology, he was not going to shackle himself with another" (*A History of Western Philosophy,* p. 848). Like other eclectics, Dewey inclined to classify any type of systematic thought under the heading of "absolutism," "dogmatism," or "theology." In any case, he was clear-sighted and candid enough to insist on the basic opposition between his own viewpoint and Marxism.

All eminent Marxists who have concerned themselves with this question, from Plekhanov through Lenin to Trotsky, have drawn a sharp line beteen pragmatism and dialectical materialism. In *Materialism and Empirio-Criticism* (chapter 6, section 4) Lenin indicates how pragmatism in the last analysis proceeds from the same subjectivist premises and arrives at the same antimaterialist conclusions as positivism.

As the scientific theory of the revolutionary movement of the working class, Marxism could not avoid clashing with Deweyism which, as the expression of middle-class preconceptions, served as an instrument of reformism, opportunism, and socialist revisionism. Their profound antagonism has been manifested by the eruption of conflicts between these tendencies within the Marxist movement itself. Every attempt to dilute or delete the revolutionary essence of Marxism in the United States has sooner or later connected its aims and ideas with those of pragmatism, or has from the start even explicitly counterposed Deweyism to dialectical materialism. This happened, for example, with Max Eastman who, before he renounced socialism at the end of the 1930s, tried to absorb Marxism into instrumentalism and represent Lenin as an unavowed disciple of Dewey in practice.

In the last year of his life, 1939-40, Trotsky engaged James Burnham in a controversy over philosophic method in connection with a deep-going political struggle which split the Socialist Workers Party. The petty-bourgeois opposition headed by Burnham and Max Shachtman rejected the method of dialectical materialism and leaned toward pragmatic impressionism; the majority under Trotsky's influence vigorously championed the validity of Marxism. A full account of this dispute can be found in Trotsky's book *In Defense of Marxism.* It contains an instructive explanation of the major differences between the two world outlooks.

Stalinism and Pragmatism

Stalinism, which has a shifty attitude toward Marxism, has shown this by its shifting attitude toward pragmatism. Stalinism itself originated in an essentially pragmatic way when the Soviet bureaucracy departed from the original Marxist principles of revolutionary internationalism, working-class democracy and methods of consistent class struggle. replacing these with an opportunistic adaptation to the reflux of the international revolution during the 1920s.

The Stalinist attitude toward Deweyism has depended not upon objective evaluation of this trend of thought in the light of historical materialism, but upon the changing requirements and diplomatic alignments of the Soviet bureaucracy. Their approach to pragmatism has been purely pragmatic and thoroughly opportunistic, depending on whether Moscow happened to be· well- or ill-disposed toward bourgeois liberalism at the given juncture.

From 1929 to 1935, when their politics had an ultraleft twist, the Stalinists stamped Deweyism as a "social fascist" philosophy, and Earl Browder, then leader of the American Communist Party, denounced Sidney Hook for trying to smuggle its ideas into the communist movement. The Stalinists softened their criticism when they swung over to their "popular front" period of support to Roosevelt's administration after 1935.

But Dewey's participation in the exposure of the Moscow Trials frame-ups in 1936-37 compelled the Stalinists to change their tune again and label him an agent of "Trotskyite fascism." During the Second World War, when they volunteered as supply sergeants for the imperialist war machine, the Stalinists sought reconciliation with the pragmatic liberals who were also, for their own reasons, marching along with the monopolists. The cold war effected still another estrangement between them. In the eyes of loyal Stalinists, the followers of Dewey, who persisted in their fidelity to American capitalism, were ideological agents of the warmongering imperialists—as some of them indeed were.

After the thaw in the cold war and the accentuated adaptation of the American CP to middle-class liberalism, its spokespeople are rediscovering hidden virtues in this peculiarly American philosophy.

Some of the Stalinized intellectuals have published appraisals of Dewey's ideas which contain valuable and correct criticisms of instrumentalism from the materialist standpoint. But their works have two major faults. First, they have to conform to the characterization of Deweyism dictated by current Soviet diplomacy and cultural policy. Thus Maurice Cornforth, parroting the Soviet ideological bandmaster Zhdanov, asserted in *Science Versus Idealism* (1955) that pragmatism, "particularly in the form which Dewey has given it, is the philosophy of American imperialism. It expresses the outlook and aspirations of American big business in philosophical form. That is its basis, the real content of all its doctrines" (p. 422).

Harry K. Wells made this same false characterization the main thesis of his book *Pragmatism: Philosophy of Imperialism* (1954): "Pragmatism is the main-line philosophy of U.S. imperialism. It is the world outlook, the theory and method, of the capitalist class" (p. 187).

Second, these writers approach Dewey in an unhistorical manner. They do not view his philosophy as a necessary phase in the evolution of American thought, and in its time and place even a progressive one, which has been rendered obsolete by new conditions. They judge it in a schoolmasterish way, from the standpoint of abstract general principles, by whether or not it fulfills a set of doctrinaire requirements. By such a standard, of course, pragmatism falls short and is easily condemned.

An important national school of philosophy has to be judged not simply by the standards of the highest development of world thought, but also in the light of specific national conditions and its connections with them. Sun Yat-senism, for example, could be rejected out of hand as unworthy of consideration because it was backward and muddled compared to the clearest expressions of revolutionary democratic, not to speak of socialist, thought in the West. However, this does not dispose of it. It was the expression of an inescapable step in the awakening of modern thought in China, a weapon against mandarinism, a bridge over which the most progressive elements passed from feudal thought to Marxism.

Croce contributed little to the advance of world philosophy. Yet his historical idealism, the expression of Italian bourgeois liberalism, helped prepare minds like the communist Gramsci and others for the reception of Marxist ideas.

Today the overall national thinking of the American people is more backward than that of either China or Italy. Deweyism must be appraised in that concrete context. It is as wrong and misleading to identify pragmatism with imperialism as it is to identify pragmatism with Marxism. Pragmatism is essentially the philosophy of middle-class individuals who are caught between capital and labor; its hallmark is the attempt to find political and ideological positions somewhere between these polar forces in American society.

Two Instructive Examples

An event that illustrates the difference between the pragmatic and Marxist approaches to an acute social problem occurred in the last years of Dewey's life. When the witch-hunters launched their campaign to bar "subversives" from teaching in the public schools, Dewey courageously opposed this undemocratic purge. In 1949 he justified his stand by saying that the motives of the witch-hunters were not clear and the specific results of their actions could not be foreseen. He said that the purge might have either good or bad results but he feared that the latter would be the case.

Thus Dewey hinged his reasoning on social indeterminateness and personal ignorance, not on considerations of principle. This purely pragmatic approach made it possible for virulent anticommunists like his disciple Sidney Hook to approve the exclusion of Communist Party sympathizers from teaching staffs as "conspirators" and agents of a foreign power.

The Trotskyists, like Dewey, opposed such persecutions, but on a different basis. They stated that the drive had completely reactionary motives and was bound to stifle democratic rights. Their arguments were premised on the role played by thought control in the struggles issuing from the *determinate* class antagonisms of American society, and on the *principle* that the interests of democracy and labor demanded an irreconcilable fight against the inquisitors.

Thus even where the positions taken by certain pragmatists and the Marxists on a specific issue coincided, they were based on different premises, animated by different class aims, and guided by different methods of social analysis. Middle-class elements and the workers can and do have certain points in common. This makes it possible and even necessary on occasion for their representatives to join in action against oppressions of the capitalist regime. But such united fronts on specific issues do not mean that the motives, programs, methods, and aims of the two are identical. They are often in fact quite different, as the further test of experience will show.

This diversity in common action was exemplified not only in the fight to defend civil liberties against the capitalist witch-hunters after World War II, but in the movement to expose Stalin's frameups of the Old Bolsheviks before it.

Although the protests against the slander and murder of Lenin's associates was worldwide, the organized effort to stay the hand of Moscow centered in the United States. Dewey headed the International Commission of Inquiry which was supported by a united front of liberal intellectuals and left-wing Socialists. This commission performed a historic service to the world working class and to the cause of justice. Its members examined the available body of information connected with the Moscow Trials of 1937–38, concluded that they were frameups, and found that Trotsky and his son Leon Sedov were not guilty of the infamous charges against them. These conclusions have stood the test of time; in 1956 Khrushchev himself partially confirmed them, although not directly and honestly.

Both tendencies backing the commission's work were interested in probing the case to the bottom, making known the truth about the accusations, and offering the exiled Trotsky the opportunity to present his defense to the public. These tasks were done, and done well. But the two allies did not have the same political motives.

Many liberals took the exposure of Stalin's crimes against the working class and its revolutionary representatives as an opportunity to strike a blow against socialism. They vaunted the superiority of bourgeois democracy over Stalinist totalitarianism by falsely identifying the policies and misdeeds of the Soviet bureaucracy with genuine communism and asserting that Stalinism was the logical outcome of Leninism.

The Marxists had different objectives. They faced the difficult dual task of exposing the crimes of Stalinism while defending the honor of Bolshevism, the traditions of Marxism, and the program of socialism against both their desecrators and detractors. The Marxists saw no reason for exalting the virtues of an imperialist democracy which was splotched with a criminal record extending from world wars to frameups of labor militants and lynchings of Blacks. They explained that the very fact that Stalin had to besmirch and slaughter an entire generation of revolutionary leaders showed how incompatible his regime was with that of Lenin's time.

Dewey himself utilized the occasion of the announcement of his Commission's verdict in 1937 not only to repledge allegiance to democratic liberalism but to denounce Trotsky's doctrines as no better than Stalin's. This uncalled-for disavowal was one of the signs of the growing reconciliation by American intellectuals with imperialism in the late thirties, which culminated in their support to its war. By 1941 the anti-Stalinist liberals found themselves together with the American Stalinists—and against the Trotskyists—on the war issue.

Class Expressions in American Philosophy

The record of their mutual relations, the testimony of their principal representatives, the difference in their class connections, the conflicts in their methods and leading principles as applied to specific cases all serve to demonstrate the fundamental opposition between pragmatism and Marxism. Whatever points they have in common are subsidiary to their major disagreements. The two are not harmonious and reconcilable but basically incompatible world-views and methods of thought.

They express the outlooks of two different social forces with opposing interests and aspirations. Marxism is the militant ideology of the revolutionary working class on its way to power and of the most advanced sections of humanity on the way to emancipation from capitalism and all forms of class domination. Pragmatism is the conciliatory philosophical instrument of the middle classes on the downgrade, trying to clutch at any means for salvation.

Three main lines of theory are set into motion and sustained by the major social trends at work in the United States today. Monopoly capitalism, with its drive toward reaction, militarism, and repression, patronizes the most backward prejudices and obsolete ideas—from religion to racism—while it tries to screen its predatory purposes behind the slogan of defending "democracy." The banner-bearers of "the free world" seek to blockade or even banish progressive social, political, and philosophical ideas as they themselves head toward obscurantism and cultural retrogression.

This is not the zone congenial to the second tendency, instrumentalism, which feels most at home in a twilight world where sharp distinctions are blurred, outlines are vague, and the precise places of things are uncertain. It is at ease so long as it can avoid choosing between sharp alternatives and can smooth or slur over differences. One of its principal characteristics is indefiniteness on major questions; it feeds on ambiguities and patchwork.

The third tendency, Marxism, is intolerant of equivocation and half-measures. It frankly and truthfully asserts that the interests of capital and labor are incompatible and that their struggle will have to be fought through to a finish. Such talk about the "irrepressible conflict" of the twentieth century sounds like the raving of a maniac, or like the crack of doom, to the pragmatic liberal, just as abolitionism did to the compromisers of pre–Civil War days.

By laying bare the necessary evolution of the basic conflicts in our society toward brutal dictatorship or socialist revolution, Marxists may offend the liberals. But they render invaluable aid to the workers and their allies. Through scientific socialism the workers can emerge from the darkness of social ignorance that has been imposed on them into the broad daylight of class understanding. They can pass from uncertainty to a firm grasp of the truth, from confusion to clarity, from shapelessness of thought to a definite viewpoint and a consistent method, from vacillation to steadiness of purpose. When shadows are dispelled, the contenders for power can be seen arrayed against each other. Only in such a clear light can action proceed with maximum vigor and effectiveness.

Marxism has to combat pragmatism and its influence not only in the direct contest of one philosophical school with another, but also inside the ranks of labor and sometimes within the revolutionary vanguard itself. Although the Marxist movement opposes the ideas and influences of bourgeois society, its adherents are not separated by impermeable partitions from them. Living side by side, they react upon one another. The empirical habits of behavior and the pragmatic modes of thought which have found generalization and justification in Deweyism continually sprout from the soil of capitalism and are nurtured by the atmosphere of middle-class life. The "petty-bourgeoi-sification" of union officials and privileged, better-paid white workers reinforces the influence of such ideas within labor circles.

The revolutionary ranks are infiltrated by pragmatic modes of thought and habits not only through the upper sections of the working class but through university-trained intellectuals who in one way or another attach themselves to the radical movement and seek to influence it.

It is possible to approach socialism, adopt its ideas, and enter its ranks on purely empirical grounds, that is, on the basis that socialism would probably work better than capitalist rule or seems to have a better program for solving current problems. Many people, especially in periods of acute social crisis, make their way to Marxism in this manner, through deductions from their personal observation or experience at a given juncture. There is nothing reprehensible, and even something inevitable, in this kind of development. This is in fact the normal route by which the masses of workers move to socialism. Confrontations and clashes with the powers that be keep them on that road until they drive through to the end.

Intellectuals may be impelled toward Marxism by the general social crises of capitalism that affect the workers. But since they occupy more sheltered and favored positions and are not integrated into industry, the direct pressure of social forces in the class struggle alone cannot suffice to keep them on the revolutionary path. If their thought is not securely moored in Marxism, their conduct is liable to vacillation. Individuals from middle-class environments are obliged to compensate for their lack of class stability and stamina with unshakable ideas.

This means that an intellectual who comes to Marxism by way of empiricism has to undergo a thorough ideological conversion. Upon becoming a socialist, it is necessary to pass from the initial point, the impact of immediate experience, to the higher stage of deep scientific insight into the problems of social life and the march of historical development—or run the risk of succumbing to alien theoretical influences.

A person who takes up socialism in a purely pragmatic way, that is, solely under the thrust of episodic circumstances in the class struggle, can as easily drop away at a new turn of events. The passage of many unreconstructed intellectuals into the radical movement during the 1930s, and then out of it en masse in the following decade, testifies to the reality of this instability.

The interplay of social forces is extremely complex. Marxism offers the best method of analyzing the many-sided movement of contemporary capitalism, enabling an individual to discern and hold on to the main line of development through all the ups and downs, twists and turns in the class struggle.

Pragmatism, on the other hand, which takes things "as they are"—without grasping the contradictory forces operating below the surface in historical perspective—sets a trap for unwary intellectuals. Deluded by appearances and overawed by episodic conjunctures of events, they too often mistake a lull in the struggle for the enduring relations of the major classes—and slide back from Marxism to the pragmatic liberalism they had earlier abandoned.

The best insurance against such backsliding is a thorough understanding of the theoretical foundations of scientific socialism combined with active participation in the organized anticapitalist struggle.

15

The Metaphysics of
Bourgeois Democracy

Some thinkers deny that philosophy has registered any cumulative achievements from its first appearance in Ionian Greece to the present day. Such an antievolutionary approach removes world philosophy, or any sector of it, from the ascent of humanity and deprives it of all genuine gains in insight into reality. So false a view has been repudiated by outstanding thinkers from Aristotle to Hegel, Feuerbach, Marx, and Dewey.

Most historians of American thought do not discern any main line of development leading to secure advances in theoretical insight and outlook as different schools and individual interpretations have succeeded one another in American philosophy since colonial times. They take a superficial, empirical, descriptive approach to its evolution.

All the same, American philosophy has progressed along with the rest of American civilization, in consonance with both its achievements and its shortcomings. As it has grown from one period of American culture to the next, the most advanced philosophical thought has shed obsolete ideas and made definitive and durable acquisitions.

When we review American philosophy from the writings of Jonathan Edwards in the early eighteenth century to the pseudo-Marxist commentaries of Sidney Hook in the middle of the twentieth century, as we have tried to do through the analysis of Dewey's works, the following questions arise: What is the upshot of these two centuries of ideological effort? Where does American philosophy objectively stand today? In what direction do the signposts of further advancement point?

It should not offend our national self-esteem to acknowledge that the major contributions to philosophic progress from the eighteenth to the twentieth centuries did not arise on this side of the Atlantic but came from thinkers in the theoretically more developed countries of Western Europe. The economy of the United States did not pass beyond colonial status until after the Civil War, although political sovereignty had been won almost a century before. From the world-historical standpoint, American philosophy has been even more immature. H. W. Schneider has accurately observed: "America was intellectually colonial long after it gained political independence and has been intellectually provincial long after it ceased being intellectually colonial" (*A History of American Philosophy,* p. viii).

Despite this backwardness, the generalized thought native to the United States has passed through a significant line of development of its own, molded by the special features of its history. American philosophy started out as an appendage to Protestant theology and remained under that tutelage for almost two hundred years. Dewey testified that when he went to college in the 1870s, "teachers of philosophy were at that time, almost to a man, clergymen; the supposed requirements of religion, or theology, dominated the teaching of philosophy in most colleges" (*Contemporary American Philosophy,* vol. 2, p. 15).

From that point of departure, the headway of the nation's philosophy can be measured by the success of a series of attempts to throw off its infantile subordination to religion and link itself with the secular scientific trends associated with the most progressive forces in modern life. This antitheological and increasingly scientific movement of thought has gone through three stages which coincide with the three main phases in the lifespan of American bourgeois-democratic ideology.

The eighteenth-century Enlightenment which inspired many leading figures of the Revolution was marked by freethinking in regard to Protestant orthodoxy. The process of liberating intellectual speculation from religion received its first impetus during this pioneer stage of the bourgeois-democratic era. But the separation of the two did not go nearly so far in the sphere of theory as it did in American government, where the division of church from state was more definitively achieved than in any other major country of the Western world.

The Transcendentalists of pre–Civil War years were in sharp conflict with the established churches, their creeds, and their wealthy, conservative pewholders. Even though Emerson, Parker, Alcott, and others counterposed their idealism to philosophical materialism, the effect of their heterodox teachings was to further loosen the hold of clericalism on more emancipated minds.

The pragmatic school, which gave theoretical expression to the liberalism of the period following the completion of the bourgeois-democratic revolution, pushed the process of secularizing philosophy and linking it with science as far as progressive middle-class thought could go. The instrumentalists, captained by Dewey, aimed at consummating the divorce of philosophy from religion by striking at metaphysics and wedding their method to a thoroughly scientific outlook.

For reasons already set forth, they were unable to deliver the goods. What these liberal thinkers projected as their goal has still to be accomplished. Twentieth-century American philosophy no longer has to kowtow before clericalism. Even though Democratic and Republican presidents fear to offend the organized churches and make ritualistic references to the divinity in their speeches on state occasions, the teacher in the university is not obligated to do so.

Yet one stronghold of fetishism, so alien to science, remains. The ultimate refuge of historical idealism in American pragmatism is its abstract metaphysics of bourgeois democracy. Pure democracy, wrenched out of historical reality and hoisted above class relations, to which all social practices must conform, is the central absolute in Dewey's thought. This idolization of an abstraction, the democratic "idea" in the Platonic sense, is the residue of several centuries of American experience.

The past two hundred years have witnessed the rise and decline of the progressive, democratic phase of capitalism and its ideology in the Western world, including the United States. In its youth and its prime, this democratic outlook was highly revolutionary. It was pitted against feudal ideas and precapitalist institutions (the church, monarchy, nobility, nonrepresentative political bodies, the Southern slavocracy) and was strongly critical of the ruling ideas of the superior classes. It was subversive of the established order, by implication if not always by intent, and an indispensable element for creating a new and freer one. It was the most effective instrument for the proclamation of the demands of the innovating forces throughout the Western world.

The tasks of all previous schools of philosophy in this country were set by the requirements of the bourgeois-democratic movement in its march forward. Radical thinkers of the seventeenth and eighteenth centuries, from Roger Williams to Thomas Jefferson and Ethan Allen, laid out a pattern of bourgeois-democratic ideas that has since shaped the course of our predominant national thought. Emerson and the constellation of idealistic New England iconoclasts who constituted the Transcendentalist movement unfolded further implications of the individualist creed of petty-bourgeois democracy during the expansion of Northern capitalism and the struggle of the free labor forces against the slave power that erupted into the Civil War.

Decades after that war was won by the Union, Dewey became the philosophical head of the protest movement that tried to assert the claims of middle-class democracy against the conservative clutch of the money magnates. The Progressives believed that the fundamental framework for the unlimited flourishing of democracy had been constructed by the Declaration of Independence, the Constitution, and the Bill of Rights. While recognizing that capitalist ownership and control of the means of production endangered democracy, they did not regard this economic reality as an insurmountable obstacle to the realization of a thoroughly democratic America.

Thus the most influential and enduring schools of American philosophy, from the rationalists of the eighteenth century to the pragmatists of the twentieth century, all undertook the defense and development of bourgeois-democratic ideology, their doctrines reflecting successive steps in perfecting it. Dewey's entire outlook was predicated on the preeminence of this mode of thought. He continually counterposed his own positions to the philosophy, logic, politics, and sociology of the pretechnological, prescientific, and hence predemocratic era.

However, this bourgeois democracy, which found its chief social support among the middle classes on the farms and in the towns, has changed its character as history has advanced. Bourgeois-democratic ideology was the radical expression of progressive capitalism. When international capitalism passed over into its monopolistic, parasitic, reactionary stage, and the modern labor movement with its socialist program and objectives came on the scene, it began to play a different role.

When it came to a showdown between the two, the liberal reformists who succeeded the revolutionary fighters for democracy gave precedence to the preservation of capitalism over the further extension of the rights of the people through militant mass action. Their loyalty to bourgeois society usually outweighed their professions of faith in democracy. In their hands the democratic ideology, once the war cry of aggressive attack on outworn institutions, became converted into a last-ditch defense for capitalist rulership.

The struggle for the promotion of democracy was hindered but not halted by the default of liberalism. Its main social base shifted from the progressive middle classes to the ranks of labor. The viable elements of the democratic ideology were absorbed into the anticapitalist program of socialism, and the tasks previously shouldered by the liberals were carried forward by the working-class movement.

This decay of bourgeois-democratic ideology has accompanied the disintegration of the capitalist system that has been proceeding on a world scale since 1917. In one country after another bourgeois liberalism has been losing ground. It is being squeezed by various forms of capitalist reaction from military dictatorship to fascism on one side, and by the socialist movement of the working class in all its diverse forms on the other. The decline of the Liberal Party in England, the classic home of parliamentary democracy, provides one conspicuous example of this process; France under de Gaulle presented another. In fourteen countries from China to Cuba bourgeois politics, liberalism included, has lost the ground under its feet with the elimination of capitalism.

The erosion of the supports of bourgeois democracy has not been so easy to see in the United States as in those parts of the world where capitalism is in more extreme difficulties or has already toppled into the abyss. Despite the memory of the 1930s depression and the beginnings of a new one, this political trend of our revolutionary epoch has not yet penetrated into the consciousness of the American masses because most of the residual strength and stability of capitalism is concentrated on this continent. The conviction persists that, at least in the United States, bourgeois democracy will be spared the blows it has received elsewhere, just as American capitalism will stand despite the crumbling of one after another of its supports abroad.

Nevertheless, the spectacle elsewhere of the eclipse of bourgeois liberalism by capitalist reaction on the right and the socialist and communist movements on the left has not left the pragmatic Progressives untouched. If they do not feel at bay or seized with panic as in 1930–33, and have even become belligerent in defense of the old creed, their consciences are disturbed. Looking at the world around them, and into the past, they are aware that all is far from well. They felt the breath of Marxism upon their necks in the thirties and the fangs of McCarthyism at their backs in the fifties. They cannot suppress the premonition that the bloom has passed from liberalism; that its predominance in advanced circles is drawing to a close; and that, if it is not yet dangerously threatened, the possibility of a fundamental challenge lurks around the next corner as the radicalization of the sixties and seventies continues to unfold.

Their uneasiness is well founded. The social, political, intellectual cause they cling to has no brilliant future in the world—and it is starting on the downgrade in this country too. The vast shifts that have taken place in the balance of social forces here work against it in the long run. The United States is dominated by three highly centralized aggregations of power—big business, big labor, and big government—say the academic political scientists. It would be more accurate to say that national policies are determined by the struggle of the first two for influence over the third—with big business on top in the present setup.

This lineup of social forces, in which monopoly capital and organized labor are in contention, has placed middle-class liberalism in a difficult position. Although it strives to act as arbiter between these mighty forces, liberalism is in the end compelled to go along with one or the other. It cannot be the deciding power; at best it serves as a makeweight to tip the balance toward one side or the other.

This new social situation calls for a new theoretical outlook and philosophic method to analyze its tendencies of development. Nevertheless, by sheer inertia, many liberal intellectuals continue to regard Deweyism as the latest word in philosophy, logic, and scientific thought, as the highest achievement of contemporary knowledge, as indispensable equipment for anyone claiming to keep in step with advanced ideas. Pragmatism is the predominant mode of thought not only among the liberal, but even among many radicalized intellectuals. The instrumentalist philosophy has become a hardened sedimentary deposit in the minds of educated Americans inside and outside the universities, and it will take explosive events to blast it out.

All the same, pragmatism is fighting a losing battle in the long-term contest of ideas. It is engaged in a defensive delaying action against rival types of thought crowding in upon its territory. On the left looms the shadow of Marxism. This is the main threat to be exorcised. While the thought controllers and witch-hunters strive to suppress the ideas of Marxism and their upholders by official and unofficial persecution, the pragmatic intellectuals try to forestall their headway by more subtle means: ridicule, indifference, distortion.

Having imbibed liberal ideas with their mother's milk, these intellectuals put up stubborn resistance to the inroads of scientific socialism and its philosophy. Despite pragmatism's avowed opposition to dogmatism of all kinds, clerical or communist, pragmatism itself has hardened into a dogma by categorically disqualifying dialectics and materialism. The only doctrines it will accredit as progressive have to come within the confines of empiricism, positivism, and pragmatism.

Although its adherents boasted that free competition in ideas was the test of freedom and the motive force of progress, the supremacy of pragmatism has coincided with a concerted boycott of its most formidable rival. For decades Marxism could not get a passport into academic circles, let alone a fair hearing; it has had to creep in stealthily and often in disguise.

Liberals uphold Dewey as the American answer to Marx. Dialectical materialism, they say, belongs to the backward countries of the Old World and the East and to the nineteenth century, whereas instrumentalism is by right the reigning philosophy of advanced America. This puts things upside down.

It is undeniable that Dewey's doctrines have deep roots in American soil; that they exert tremendous attraction upon the educated elite; that they contain valid insights. But instrumentalism reflects the American past more than its future; the ideas, interests, and outlook of the receding middle classes and not the ascending workers; a last hope of salvaging the rickety structure of capitalism instead of creating the new world of socialism. As tools of thought for probing into the processes of nature, society, and the intellect, the ideas of instrumentalism are no less inferior to Marxism than the naked eye is to the electron microscope and the telescope.

These two philosophies collide over the question of democracy.

In principle both are committed to democratic aims. But they disagree on their whole approach to the question. How did democracy come into this world? How can it be preserved and extended under present conditions? What forces in our society are its protectors and promoters? Marxism answers these questions one way; Deweyism another.

Liberalism refuses to recognize the significance of the fact that democracy entered history, including American history, not in a peaceful and gradual manner but through revolution. Insofar as the liberals take cognizance of this fact, they dismiss it as accidental and irrelevant.

For Marxists, on the contrary, democracy has been the political product of class struggles waged by economically rising social forces from the time of its first appearance as mercantile slave democracy in the Greek city-states of the sixth and fifth centuries B.C. to its development along bourgeois lines in North America since the eighteenth century. Revolution, as the supreme expression of class struggle, has been the midwife of democracy throughout its progress.

How does this historical generalization apply to the problem of democracy in our own time? The development of class relations poses the issue in the following specific terms: Are the capitalists or the workers the most reliable guardians of democracy? Does capitalist enterprise or a socialist planned economy provide the best soil for the flourishing of democracy in everyday life?

The spokesmen for the capitalists forthrightly identify the cause of democracy with their own rulership. They claim that "free enterprise" based on private property and profit is the indispensable foundation for political freedom—and they do not refrain from taking punitive measures against dissenters from this doctrine.

Scientific socialists assert that capitalism, which in its revolutionary antifeudal youth propelled democracy forward, has now in its monopolist old age become democracy's deadliest enemy. Through antilabor legislation, thought-control laws, and daily discrimination against the oppressed nationalities, capitalism strives to abridge democracy at home while professing to be its foremost exponent in the "free world." The only firm and consistent social bulwark of democracy is the working people, whose rights and welfare are continually being imperiled by the capitalist regime.

The democratic rights and traditions inherited from past

struggles in this country are precious possessions. But they can be maintained and extended only by constant resistance to the aggressions of the rich and their official agents. In the course of their struggles to defend and extend the rights of labor, Afro-Americans, and other abused and exploited sections of the nation it will become clearer to more and more people that capitalism itself is the breeding ground of the antidemocratic plague. This system will have to be thoroughly cleaned out in the interests of social sanitation and salvation. A workers' government that takes the national resources out of monopolist hands and uses them for the public good is the only secure guarantee for the preservation of democracy. The establishment of such a people's government will be the next great step in the advancement of democracy in this country. Such is the program and perspective of revolutionary socialism.

Although they are vociferous democrats with both a small and a big "d," the pragmatic liberals do not have any clear and consistent position on the relation of democracy to the incompatible economies of capitalism and socialism. All shadings of opinion on this crucial question are to be found among them. These range from the bourgeois identification of political liberty with free competition to recognition of the need for public ownership and a planned economy as the substructure for genuine democracy. At one time the liberals imply that a reformed capitalism is the best framework for democracy; in a more radical mood they will grant that political democracy is a sham without industrial democracy which requires workers' control over publicly owned means of production.

Dewey himself occasionally inclined to the latter alternative, although he made no lasting commitment to it. In any case, like his fellow liberals, he believed that the partnership of all classes, and not the triumph of the working class, would lift American democracy to a higher stage.

Dewey could not see any *necessary* connection between the economic foundations and the political system of American society. For him democracy as an ideal stood above property forms and contending classes. This separation of the state from society, and in particular the structure of the economy, is a typical misconception of liberalism.

C. Wright Mills pointed out that the "power elite" ruling this country has not needed to create any special conservative ideology. Its defenders have continued to use "the liberal rhetoric which is the common denominator of all proper and successful spokesmanship. . . . They have not had to confront any opposition based upon ideas which stand in challenging contrast to the liberal rhetoric which they employ as standard public relations" (*The Power Elite,* pp. 229–30).

Taking this retarded state of national political development as fixed and final, the liberals believe that Locke and Jefferson will forever keep Marx and Lenin from our shores, although Castro's Cuba is already only ninety miles away!

The pragmatists have given up traditional theology, timeless standards in morals, and eternal truths in their theory of knowledge. After having forsaken all these absolutes so dear to orthodox idealism, they hug all the more tightly one cherished abstraction. This is the ideal of an ethereal democracy as envisioned by Jefferson and Lincoln. Here metaphysics and mysticism make a last stand in pragmatic thought.

Dewey derived his basic stance toward democracy not, as he contended, from a scientific investigation of the history of society and a realistic analysis of American conditions, but rather from a tradition that was rooted in the mystical equality promised by the Christians. He accused the dualistic idealist philosophers of Greek and modern times of "operating with ideal fancies" instead of dealing with the given facts. Yet he committed the same error of metaphysical abstraction in the pivotal question of his whole philosophy: the origin, meaning, and application of democracy. He approached democracy not in its concrete manifestations throughout class society, but as an abstraction to be stuffed with the content he preferred to give it. Democracy to him was less a historical phenomenon than a secular religion.

As a humanist, Dewey had abandoned belief in God, Christ's divinity, and immortality. Yet he wanted to retain the gist of the religious experience, which he defined as the active relation of the ideal to the actual, by means of "a common faith" of the American people. The substance of this creed that he sought to substitute for the content of traditional religion was a disembodied, classless democracy.

By exposing the class nature of all the historical forms of democracy from ancient Greece to modern America, Marxism invades the sacred shrine of liberalism and tears the veil of mystery from the idol worshipped therein. It can then be seen to have the features of a gentleman of middle-class origins who has seen better days.

The liberals resent such vigorous iconoclasm toward their holy of holies. For them democracy is supposedly invested with a classless content. But this is myth, not history; metaphysics, not fact. The bourgeois embodiment of democracy is only one of the forms this type of government has assumed in the course of its career, and it is not the last. In the past, various forms of political democracy have grown out of commercial slave society, medieval trade and craftsmanship, and then out of bourgeois conditions. Now it has to find a new economic basis in public ownership, a firm social support in the working class, a new type of popular representation and rule in the workers' councils.

All this is rank heresy to the liberal mind, which cannot picture democracy in any higher form than it acquired through the bourgeois revolutions of yesteryear. Their outlook in politics is as restricted and retrograde as that of a natural scientist who rejects Einstein's relativity because of an inability to think of physical laws except in their Newtonian form, or of a mathematician who cannot accept any kind of geometry but Euclid's, or an economist who believes working people can earn their livelihood only by receiving wages from private owners of the means of production.

16

A New Road For
American Philosophy

The problems and prospects of American labor nowadays seem light-years removed from the current concerns of American philosophy. Will the mutual alienation of these two departments of our national life go on indefinitely? This would certainly be so if the conditions which produced their estrangement were to persist unchanged.

However, the remainder of this century promises to be even less calm than the first three-quarters, marked by wars, revolutions, counterrevolutions, and colonial uprisings. Multiple crises are maturing in American life. The American people are already gripped by unemployment and inflation rates rivaled only by the Great Depression. Hanging over them is the constant threat of new wars in a world armed to the teeth with nuclear weapons. America's ruling class is faced with the challenge of the workers' states and with recurrent emergencies that require it to shore up the sagging structure of international capitalism. The gap between its democratic pretensions and undemocratic practices, exposed in particular by the Vietnam war, CIA machinations abroad and systematic racism at home, can only widen as the international conflict between capital and labor intensifies and penetrates further into American industry itself.

The intellectual life of the country is bound to be affected by developments of such gravity, which are already of concern to every thoughtful person. How long, then, could philosophy, which is supposed to be the consummation of informed and scientific intelligence, remain oblivious to their impact and implications?

The professionals who study the thought process can, of course, continue to rationalize their indifference to burning social issues by pretending to be preoccupied with loftier subjects. Such snobbish self-deception shirks the primary task of philosophy, which is to come to grips with all areas of reality. To be consistent with its highest aims, to be truthful, to be a beneficial influence in the lives of people, philosophy must analyze the social reality within which it functions. American philosophy cannot turn away from the arena of class conflict without widening its separation from the most vital concerns of the American people and the fate of humanity itself.

There have been two different traditions in American thought on the relations between philosophy and social questions. One enjoins the philosopher to view the universe "from the standpoint of eternity" and not become too much absorbed in the passing show. The most extreme and exotic illustration of this other-worldly attitude was given by Santayana, who professed utter indifference to the kind of government and economy he lived under; bourgeois democracy, fascism, and communism were all one to him. Other academicians practice aloofness by burying themselves in technical and historical problems, letting the rest of the world go by. But however much they ignore politics and the class struggle in the name of pure reason and scientific research, these realities will not leave them alone. As the German scholars who believed they could ignore Hitlerism found out, the claws of reaction can reach into the most sheltered academic hideouts.

The opposite current, whether its program be reformist or revolutionary, seeks to establish close ties between the ideologists and the mass of participants in social and political movements. This vigorous tradition goes back to the first American revolution. In the days of Franklin, Jefferson, Adams, Paine, and Ethan Allen, generalized theory was more closely associated with political practice than it has been ever since.

In this century American philosophy came closest to the progressive trends in our political life through pragmatism. Dewey waged unrelenting war upon all the theorists of political indifferentism. He insisted: "Philosophy recovers itself when it ceases to be a device for dealing with the problems of philosophers, and becomes a method, cultivated by philosophers, for dealing with the problems of men."

However, the movement of Progressivism, based upon the

middle classes, has had its day. The social development of the United States over the past half century has witnessed the tightening of the economic and political domination of corporate wealth followed by the ascent of a union movement over twenty million strong. As these two titanic social forces have thrust forward, they have pushed the other strata more and more into the background. The interaction of monopoly capital and organized labor decides the most important issues, whereas the influence of intermediate groupings merely conditions them.

Nowadays the monopolist "power elite" is the powerhouse of reaction, as was the slaveholding class in the decades before the Civil War. The working class is the principal defender of political democracy and the driving force of social progress.

This situation poses the following question to philosophy, whether or not this is recognized by any of the professional philosophers: Can philosophy get out of its scholastic blind alley without consciously aligning itself with the progressive forces in our national life and divorcing itself from reaction and obscurantism?

The main body of academic philosophers can continue in its surrey with the fringe on top. But not all the critical minds among the younger generation will be satisfied with lagging so far behind the intellectual requirements of their own time.

American philosophy is compelled by the whole evolution of the twentieth-century world to find a way to league itself with the hosts of labor, on penalty of continued sterility. But that is only one side of the situation. The workers' movement itself needs the enlightenment and guidance of a scientific philosophy in order to overcome its present handicaps. This two-sided problem now confronts the most progressive elements in both the field of philosophy and the ranks of labor.

American philosophy has arrived at a crossroads along with American labor. It cannot continue to mark time at the pragmatic stage. If it is not to stagnate and retrogress, it has to find a new road.

This road has been marked out by the disintegration of world capitalism and by the reactionary course of U.S. imperialism, which are bound to provoke a crisis of perspective in the American labor movement. The ideological quandary of the working class runs parallel to the quest for a new orientation in philosophical circles. Both have been engendered by the new demands of America's development.

Although it was ushered in under the sign of domestic reaction, the present half century has already begun to see the revolutionary influences that girdle the globe more and more extended into the home grounds of American imperialism. The progressive forces of our country will require a broader historical outlook and a better method of thought to cope with these radical changes. The theoreticians of the oncoming generation will be called upon to supply these. Where shall they turn for sustenance and inspiration?

None of the popular philosophies of the past will prove adequate to the needs of the revolutionary period ahead. The best of these, pragmatism, was incapable of offering labor a proper long-range goal or dealing satisfactorily with the major social crises of the first three-quarters of the twentieth century. Can it do any better with the deeper crises in store for capitalism in the last quarter?

At an earlier time of national need, in the second half of the eighteenth century, the heralds and leaders of the independence movement drew their philosophies and political ideas from abroad. The developing American radicalism will likewise have to import its theory from the more philosophically advanced nations in other parts of the world—not England and France this time, but the Germany of Marx and Engels and the Russia of the Bolsheviks.

What would be thought of airplane pilots who refused to use the latest technical devices for navigation perfected elsewhere, and preferred to steer their craft "by guess and by God"? The course of American labor is now being steered in no less primitive a manner, even though superior instruments are at its disposal. Without the aid of Marxism it is thrown back upon day-to-day experience and rule-of-thumb procedures; it has no science of society, no political guidelines, no philosophic method to go by.

The new problems of the new age cannot be handled with the obsolete ideas and hit-or-miss methods of the horse and buggy days. The provincial pragmatists who believe that the United States will always find its own special path of development apart from the rest of the world don't know wha. the score is in this epoch of transition from capitalism to socialism.

American capitalism, as the mainstay, manager and master of a decaying social order, has dragged American labor, whether it likes it or not (and whether it knows it or not), into the vortex of the world maelstrom. American labor can no longer get its bearings unless it acquires a systematic scientific conception of the historical process, one that explains this novel situation and its own place and part in it. Fortunately, such a theory does not have to be improvised. It already exists in the doctrines of Marxism.

It is widely argued that Marxism and its twentieth-century extensions, Leninism and Trotskyism, have little or no relevance to American life because they originated from European conditions and culture. This appeal to national prejudice has no historical validity. Most of the institutions and ideas dear to our patriots, from Christianity to capitalism, have been borrowed from the Old World.

Even our population was largely drawn from across the Atlantic. With them, along with many other useful things, came the sciences, from mathematics to physics. More recently, before the atom bomb could be fabricated here, much of the necessary nuclear theory was created by such European scientists as Einstein, Fermi, Bohr, and others. Philosophy itself is not a native product. Pragmatism, the most indigenous of our schools of thought, was an offshoot of English empiricism adapted to American circumstances.

Moreover, the time for parochial national philosophies has passed, along with the period of insulated national states. Today there can no more be a purely national philosophy, as Dewey tried to devise, than a purely national physics or sociology. The efforts to produce one would turn out to be as hopelessly reactionary as Hitler and Mussolini's attempts to organize an autarchic national capitalist economy or Stalin's program of socialism in one country.

Methods of thought are as cosmopolitan as methods of production or union organization. They are transportable from the place of their origin to other lands when the need for their introduction becomes urgent, regardless of previous national ignorance and indifference. The spread of socialist ideas throughout the colonial countries demonstrates this.

The opponents of Marxism utilize this latter fact to buttress their contention that Marxism as a philosophical instrument is especially or solely suited for backward peoples. In reality, it is most applicable in the most advanced countries.

Marxism is not a new philosophy; indeed, it is older than pragmatism. But it must be admitted that in the century since its birth it has never secured a firm foothold in American thought. It has been rejected as an exotic and irrelevant system of ideas even by the best representatives of the Progressive school, like Parrington, Beard, and Veblen—who have not hesitated, however, to borrow whatever they could use from its treasury.

The latter-day pragmatists argue that American life and thought have gone beyond Marxism. The philosophy of socialism, they say, may have been proper for less developed countries or justified by the conditions of the nineteenth century. But it has been outmoded by the progress of American society.

This is a puerile and superficial estimate. *The truth is: American life and thought have neither bypassed nor gone ahead of Marxism; they are only now beginning to grow up to it!* The belief that Marxism has become antiquated and inapplicable to the peculiar conditions of the United States only testifies to the theoretical and political immaturity of American life.

Pragmatism claims to be untrammeled by past conditions and to leave the door open to any possibilities. But when it comes to basic problems of social development the pragmatic liberals are so enthralled by America's past that they take a blinkered view of future possibilities.

Because the United States has been so powerful, prosperous, and preeminent, they believe that it will always be so privileged; because democratic traditions are so deep-rooted, they believe they will remain invulnerable to the assaults of capitalist reaction; because the workers have so long been captive to the two-party system, they assume that any independent political course by labor is out of the question; because the socialist movement has been so dwarfish, they deny its potential for becoming a gigantic force. Finally, because pragmatism has ruled the roost in their lifetime, Marxism has no prospect of dislodging it.

Since all of the developments mentioned above have arisen elsewhere in the contemporary world, no exceptional prevision is required to anticipate their eventual appearance on the American scene as well. Nonetheless, the pragmatists proceed on the tacit supposition that whatever has prevailed up to now in American life will persist indefinitely. Despite their alleged receptivity to innovation, the pragmatists fail to see that changing conditions and new alignments of forces in the world and the nation will undermine worm-eaten institutions and familiar ideas, creating a demand for radically new departures in politics and philosophy.

World history is only now setting the stage for the large-scale entry of socialist ideas into American life and culture. Hitherto, for reasons beyond anyone's control, the doctrines of scientific socialism have been accepted and cultivated by a very small fraction of Americans. By and large there has been a split, and even opposition, between the organizations and concerns of the masses and the advocates of Marxism. This has been mirrored in the divorce between the Marxists and the mainstream of American scholarship.

With some exceptions, Marxism and the mass movement have in large measure developed apart and at odds with one another. Both have suffered from this separation. The main body of the masses have limped along empirically without the help of scientific socialism, while the inescapable isolation of the Marxists as a tiny minority within the mass movement has prevented them from demonstrating the inherent power of their ideas.

Radical circles recurrently talk about the need to Americanize Marxism. This task has to be carried through by applying the methods and ideas of scientific socialism to the problems of American development in all fields.

In philosophy, this cannot be done without a thoroughgoing critical appraisal of instrumentalism, Marxism's predecessor as the most progressive school of American thought. The reckoning with Deweyism will have to be performed in a dialectical way, taking into account its merits and positive accomplishments as well as its outmoded character.

Fundamentally, pragmatism is incompatible with dialectical materialism; their methods and doctrines cannot be reconciled. The theory of revolutionary socialism cannot be assimilated in any ideological mishmash with the school of liberal reform. It is imperative to choose between these two opposing outlooks. Marxism has declared war to the finish not only against all feudal and bourgeois philosophies but also against all petty-bourgeois modes of thought—and pragmatism is quintessentially petty-bourgeois in all its fundamental aspects.

At the same time, pragmatism cannot be condemned as utterly wrong and worthless and thrown out *en bloc*. It was not a philosophical aberration foisted upon the nation by thinking representatives of the middle classes. It arose from tendencies deeply rooted in the history and habits of the American people. It was, like bourgeois democracy itself, a historically inescapable and progressive phase in the growth of American views and institutions.

As a mixture of tendencies reflecting advanced as well as immature and regressive currents of America's social development, it contained numerous valid and valuable insights amidst its errors and structural inadequacies. Pragmatism performed important services in weakening the grip of clericalism, throwing off traditional idealism and the worst vices of academic rationalism, and holding up scientific practice as the model of knowledge. It helped bring philosophy, which had been the preserve of the professorial caste, remote from popular concerns, into closer communion with the needs of everyday life. It sought to bring philosophy down to earth, to orient it toward the solution of the social problems of the American people.

In formulating the demands of the plebeians, the instrumentalist intellectuals seized upon some of the healthiest trends in American life. The high place Deweyism accorded to technique; its emphasis upon the value of conquering nature for the sake of increasing humanity's social powers and common wealth; its stress upon the primacy of practice in human life and thought; its insistence that ideas verify their truth and worth by submitting to the test of practical consequences; its utilitarianism which, in its boldest representatives, verged upon materialism; its evolutionary optimism; its disdain for absolutes of any kind; its democratism; its demand that philosophy participate in social improvement—all these contributions of instrumentalism are permanent acquisitions of American thought.

To be sure, none of these points is alien or unknown to Marxism. Scientific socialism had either already incorporated them into its outlook or can easily assimilate them and, in fact, give more rounded expression to them.

Thus, despite their essential opposition, instrumentalism has certain elements and inclinations which can provide a bridge toward dialectical materialism. Indeed, at the limits of its growth instrumentalism tended to negate itself and seek an alliance on the left with Marxism. This caused some misguided intellectuals like Sidney Hook and Corliss Lamont to confuse and identify the two, and even to subordinate dialectical materialism to Deweyism.

The radicalism inherent in instrumentalism arises out of its demand that general ideas prove their validity in social practice.

However, this requirement can be fully realized only through the scientifically guided revolutionary movement of the working class. Thus it is possible under certain circumstances for pragmatists to pass over, by way of an inner revolution, to Marxist positions, just as advanced sections of the labor movement can, through the lessons of their own experience, break with traditional empiricism and become Marxist. How firmly they hold on to their new convictions is another matter.

The Americanization of Marxism is a two-way process. Not only does Marxism have to be naturalized by its application to special American conditions; it is no less necessary to "Marxize" the activity of labor's vanguard and the mentality of the intellectuals associated with it.

Pragmatism, speaking through John Dewey, acquired its sustained influence by expressing the demands of the plebeian forces at a specific stage of national development. The key role in this process was performed by militant middle-class intellectuals. Through pragmatism they subjected philosophy to their class needs, using it to mediate between the ruling plutocracy above and the working class below.

It is now the turn of the militants among the working masses, and the task of their cooperating intellectuals, to take the lead in the further development of the country's philosophy as well as its politics and economy. The primacy of the middle class and its ideologists can no longer be maintained in the decisive departments of American life.

The struggle to displace plutocratic and petty-bourgeois influences in favor of working-class forces is the dominant movement of our time on a world scale. It has to be conducted on the ideological as well as the political and industrial fronts. To combine all these into a single integrated process is a job that cannot be carried through except by an organized vanguard imbued with the ideas of scientific socialism.

The further course of the anticapitalist struggle in the United States will tend to reverse many things. It will call for a new type of leadership which can overcome the cleavage between theory and practice that has held American labor back for so long. As the banner-bearers of socialism penetrate more deeply into the thick of the working masses, their activity will have to be permeated with a greater thoughtfulness. The magnificent endowments for action and organization shown by the workers will have to be reinforced and rounded out by solid theory, firm class principles, and a grand historical vista.

The deficiencies of earlier American experience and the bad habits issuing from them can be corrected only by learning the value of scientific principles in political practice. The theoretical achievements of European culture and labor codified in the teachings of Marxism can compensate for the underdevelopment of our own labor movement in this respect. What an unbeatable combination can emerge from the fusion of scientific socialism with the vigor and inventiveness characteristic of the American workers!

All will benefit from their mutual interpenetration. The labor movement will be enlightened by a clearer conception of its tasks and goals. American philosophy will be rescued from stagnation and lifted to a higher stage. Marxism itself will receive fresh nourishment and amplification, for, although based upon a definite and tested body of principles, it is not a revelation imparted once and for all by a few geniuses. It is an evolving view of world development which grows and widens along with the discoveries of the sciences and the advances of the world social movement that sustains it.

In the 1930s Trotsky predicted that the dawn of a new independent class movement of the American workers would also witness a resurgence of genuine Marxism. "In this too, America will in a few jumps catch up with Europe and outdistance it. Progressive technique and a progressive social structure will pave their own way in the sphere of doctrine. The best theoreticians of Marxism will appear on American soil. Marx will become the mentor of the advanced American workers," he wrote (*Marxism in Our Time,* p. 38).

How is this forecast, still unfulfilled, likely to be realized? Though they do not proceed simultaneously or harmoniously and are not sustained by the same social forces, American labor and American philosophy will have to converge toward the same ends. Just as pragmatism was bound up with middle-class Progressivism, so the future of American philosophy is linked with the struggles of the labor movement.

This imposes certain obligations upon philosophy. It will have to move out of the university halls and become active in union halls. The musty atmosphere of stale technical controversies will have to be cleansed by permitting the purer currents of a materialist humanism to circulate in the classrooms. Through

Marxism, philosophy can be placed at the service of the workers in their strivings for better organization, enlightenment, and emancipation.

Philosophy in this country has too long been the property of pedants. It must—and will—become the guide of the people, popular in the best sense of the word, not by debasing itself to vulgar tastes or profiteering parasitism, but by helping to raise inquiring minds to the level of a scientific understanding of the world around them.

In doing so, it will, incidentally, for the first time realize the promise held out by pragmatism itself. Dewey tried to take philosophy out of the libraries and lecture rooms and make it an instrument for better education, for the enlightenment of the people, for the reform of our social relations. This progressive aim belongs to the finest traditions of our country's intellectual activity; Marxism will build upon it.

But Dewey's outlook induced him to search in the wrong places and among the wrong forces to carry through this job. The leaders of America up to now have been mostly clergymen, lawyers, businessmen, and generals. Dewey expected that the educated middle classes—and their educators—would, on behalf of the people, take over the leadership, oust the monopolists from power, and remake American life. But the staffs of the schools and colleges cannot furnish the forces needed for so immense an assignment. They are not rooted in the productive apparatus and not driven en masse to oppose the ruling class. As a social grouping they can follow but they cannot give the lead.

The Technocrats saw the engineer, exalted above the petty strife of capital and labor, as the magician-hero who would release industry from bondage to money and transform it into an automated, planned economy run for everyone's benefit. Liberals hoped that leadership would come from the laboratories, as Sinclair Lewis predicted in his novel *Martin Arrowsmith*. But the advent of nuclear weapons has demonstrated how little can be expected from this quarter. The best of the physicists stand aghast at the cruelly contradictory consequences of their own work and their total lack of control over it. In *The Bulletin of the Atomic Scientists* they can do no more than register their protest against the misuse of their achievements by the militarists and monopolists. But by themselves they are helpless to organize any movement to combat them.

The same is true of other professions. Teachers, scientists, writers, artists, and intellectuals of all types can make valuable contributions to the movement for emancipating America from capitalism. But they cannot provide the basic forces to lead the great upheaval in the making. The bulk of the fighting forces will come not from the intermediate elements of the population, but from the lower depths of present-day society, from what Jack London called "the social pit."

The forces creative of the future will come from the factories, the mines, the transportation facilities, the mills, the fields, from the slum neighborhoods and the ghettos, from the ranks of the most exploited and oppressed. The industrial workers at the head of all the oppressed will be the trailblazers to the future. And the philosophy of that future can only be scientific socialism, which formulates their aspirations for a secure, cooperative, and peaceful world and can direct their footsteps toward that goal.

Marxism is the only philosophy in the world, and the only world outlook, that systematically seeks to connect itself with the toiling masses. Its conscious program and aims coincide with the strivings of the working class for a better life. From their side, the most forward-looking forces among the insurgent masses instinctively strive to attain a comprehension of their place and prospects in the march of events. As Cuba has demonstrated, this inclines them toward the positions of Marxism and the acceptance of its approaches and conclusions.

The juncture of Marxism with the labor movement is a worldwide tendency. It has already taken place in other countries at critical turning points in their history. But the manner of their coming together is extremely irregular; it has varied widely from country to country and from one generation to another. It happened in Germany as early as the 1880s—although the West German social democrats suffered a relapse in the 1950s when they eliminated Marxism from their official program. Scientific socialism won the day in Russia in the first two decades of the twentieth century Its ideas, however disfigured, spread through China after the Second World War and are now penetrating one colonial country after another. Socialist ideas have likewise had a tremendous expansion in Japan since the end of World War II.

The United States is the most primitive and laggard of all the industrialized countries in this respect. This resistance to Marxism, coupled with a clinging to pragmatism, expresses the prolonged subjection of the American mind to essentially bourgeois modes of thought.

No prejudice is more powerful in this country than the illusion that the United States has followed a unique path of evolution and will continue to have a self-centered national development fundamentally different from that of less favored sectors of the globe. It follows that the inner experiences of other countries and continents seem to furnish no anticipations of America's future and very little of decisive importance for Americans to learn about their own prospects. This arrogant outlook upon the history and destiny of the American people, which has been cultivated by the liberal intellectuals, is shared by all classes.

It is true that American history has been marked by immense peculiarities. Indeed, as we have tried to show, the predominance of pragmatism is a philosophical sign and summary of them. But it should not be overlooked that all these peculiarities have been located within the framework of the world capitalist system and its evolution. North America was discovered, invaded, explored, and settled as a result of the rise of capitalism in Western Europe and its expansion overseas. Even such an anomalous institution as Black slavery was planted on American soil as an agricultural branch of commercial capitalist enterprise, to grow staples for its world market. The rise of merchant capitalism was the principal motive force behind the War of Independence in the eighteenth century; the impetuous rise of industrial capitalism set the stage for the Civil War in the nineteenth century. The size and vigor of its multinational monopolist enterprises endows the United States with its predominance in the world today.

If the American nation has been an integral part of the expansion of the capitalist system on a world scale from its early days, and the ultimate beneficiary of its conquests, then how can it escape the effects of its contraction and decline? The most that can be realistically expected is that the path and forms of its participation in the disintegration of capitalist civilization will take on distinctive features conditioned by America's history, its special social structure and cultural characteristics, and its key role in world affairs.

Of course, if the United States were somehow predestined to pursue a course outside the struggle between capitalist and socialist forces that dominates the rest of this planet, then the main lines of its ideological development would be unique. But it is up to its neck in world affairs. Its further economic and social evolution will be even more compulsively determined by the ill fortunes of world capitalism in the future than it was by capitalist prosperity in the past. These developments in turn will set their stamp on the next stage of philosophical thought.

Thus the fundamental problems that American philosophy is called upon to solve in its further development are not posed by the random speculations and purely individual inclinations of isolated thinkers. They are primarily brought forward by the deepest and most urgent demands of national progress, which are in turn an outgrowth of international conditions. They come to the fore in response to the need of the people, or the most progressive and dynamic elements among them, for a superior, more scientific theoretical outlook.

The crisis in American philosophy comes about as a result of the entire preceding course of American history, the social contradictions shaking and shaping the nation, and the requirements of the next stage of evolution. The issues at stake are not merely of theoretical interest to scholars and intellectuals; they concern the entire people and its constituent classes.

Are the money barons or the workers to be the leaders of America? Is shaky bourgeois democracy to be supplanted by workers' democracy before it yields to reactionary dictatorship? How can the oppressed nationalities achieve self-determination? Will capitalism maintain its stranglehold over the resources and lives of our people or will we go forward to the building of socialism together with the rest of humanity?

These momentous questions facing the United States are first of all social and political questions. But they must also find their formulation and resolution in the field of general ideas. Just as Deweyism was the ideological instrument of Progressivism, so the coming American philosophy must strive to perform the same tasks in a more conscious and comprehensive manner for the cause of labor's emancipation through socialism.

It may be objected that neither the philosophers in the universities nor the official heads of the unions are disposed to effect such an alliance or even see its necessity. This is so. If gradualism governed the march of history, and labor remained as fixed and laggard in its thinking as philosophy has in its practice, many generations would have to pass before the two could approach each other and come abreast of the tasks of the times.

However, this inherited backwardness is not a permanent and irreparable obstacle. From its birth the American people has shown itself able to take sudden leaps in which obstacles were

cleared and distances covered that appeared insuperable before-
hand. American imperialism, which stayed behind the European
powers for decades, has undergone an explosive worldwide
expansion since 1940. Our labor movement, too, lagged far
behind European organization and the needs of the industrial
workers until its mighty surge forward during the 1930s.

Leaps of this magnitude have not been and will not be confined
to economics and politics. They also take place in the consciousness of the most advanced social forces. The idea of independence
from Great Britain, nursed by only a few rebels, swept the
colonists in a few months when the time came in 1775–76. The
same was true of the abolition of the slave power eighty-five
years later. The need for the conjunction of philosophy and labor
through the doctrines of scientific socialism will force its way to
recognition under similar revolutionary circumstances.

The regenerated movement of radicalism will enlist the services
and require the collaboration of intellectuals and workers of a
different type, a type not common—but not unknown—in this
country before: on one hand, intellectuals who place themselves
unreservedly at the service of revolutionary labor and the
oppressed nationalities and bring to them not the leavings of
bourgeois theorizing but the fertile seeds of scientific socialism;
on the other hand, workers who have come to understand the
necessity for guiding their activities by a correct method. The
creators of our wealth, the operators of our machines, the builders
and defenders of our unions, and especially the militants among
the Blacks, Chicanos, and Puerto Ricans are the ones who will
sweep away the rotting old order and construct a new one. They
cannot do this work without the best tools and the most efficient
weapons in all fields of struggle. They will find these nowhere
else but in the traditions and teachings of revolutionary socialism.

Not least among these is the conception of a multiracial
revolutionary workers' party, internationalist in outlook and
program, as the indispensable political instrument for uniting all
the progressive forces in the nation to combat capitalism and
realize socialism.

For these reasons the next great step in the advancement of
American labor ought to coincide with a blossoming of socialist
thought which will help lift that movement onto a higher plateau
of theoretical insight and world-historical outlook. From being
the least oriented to theory among the industrialized countries,

American labor can through its Marxist contingent become one of the most highly developed.

Today in industry the American workers wield the best tools and make many of the finest machines in the world. They have created the largest and most solidly organized unions. They must now equip themselves with equally superior weapons of thought in order to displace the magnates of capitalism and go forward to reconstruct America.

The prerequisite for this is the firm fusion of scientific socialism with the independent class movement of the workers. As Ferdinand Lassalle observed at an early point in the life of the German labor movement: "When science and the workers, those two opposite poles of society, shall embrace, they shall crush in their arms all social obstacles."

Bibliography

Adams, George P., and Montague, William P., eds. *Contemporary American Philosophy: Personal Statements*. New York: Macmillan, 1930.

Ayer, A.J. *Philosophical Essays*. London: Macmillan, 1954.

Bacon, Francis. *The Works of Francis Bacon*. Ed. by Spedding, Ellis, and Heath. Boston: Houghton Mifflin, 1857.

Beard, Charles A., and Beard, Mary R. *The Rise of American Civilization*. New York: Macmillan, 1944.

Berle, A.A. *Economic Power and the Free Society*. New York: Fund for the Republic, 1957.

Bourne, Randolph S. *Untimely Papers*. New York: B.W. Huebsch, 1919.

Burnett, Charles T. *Hyde of Bowdoin*. Boston: Houghton Mifflin, 1931.

Cohen, Morris. *American Thought: A Critical Sketch*. Glencoe, Ill.: Free Press, 1954.

Cornforth, Maurice. *Science Versus Idealism*. London: Lawrence & Wishart, 1955.

Counts, George S. *Dare the School Build a New Social Order?* New York: John Day, 1932.

Dunham, Barrows. *Giant in Chains*. Boston: Little, Brown, 1953.

Dykhuizen, George. *The Life and Mind of John Dewey*. Carbondale and Edwardsville: Southern Illinois University Press, 1973.

Edwards, Paul, ed. *The Encyclopedia of Philosophy*. 4 vols. New York: Collier-Macmillan, 1972.

Feldman, W.T. *The Philosophy of John Dewey*. Baltimore: Johns Hopkins Press, 1934.

Feuer, Lewis S., ed. *Basic Writings in Politics and Philosophy,* by Karl Marx and Friedrich Engels. Garden City, N.Y.: Doubleday, 1959.

Gramsci, Antonio. *Writings*. Trans. and introd. by Quintin Hoare and Geoffrey Nowell-Smith. London: Lawrence & Wishart, 1970.

Greeley, Horace. *Hints Toward Reform*. New York and Boston: Fowlers & Wells, 1857.

Harris, Marvin. *The Rise of Anthropological Theory*. New York: Crowell, 1968.

Hook, Sidney. *Reason, Social Myths and Democracy*. New York: John Day, 1940.

Hume, David. *Enquiries Concerning the Human Understanding*. Ed. by L.A. Shelby-Bigge. London: Oxford University Press, 1966.

James, William. *Essays in Radical Empiricism*. New York: Longmans, Green, 1958.

———. *Essays on Pragmatism*. New York: Hafner, 1948.

———. *The Meaning of Truth*. New York: Longmans, Green, 1927.

———. *Pragmatism*. New York: Longmans, Green, 1907.

———. "Philosophical Conceptions and Practical Results." In William James,

Collected Essays and Reviews, ed. by Ralph Barton Perry. New York: Longmans, Green, 1920.

————. *The Will to Believe and Other Essays in Popular Philosophy.* London: Longmans, Green, 1897.

Kadushin, Charles. *The American Intellectual Elite.* Boston: Little, Brown, 1974.

Lamont, Corliss, ed. *Dialogue on George Santayana.* New York: Horizon, 1959.

Lenin, V.I. *Materialism and Empirio-Criticism.* In *Collected Works,* vol. 14. Moscow: Progress, 1962.

————. *Philosophical Notebooks.* In *Collected Works,* vol. 38. Moscow: Progress, 1961.

Locke, John. *An Essay Concerning Human Understanding.* London: Routledge & Sons, n.d.

Lovejoy, A.O. *The Thirteen Pragmatisms and Other Essays.* Baltimore: Johns Hopkins Press, 1963.

McKeon, Richard, ed. *The Basic Works of Aristotle.* New York: Random House, 1941.

Mead, George H. *Movements of Thought in the Nineteenth Century.* Chicago: University of Chicago Press, 1936.

————. "The Philosophical Basis of Ethics." *International Journal of Ethics,* vol. 18 (1908).

Millikan, Robert A. *The Autobiography of Robert A. Millikan.* New York: Prentice-Hall, 1950.

Mills, C. Wright. *The Power Elite.* New York: Oxford University Press, 1959.

Morris, Lloyd R. *William James: The Message of a Modern Mind.* New York: Charles Scribner's Sons, 1950.

Muelder, Walter G., and Sears, Lawrence. *The Development of American Philosophy.* Boston: Houghton Mifflin, 1960.

Mumford, Lewis. *The Golden Day.* New York: Boni & Liveright, 1926.

Oakeshott, Michael. *Experience and Its Modes.* Cambridge: Cambridge University Press, 1966.

Paine, Thomas. *The Complete Writings of Thomas Paine.* Ed. by Philip S. Foner. New York: Citadel, 1945.

Parker, Theodore. *The World of Matter and the Spirit of Man.* Boston: American Unitarian Association, 1907.

Peirce, Charles S. "How to Make Our Ideas Clear." In *Collected Papers of Charles Sanders Peirce,* vol. 5. Cambridge, Mass.: Harvard University Press, 1965.

Perry, Ralph Barton. *The Thought and Character of William James.* Boston: Little, Brown, 1935.

Riesman, David. *Constraint and Variety in American Education.* Lincoln: University of Nebraska Press, 1956.

Rorty, Amelie, ed. *Pragmatic Philosophy.* Garden City, N.Y.: Doubleday, 1966.

Rosenfield, Leonora Cohen. *Portrait of a Philosopher: Morris R. Cohen in Life and Letters.* New York: Harcourt, Brace & World, 1962.

Rucker, E.D. *The Chicago Pragmatists.* Minneapolis: University of Minnesota Press, 1969.

Rugg, Harold O. *Foundations for American Education.* Yonkers, N.Y.: World, 1947.

Russell, Bertrand. *A History of Western Philosophy.* New York: Simon & Schuster, 1945.

Santayana, George. *Character and Opinion in the United States.* New York: Norton, 1967.

Schilpp, Paul A., ed. *The Philosophy of John Dewey.* Evanston and Chicago: Northwestern University Press, 1939.

Schlesinger, Arthur M., Jr. *A Thousand Days.* Boston: Houghton Mifflin, 1965.

Schneider, Herbert W. *A History of American Philosophy.* New York: Columbia University Press, 1946.

Sellars, Roy Wood. *The Philosophy of Physical Realism.* New York: Russell & Russell, 1966.

Sinclair, Upton. *The Goose-Step.* Los Angeles: the author, 1923.
———. *The Goslings.* Pasadena: the author, 1924.
Smith, T.V. *A Non-Existent Man: An Autobiography.* Austin: University of Texas Press, 1962.
Sward, Keith. *The Legend of Henry Ford.* New York: Rinehart, 1948.
Thayer, H.S. *Meaning and Action: A Critical History of Pragmatism.* Indianapolis and New York: Bobbs-Merrill, 1968.
Trotsky, Leon. *In Defense of Marxism.* 2nd ed. New York: Pathfinder, 1973.
———. *Marxism in Our Time.* New York: Pathfinder, 1970.
Wells, Harry K. *Pragmatism: Philosophy of Imperialism.* New York: International, 1954.
White, Morton G. *The Origin of Dewey's Instrumentalism.* New York: Columbia University Press, 1943.
———. *Science and Sentiment in America.* New York: Oxford University Press, 1973.

Works by Dewey Cited in the Text

A Common Faith. New Haven: Yale University Press, 1934.
Creative Intelligence: Essays in the Pragmatic Attitude. (With others.) New York: Holt, 1917.
Essays in Experimental Logic. New York: Dover, n.d. (Reprint of 1916 ed. pub. by University of Chicago Press.)
Ethics. (With James Hayden Tufts.) New York: Holt, 1908.
Experience and Nature. New York: Dover, 1958. (Reprint of 1929 2nd ed. pub. by Norton.)
The Influence of Darwin on Philosophy and Other Essays in Contemporary Thought. New York: Holt, 1910.
Intelligence in the Modern World: John Dewey's Philosophy. Ed. by Joseph Ratner. New York: Random House, 1939.
Knowing and the Known. (With Arthur F. Bentley.) Boston: Beacon, 1949.
Liberalism and Social Action. New York: G.P. Putnam's Sons, 1935.
Logic: The Theory of Inquiry. New York: Holt, 1938.
On Experience, Nature and Freedom. Ed. by Richard J. Bernstein. Indianapolis and New York: Bobbs-Merrill, 1960.
Philosophy and Civilization. New York: Minton, Balch, 1931.
The Quest for Certainty: A Study of the Relation of Knowledge and Action. New York: G.P. Putnam's Sons, 1960. (Originally pub. 1929 by Minton, Balch.)
Reconstruction in Philosophy. New York: New American Library, 1950. (Enlarged ed. of 1948, originally pub. by Beacon.)
The School and Society. 2nd ed. Chicago: University of Chicago Press, 1915.
Studies in Logical Theory. Chicago: University of Chicago Press, 1903.
"The Development of American Pragmatism." In *Studies in the History of Ideas,* vol. 2. Ed. by Department of Philosophy, Columbia University. New York: Columbia University Press, 1925.
"Education and Social Change." Social Frontier, vol. 3 (May 1937).
"From Absolutism to Experimentalism." In *Contemporary American Philosophy,* vol. 2. Ed. by George P. Adams and William P. Montague. New York: Macmillan, 1930.
"My Pedagogic Creed." *School Journal,* vol. 54 (January 1897). Reprinted in *John Dewey on Education.* Ed. by Reginald D. Archambault. New York: Modern Library, 1964.
"Nature in Experience." *Philosophical Review,* vol. 49 (1940).
"Social as a Category." *Monist,* vol. 28 (April 1928).
"Some Implications of Anti-Intellectualism." *Journal of Philosophy,* vol. 7 (September 1910).

"William James as Empiricist." In *In Commemoration of William James, 1842-1942.* New York: AMS Press, 1942.

For Further Study of Dewey

The most complete and detailed listing of all Dewey's known writings is the *Guide to the Works of John Dewey,* edited by Jo Ann Boydston (Carbondale and Edwardsville: Southern Illinois University Press, 1970). This volume contains almost a thousand items of his work arranged in twelve categories, each section introduced with an essay by a Dewey specialist.

There is an earlier chronological study by M.H. Thomas, entitled *John Dewey: A Centennial Bibliography* (Chicago: University of Chicago Press, 1962).

The Philosophy of John Dewey, edited by Paul A. Schilpp (Evanston, Ill.: Northwestern University Press, 1939), includes an exhaustive bibliography of Dewey's writings from April 1892 to October 1939.

The Early Works of John Dewey, 1882-1898 is being issued in five volumes by Southern Illinois University Press. This will be the first part of the projected *Collected Works* under the same auspices.

The Life and Mind of John Dewey, by George Dykhuizen (Southern Illinois University Press, 1974) is the first full-scale biography since Dewey's death in 1952.

Over the decades hundreds of books and articles have been published on various aspects of Dewey's thought. Extensive references will be found in *Pragmatic Philosophy,* edited by Amelie Rorty (Garden City, N.Y.: Doubleday, 1966) and in *Meaning and Action: A Critical History of Pragmatism,* by H.S. Thayer (Indianapolis and New York: Bobbs-Merrill, 1968).

Index

Mead, George Herbert, 73, 125, 162-63, 191
Metaphysical thought, 115. *See also* Idealism
Mexico, 221
Michigan, University of, 52, 58, 116
Middle class, 144; Dewey as voice of, 40-41, 60, 61, 220, 268, 285; and democracy, 285 (*see also* Democracy); as force for change, 303-4; and inconsistency of pragmatism, 276, 280-81; and Progressivism, 34, 35-36, 38, 78-79, 82; and workers, 273, 277
Midwest, 34, 36. *See also* "Chicago school"
Mill, John Stuart, 59, 62, 118, 119, 156
Millikan, Robert A., 29, 48
Mills, C. Wright, 206-7, 209, 290-91
Monopoly, 36, 37, 264. *See also* Capitalism
Morality. *See* Ethics
Morris, George S., 58
Moscow Trials, 53, 271, 274, 277
Mumford, Lewis, 80, 262
Mussolini, 216, 297

The Nation, 260
Naturalism, 112, 120
Nature: and experience, 77, 86-88; materialism on, 113; primary and secondary characteristics of, 103. *See also* Being; Object; Reality
Necessity. *See* Determinacy; Dewey on probability; Laws
Negation and affirmation, 140-42, 147-49
Neo-Hegelians, 118
New Deal, 233, 262
New Harmony, Ind., 222
The New Republic, 260
New School, 53
Newton, Isaac, and Newtonian system, 100, 101, 102, 148-49
Nixon, Richard M., 17, 272

Object: and object of knowledge, 188-92; and subject, 168, 169. *See also* Experience; Knowledge
Ontology. *See* Being
Oppressed nationalities, 306, 307. *See also* Blacks; Chicanos; Puerto Ricans
Ostwald, Wilhelm, 63
Owen, Robert, 222

Pacifism, 262. *See also* Dewey and war; Peace plans
Paine, Thomas, 24, 43, 208, 294
Palmer, George Herbert, 48
Papini, Giovanni, 67
Parker, Francis, 226, 230
Parker, Theodore, 46, 47, 284
Parrington, Vernon L., 40
Particular, the, 138-39
Peace plans, 215-17
Peirce, Charles R., 50, 57, 67-68, 138, 177-78, 193
People's Lobby, 261
Perry, R. B., 71
Pestalozzi, Johann, 221
Petty bourgeoisie. *See* Middle class
Philosophy: American, development of, 11-12, 282-85, 297, 306; and economic system, 8-9; and labor movement, 293, 295, 302-3, 306; profession of, 50-52, 53; and religion, 42-43, 283, 284; and science, 166, 167, 188-89, 201; social role of, 200-203, 254-55, 294
Piatt, Donald, 82, 191
Plan to Outlaw War, 216-17
Plato, 128, 165
Plekhanov, Georgi, 273
Poincaré, Jules, 63
Populism, 35, 36. *See also* Progressivism
Positivism, 62-64
"Power elite," 209, 290-91
Practice: as purpose of knowledge, 193; as spur to inquiry, 194-95; as test of ideas, 195, 266; and theory, 156, 166, 167, 192-97
Pragmatism, 7, 17. *See also* Dewey; Empiricism; Instrumentalism; Liberalism; Progressivism
—and American life, 12, 18
—on being, 76
—as bourgeois ideology, 259
—and capitalism, 54, 246, 268
—on contradiction, 75
—in crisis of 1930s, 261-62
—and democracy, 24, 258, 291
—as dogma, 288
—durability of, 266-68, 287-88
—and empiricism, 55-58
—on experience, 168-71
—inconsistency of, 82-83, 165, 276, 280-81
—and indeterminism, 155
—on knowledge, 56-58
—and liberalism, 8, 260

Socialist Party (U.S.), 271. *See also* Thomas, Norman
Socialist Workers Party, 274
Social studies, teaching of, 233-34
Society: American, flexibility of, 30-31; instrumentalist theory of, 66, 265; pluralistic view of, 205-9. *See also* Classes; "Power elite"
Socrates, 243
Sophists, 243
Soviet Union, 37, 145, 221, 241-42, 246, 258, 259-60, 262. *See also* Russian revolution
Spanish-American War, 35, 215
Spencer, Herbert, 48, 62-63, 64, 244
Spinoza, 92, 124, 176
Stalinism, 145, 297; identified with Marxism, 267-68, 271, 277-78; on pragmatism, 274-76
State: as public· servant, 205; and society, 205-9; as umpire, 208-9
Stimson, Henry L., 216
Studies in Logical Theory, 59, 85, 117
Subject and object, 168-69
Sun Yat-senism, 275
Survey, 260
Syllogism, 119, 121, 123, 137-38

Teachers: authoritarian, 224, 227; freedom df, 233-34; "impartiality" of, 232; progressive, 229. *See also* Education; Schools
Technocrats, 303
Teleology, 96, 130
Thales, 103
Theory: in American culture, 23, 26, 28, 296; and practice, 23, 156, 166, 167, 192-97, 294; and science, 197-98
Thomas, Norman, 240, 261, 263
Thoreau, Henry David, 45, 47, 49
Tools: and causation, 97; ideas as, 30; and language, 124-27
Transcendentalists, 11, 12, 44, 47, 284, 285
Trotsky, 14, 273, 274, 277, 278, 304
Trotskyists, 276
Truman, Harry S., 264
Truth: coherence theory of, 176; consensus theory of, 178; correspondence theory of, 176, 179; and error, 175-80; idealists on, 176; objective and subjective elements of, 177; pragmatists on, 69-71, 136, 175-84; relative and absolute, 180-83; and usefulness, 112, 179,

195-96; as warranted assertion, 136, 178, 179. *See also* Knowledge
Tufts, J. H., 73, 244, 245-46, 247
Turkey, 221

United States: Marxism in, 270-71, 297, 301; political immaturity of, 304; pragmatism as philosophy of, 12, 30-31, 32, 297; theory in, 23, 26, 28, 296; uniqueness of, 305. *See also* Capitalism; Civil War; Democratic ideology; Depression; Midwest; Philosophy, American; Pragmatism; Progressivism; Revolution; Slavery
Unity of opposites, 150-51, 153
Universal, the, 138-39
Universities. *See* Colleges

Vaihinger, Hans, 63
Value, economic, 105-6
Veblen, Thorstein, 40, 73, 270, 272, 298
Vietnam war, 251-52, 268, 293
Violence, 83, 249

Wallace, Henry A., 35, 39
Walling, W. English, 271
War, attitude toward, 38, 77, 215-18, 256-59, 278
"War and the Intellectuals" (Bourne), 257
Washington, George, 43
Weaver, General James B., 36
Wells, Harry K., 275
Whewell, William, 118
Whitman, Walt, 75
Williams, Roger, 285
Wilson, Woodrow, 35, 216, 256, 260, 263, 264
Witch-hunt: post-World War I, 260; post-World War II, 233, 264, 276-77. *See also* McCarthyism
Working class, 25-26, 34, 36, 211, 279-80; and democracy, 214, 286, 290; as force for change, 304; and Marxism, 279-80, 302, 304; and middle class, 273, 277; and philosophy, 301; pragmatism in, 280. *See also* Classes;· Labor movement
World Court, 216
World War I, 35, 216, 244, 256-58
Wright, Richard, 231

Zeno, 128
Zhdanov, Andrei, 275

In Defense of Marxism
THE SOCIAL & POLITICAL CONTRADICTIONS
OF THE SOVIET UNION

LEON TROTSKY

In Defense of Marxism

The Social and Political Contradictions of the Soviet Union

Leon Trotsky

Leon Trotsky replies to those in the revolutionary workers movement at the close of the 1930s who were beating a retreat from defense of the degenerated Soviet workers state in face of looming imperialist assault. He explains how the rising pressures of bourgeois patriotism in the middle classes during the buildup toward U.S. entry into World War II were finding an echo even inside the communist movement, and why only a party that fights to bring growing numbers of workers into its ranks and leadership can steer a steady revolutionary course. $24.95

The Struggle for a Proletarian Party

James P. Cannon

In a political struggle in the late 1930s with a petty-bourgeois current in the Socialist Workers Party, Cannon and other SWP leaders defended the political and organizational principles of Marxism. The debate unfolded as Washington prepared to drag U.S. working people into the slaughter of World War II. A companion to *In Defense of Marxism* by Leon Trotsky. $19.95

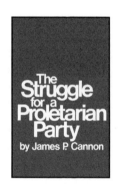

February 1965: The Final Speeches

Malcolm X

Speeches from the last three weeks of the life of this outstanding leader of the oppressed Black nationality and working class in the United States. A large part is material previously unavailable, with some in print for the first time. $17.95

Cosmetics, Fashions, and the Exploitation of Women

Joseph Hansen, Evelyn Reed, and Mary-Alice Waters

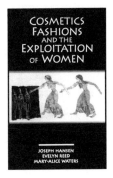

How big business promotes cosmetics to generate profits and perpetuate the oppression of women. In her introduction, Mary-Alice Waters explains how the entry of millions of women into the workforce during and after World War II irreversibly changed U.S. society and laid the basis for a renewed rise of struggles for women's equality. $12.95

Lenin's Final Fight

Speeches and Writings, 1922–23

V. I. Lenin

The record of Lenin's last battle to maintain the proletarian course with which the Bolshevik Party led the workers and peasants to overthrow the power of the landlords and capitalists of the former tsarist empire and initiate a world communist movement. Includes several items appearing in English for the first time. $19.95

Teamster Rebellion

Farrell Dobbs

The 1934 strikes that built an industrial union and a fighting social movement in Minneapolis, recounted by a leader of that battle. The first in a four-volume series on the Teamster-led strikes and organizing drives in the Midwest that helped pave the way for the CIO and pointed a road toward independent labor political action. $16.95

A Packinghouse Worker's Fight for Justice

The Mark Curtis Story

Naomi Craine

The story of the victorious eight-year battle to defeat the political frame-up of Mark Curtis, a union activist and socialist sentenced in 1988 to twenty-five years in prison on trumped up charges of attempted rape and burglary. The pamphlet describes what happened to Curtis on the day of his arrest, the fight to defend immigrant rights he was a part of, and the international campaign that finally won his freedom in 1996. $6.00

by KARL MARX and
FREDERICK ENGELS

The Communist Manifesto *Karl Marx, Frederick Engels*
Founding document of the modern working-class movement, published in 1848. Explains why communists act on the basis not of preconceived principles but of *facts* springing from the actual class struggle, and why communism, to the degree it is a theory, is the generalization of the historical line of march of the working class and the political conditions for its liberation. Booklet $3.95

Capital *Karl Marx*
Marx explains the workings of the capitalist system and how it produces the insoluble contradictions that breed class struggle. He demonstrates the inevitability of the revolutionary transformation of society into one ruled for the first time by the producing majority: the working class. Volume 1, $14.95; volume 2, $13.95; volume 3, $14.95

Anti-Dühring *Frederick Engels*
Modern socialism is not a doctrine, but a movement of the working class that arises as one of the social consequences of the establishment of large-scale capitalist industry. This defense of materialism and the fundamental ideas of scientific communism explains why. A "handbook for every class-conscious worker"—V.I. Lenin. In Marx and Engels *Collected Works*, vol. 25, $25.00

The Poverty of Philosophy *Karl Marx*
Written by the young Marx in collaboration with working-class fighters in the League of the Just, this polemic against Pierre-Joseph Proudhon's middle-class socialism gave Marx the opportunity to "develop the basic features of his new historical and economic outlook," Frederick Engels notes in his 1884 preface. $9.95

AVAILABLE FROM PATHFINDER

Works by GEORGE NOVACK

Polemics in Marxist Philosophy

Novack defends scientific socialism, answering those who, parading as the true interpreters of Marx, have provided a "philosophical" veneer for the anti-working-class political course of Stalinist and social democratic misleaderships around the world. $19.95

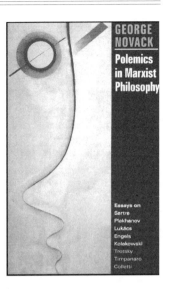

The Origins of Materialism

The rise of a scientific world outlook in ancient Greece, and the development of agriculture, manufacturing, and trade that prepared the way for it. $19.95

Democracy and Revolution

The limitations and advances of various forms of democracy in class society, from its roots in ancient Greece through its rise and decline under capitalism. Discusses the emergence of Bonapartism, military dictatorship, and fascism, and how democracy will be advanced under a workers and farmers regime. $18.95

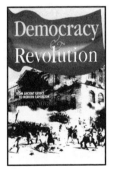

An Introduction to the Logic of Marxism

Marxism is dialectical, Novack explains. It considers all phenomena in their development, in their transition from one state to another. And it is materialist, explaining the world as matter in motion that exists prior to and independently of human consciousness. $12.95

- **Understanding History** $15.95
- **America's Revolutionary Heritage** $21.95
- **Empiricism and Its Evolution** $13.95
- **Pragmatism versus Marxism**
An Appraisal of John Dewey's Philosophy $19.95

PATHFINDER

New International

A MAGAZINE OF MARXIST POLITICS AND THEORY

New International no. 10

Imperialism's March toward Fascism and War *by Jack Barnes* • What the 1987 Stock Market Crash Foretold • Defending Cuba, Defending Cuba's Socialist Revolution *by Mary-Alice Waters* • The Curve of Capitalist Development *by Leon Trotsky* $14.00

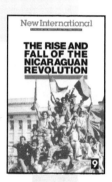

New International no. 9

The Triumph of the Nicaraguan Revolution • Washington's Contra War and the Challenge of Forging Proletarian Leadership • The Political Degeneration of the FSLN and the Demise of the Workers and Farmers Government $14.00

New International no. 8

The Politics of Economics: Che Guevara and Marxist Continuity *by Steve Clark and Jack Barnes* • Che's Contribution to the Cuban Economy *by Carlos Rafael Rodríguez* • On the Concept of Value *and* The Meaning of Socialist Planning *two articles by Ernesto Che Guevara* $10.00

New International no. 7

Opening Guns of World War III: Washington's Assault on Iraq *by Jack Barnes* • Communist Policy in Wartime as well as in Peacetime *by Mary-Alice Waters* • Lessons from the Iran-Iraq War *by Samad Sharif* $12.00

New International no. 6

The Second Assassination of Maurice Bishop *by Steve Clark* • Washington's 50-year Domestic Contra Operation *by Larry Seigle* • Land, Labor, and the Canadian Revolution *by Michel Dugré* • Renewal or Death: Cuba's Rectification Process *two speeches by Fidel Castro* $10.00

New International no. 5

The Coming Revolution in South Africa *by Jack Barnes* • The Future Belongs to the Majority *by Oliver Tambo* • Why Cuban Volunteers Are in Angola *two speeches by Fidel Castro* $9.00

New International no. 4

The Fight for a Workers and Farmers Government in the United States *by Jack Barnes* • The Crisis Facing Working Farmers *by Doug Jenness* • Land Reform and Farm Cooperatives in Cuba *two speeches by Fidel Castro* $9.00

New International no. 3

Communism and the Fight for a Popular Revolutionary Government: 1848 to Today *by Mary-Alice Waters* • 'A Nose for Power': Preparing the Nicaraguan Revolution *by Tomás Borge* • National Liberation and Socialism in the Americas *by Manuel Piñeiro* $8.00

New International no. 2

The Aristocracy of Labor: Development of the Marxist Position *by Steve Clark* • The Working-Class Fight for Peace *by Brian Grogan* • The Social Roots of Opportunism *by Gregory Zinoviev* $8.00

New International no. 1

Their Trotsky and Ours: Communist Continuity Today *by Jack Barnes* • Lenin and the Colonial Question *by Carlos Rafael Rodríguez* • The 1916 Easter Rebellion in Ireland: Two Views *by V.I. Lenin and Leon Trotsky* $8.00

Distributed by Pathfinder

Many of the articles that appear in **New International** are also available in Spanish in **Nueva Internacional,** in French in **Nouvelle Internationale,** and in Swedish in **Ny International.**